Daydream Believer

'As a young boy, the author of this enchanting memoir used to fantasise that he was a cricketing and military hero called "Sir John Julian Bruce, Bart, MA, OBE, VC, the great all-rounder". This distinguished person would dictate his memoirs to a Boswell named J. R. Tegberry, "a Surrey stalwart, whose prose style owed rather more, alas, to the sports journalese of the day than to the magisterial cadences of E. W. Swanton in *The Daily Telegraph*". When one of his half-brothers discovers the notebooks in which these exploits are recorded, the author is accused of "Walter Mitty daydreaming".

The whole book is really an extended and artful repetition of this childhood humiliation – although here the grown-up mocking the "daydream believer" is none other than the dreamer himself. It is a brilliant comic device, which allows Hugh Massingberd the chance not merely to send himself up, but to explore a much more interesting general phenomenon – the discrepancy between our perceptions of the world and what might cautiously be called reality.'

A. N. Wilson, *Country Life*

'One of the few books of the past decade that I would label sublime. Massingberd's disarming honesty about himself and the mixture of romance, snobbery and love of history that actuates him is told with modesty and wit.'

Andrew Roberts, *The Week*

'As he wrote this book I can imagine Hugh blushing at his outrageous presumption in daring to write the autobiography of one so thoroughly insignificant. But he needn't have worried. Although en route we do meet plenty of people more famous . . . none of them can begin to match the charm of the book's bumbling narrator in his Dickensian progression from weedy daydreamer to failed solicitor, country squire, genealogist, obituarist and lurker at stage doors of Andrew Lloyd Webber musicals. This man is an institution, one of the great English eccentrics of our time.'
James Delingpole, *Literary Review*

'His often amusing memoirs have an undercurrent of sadness . . . What there is of self-revelation is oblique, or dropped into piercing little parentheses. But what parentheses they are: the comfort-eating, the nervous breakdown, the tiny humiliations accepted but not forgotten . . . there are nuggets of wonderful gossip throughout.'
Sam Leith, *Daily Telegraph*

'It is an ode to the failure of Fifties' England, a love letter to hopelessness . . . a more general elegy about the frayed fabric of old England, a regret at the passing of a more varied society in which people had less mundane, though not necessarily happier lives.'
Quentin Letts, *Daily Mail*

'Perhaps the most remarkable thing about *Daydream Believer* is its knowing unreconstructedness, so thorough as to be virtually subversive . . . His loving documentation of their uselessness is delivered in an attractively desultory manner . . . this surprisingly charming and disarming book.'

Philip Hoare, *Independent*

'Funny, revealing, sad, sometimes painfully honest, often hilarious.'
Robert Innes-Smith, *Derbyshire Life*

Hugh Massingberd was born at Cookham Dean, Berkshire, in 1946. His father was in the Colonial Service, and later worked for the BBC; his mother was a schoolmistress. He boarded at Port Regis Preparatory School in Dorset, and Harrow. After an unsatisfactory stint as a solicitor's articled clerk in Lincoln's Inn, he gained a place to read History at Cambridge, only to pull out before matriculating. He then drifted into publishing and journalism, where he has made desultory attempts to keep afloat for the last 35 years.

Altogether he has written or edited some 40 books, including works of genealogical reference, studies of royalty and social history as well as a series of illustrated volumes covering palaces, grand hotels and country houses, great and small. His five volumes of collections from the Obituaries page of *The Daily Telegraph* (which he created in 1986 and edited for eight years), and a further volume covering *The Very Best of The Daily Telegraph Books of Obituaries*, are all available as Pan paperbacks. The fifth volume was shortlisted for the inaugural Bollinger Everyman Wodehouse Prize for Comic Writing in 2000.

In addition to being Obituaries Editor of *The Daily Telegraph*, he was also that newspaper's Heritage columnist and TV critic. He has two children from his first marriage and, following a sojourn in his ancestral county of Lincolnshire, now lives with his second wife in London. He has listed his recreations as gluttony, sloth, watching cricket at the Oval and hanging round stage-doors and unsaddling enclosures.

ALSO BY HUGH MASSINGBERD

The Monarchy

The British Aristocracy
(with Mark Bence-Jones)

The London Ritz
(2 edns, with David Watkin)

Her Majesty The Queen

Great British Families

Royal Palaces, Castles
and Homes
(with Patrick Montague-Smith)

Diana – Princess of Wales

Heritage of Royal Britain

Royal Palaces of Europe

Blenheim Revisited

Queen Elizabeth
The Queen Mother

Family Seats

With Christopher Simon Sykes

Great Houses of England
and Wales *(2 edns)*

Great Houses of Scotland
(2 edns)

Great Houses of Ireland

English Manor Houses

Edited by Hugh Massingberd

The Landed Gentry

Guide to The Royal Family

Presidential Families of
the USA *(2 edns)*

Irish Family Records

Family Index

Royal Families of the World
(2 vols)

Guide to Country Houses
(4 vols)

The Disintegration of a Heritage

Lord of the Dance:
A Moncreiffe Miscellany

The Daily Telegraph
Record of the Second World War

The Daily Telegraph
Books of Obituaries *(5 vols)*

The Very Best of
The Daily Telegraph
Books of Obituaries

HUGH MASSINGBERD

Daydream Believer

Confessions of a Hero-Worshipper

PAN BOOKS

First published 2001 by Macmillan

This edition published 2002 by Pan Books
an imprint of Pan Macmillan Ltd
Pan Macmillan, 20 New Wharf Road, London N1 9RR
Basingstoke and Oxford
Associated companies throughout the world
www.panmacmillan.com

ISBN 978 0 230 76824 6

Typeset by SetSystems Ltd, SaffronWalden, Essex
Printed and bound by CPI Group (UK) Ltd, Croydon, CR0 4YY

All Pan Macmillan titles are available from
www.panmacmillan.com
or from Bookpost by telephoning 01624 677237

For M.D.N.

Acknowledgements

'The Wind Beneath My Wings' Words and music by Larry Henley and Jeff Silbar © 1984 Warner House of Music and WB Gold Music Corp, USA Warner/ Chappell Music Ltd., London W6 8BS. Lyrics reproduced by kind permission of IMP Ltd. All rights reserved.

Extract from *Summoned by Bells* by John Betjeman is used by generous permission of John Murray (Publishers) Ltd.

Patrick Barrington's 'Songs of a Sub-Man' first appeared in *Punch* in the 1930s.

'Prima Donna' from *The Phantom of the Opera* Music by Andrew Lloyd Webber. Lyrics by Charles Hart. Additional lyrics by Richard Stilgoe © 1986 The Really Useful Group, Ltd., London. Reproduced by generous permission.

Lyrics from 'The Family Solicitor' (Words by Douglas Furber/ Music by Noël Gay) © 1937 Cinephonic Music Co Ltd./ Richard Armitage Ltd. All rights reserved. International copyright secured. Reproduced by kind permission.

Extract from Mike Hugg's theme song for *Whatever Happened to the Likely Lads* is reproduced by generous permission of Palam Music Publishing Ltd.

Every effort has been made to trace all copyright holders, but if any have been inadvertently overlooked, the author and publishers will be pleased to make the necessary arrangement at the first opportunity.

Contents

Special thanks to Gillon Aitken, Antony Alderson, Andrew Barrow, Stefanie Bierwerth, Michael Bloch, Craig Brown, Christine Comonte, Simon Courtauld, the late Lesley Cunliffe, David (Lewis) Jones, Mary Killen, Cynthia Lewis, Candida Lycett Green, Georgina Morley, Patrick O'Connor, the late Lady Violet Powell, Lesley Shaw, Tess Tattersall, Hugo Vickers and A. N. Wilson.

ONE

Everything I Would Like to Be

'*D*ID YOU EVER *know that you're my hero,*' warbles
Bette Midler in 'The Wind Beneath My Wings', *'and
everything I would like to be . . .'* As a boy in the 1950s
and an adolescent in the 1960s I would cover the walls of
my suburban bedroom with graven images – cut-out press
photographs of cricketers, jockeys, actors, satirists, authors,
aristocrats. These were my heroes, an idiosyncratic
mixture of idols who appeared to exude the insouciant
self-confidence, style, glamour, panache (however flash
and counterfeit) that I so conspicuously lacked.

Blushing, buttoned-up, painfully shy and acutely self-
conscious, I constantly escaped into a fantasy world where
I would be transmogrified into one or other of these heroes
– sometimes, with careful editorial adjustments, an amalgam of several. This was not an idle whim or fancy but a
way of life. In the title of another cheesy pop song, I was
a 'Daydream Believer' – or should that be 'Deceiver'?
Facts, figures, rejigged curriculum vitae, timetables and
schedules, detailed menus (these took up an inordinate
amount of my time), decorative schemes, even lists of
favoured tradesmen were copiously compiled to provide a
framework within which the imagination could take flight.
After hours of annotation would come days of solitary
play-acting, occasionally supplemented by such props as
stripy caps and cricket bats, riding whips, batons and
pretend microphones. The heroes would be 'stalked' outside stage doors, changing rooms, unsaddling enclosures.

The object was not so much the collecting of autographs – meaningless scrawls soon discarded – as the opportunity to be close to the idol, to bask in his aura, to overhear his voice and drink in every detail of his being.

Such 'trainspotting' might be regarded as a fairly harmless diversion in a teenage fan, something, surely, that he will naturally grow out of. Yet, as I approach my sixties and face up to impending mortality (hastened by a heart condition), I confess that I have not grown out of it. Far from it.

It would be comforting to claim that the obsessive creep who emerges from these pages is, to borrow the title of my hero James Lees-Milne's romantic memoirs, *Another Self*. Yet to this day – though I like to think I have shed some of my worst traits – I still loiter at stage doors, still spend most of my time transported in day-dreams underpinned by painstaking research, still worship an ever-expanding gallery of heroes – now often far younger than myself.

It has taken me a long time to realize that there is something, well, sad (in both the old-fashioned and modern sense) as well as funny (peculiar and ha-ha) about all this. Only recently did I grasp the fact that the word 'fan' derives from 'fanatic'. Yet plenty of hints have been dropped along the way.

For instance, my uncle Hugh – an unconventional diplomatist from an Ulster family, who won the MC in the Great War and later became a Catholic and a Mon-signor – found himself intensely irritated by my syco-phantic desire to sit at his feet during a bizarre Grand Tour on which he conducted me around the Continent in order to qualify for membership of his comfortingly gloomy club. In between castigating me to other occupants of railway compartments as '*Puritano inglese*', he denounced my daydreaming and hero worship as 'unhealthy and unchristian'.

The belief that one will somehow endear oneself to a hero by laboriously reciting his achievements is one of the fallacies of fandom. After all, why on earth should he be interested, or impressed, by hearing a litany of material he himself knows only too well? None the less, my urge to sit at my heroes' feet, to purr like a cat in their laps, to place their idealized images on a pedestal and bow down before them – to obliterate my own insignificant personality in their magical glow – remained paramount.

The consequences have been dire, embarrassing, frequently farcical. The first time I met my chief hero, Anthony Powell, I persisted in demonstrating the extent of my tabulation of his novels and characters to the point where he felt compelled to protest 'My dear boy . . .' He merely wished to pursue our shared interest in genealogy, but I was incapable of thinking myself worthy of conversing with the Sage of the Chantry on equal terms and kept on harking back to the foibles of Widmerpool or Major Fosdick.

James Lees-Milne (who inspired me to search out the dimmer sort of squirearchical seat) has recorded in his diaries how my excessively deferential and polite attitude towards him induced 'a state of acute nervousness. I could hardly bear it I was made so shy . . . such overt treatment makes me very uneasy.' Later, after I had scribbled a series of intensely flattering profiles, Jim complained that they made him '*squirm*'.

Such reactions gave me pause but I could not restrain myself. For the truth was that I hero-worshipped with blind passion. The thrill of, say, spending an afternoon in the Coach and Horses in Soho with James Villiers and Ronald Fraser, two of my favourite fruity actors, prompted me to exclaim that this was one of the most enjoyable days of my life – and, alas, to ignore their pathetic pleas for me to write them a script. Similarly, lunching upstairs in the same Soho pub with the senior satirical prefects of *Private Eye*, or in Doughty Street with the assorted fogeys and raffish cards of the *Spectator*, proved excitement beyond my imaginings.

As a reclusive teenager and articled clerk I never expected to meet any of my heroes and, lacking, as I did, social graces or charm, remained ill-equipped to do so. All I had to offer was dog-like devotion and slavish obeisance. My contribution to the conversation was unlikely to rise above the level of stating useless information in a dull, virtually inaudible monotone; my manner must have seemed like a parody of a gauche, middle-class snob.

To my continuing surprise, though, I found myself – despite my pathological avoidance of social gatherings – coming into direct contact with heroes I had only fantas- ized about during my days as a commuter on the 8.12 from Cookham-on-Thames, near Maidenhead. Some of the encounters amounted to little more than the type recalled by my idol P. G. Wodehouse in connection with his meeting Clem Attlee at Westminster: 'How d'you do?' 'How d'you do?' (End of story.) Others yielded comic and ultimately instructive exchanges.

Quite a few heroes met in the flesh proved a grave disappointment. Cavalier cricketers worshipped from the boundary came into focus as dim, narrow-minded bores and philistines. Telly pundits such as Norman St John-Stevas, whose exotic attire and flamboyant campery had intrigued me as a callow youth, fell absurdly short of expectations in real life. Admiral of the Fleet Earl Mount-batten of Burma, who enlisted me in one of his tireless campaigns for vainglory, showed himself to be a prepos- terous fraud. Journalists admired from afar turned out, on closer inspection as colleagues, to be all too eager to toady to the power mania of politicians and proprietors.

Many of the heroes, however, only increased in statue on acquaintance. The gentle William Trevor, the acerbic V. S. Naipaul and the pellucid Kazuo Ishiguro invoked the appropriate sense of awe and reverence felt by the hack for the true creative artist. Peter Cook, the eternal undergraduate, was everything I had imagined with his anarchic humour and unbridled generosity of spirit. His straightforward invitation to join him – after a riotous lunch – in front of the golf on television, though, caught me unawares. I did not have the confidence to accept, and have regretted it ever since. Stephen Fry was the soul of tolerance as I idiotically parroted the best lines of a part he had played in *Forty Years On* by yet another principal hero in my pantheon, Alan Bennett. In the company of the endearingly insecure Hugh Laurie, I longed to shed the inhibitions that had crippled me since my days at prep school (when the repressed headmaster, a school friend of Christopher Isherwood's, publicly admonished me for innocently kissing a classmate) and enfold the Etonian rowing Blue in a chaste embrace.

As such confessions may indicate, I have – at the risk of exposing myself as a ghastly combination of Mr Collins, Uriah Heep and Kenneth Halliwell – sought to be as honest as I dare in attempting to exorcize the demons of my daydream believing. A handful of names have been altered to protect the innocent. Yet this is not an autobiography, merely an exercise in confronting the way fantasy and reality have overlapped in my tiptoeing odyssey round the outskirts of life.

To write about oneself is to reveal more than one intends. Self-deprecation, for example, is often a transparent mask for self-regard ('The Wind Beneath My Wings' is indeed a case in point), and snide score-settling usually blows up in your face. It is not for me, then, to analyse what follows. For all I know, it may well read like the ravings of a maniac, or perhaps it may even strike a chord or two of identification.

TWO

Sir John Julian

'HERE'S A SKYER for little Lovey-Boy!' Up would go the shout from my half-brother Antony (my first hero) and up, up, up would go the hard, red ball, high above the tall, thick hedges surrounding the spacious green-belt suburban lawn where the fearsome family fielding practices took place. The ball always seemed to be suspended in mid-air as if in freeze-frame, and certainly long enough for everyone present – grandparents, parents, assorted aunts, cousins, half-siblings and so forth – to focus their attention on the blushing, nervous, curly-headed youth underneath it.

'Butterfingers!' came the hearty chorus in unison, as the ball, having suddenly plummeted with unexpected ferocity, popped out of my fumbling grasp.

Following such habitual humiliations, I would retire, in a furious and tearful sulk, to Antony's 'den', an outbuilding to Rondels (an allusion to its round windows), our grandparents' rambling, pebble-dashed Edwardian villa above the Thames at Cookham Dean. There I would escape from the embarrassment of failure into a dream world of games-playing glory. The den, redolent of linseed oil and sweaty batting gloves, was hung with a dazzling assortment of stripy caps, some earned by Antony (or 'A. S. R. de W. Winlaw', as he appeared on the framed scorecards on the wall), others by his father, R. de W. K. Winlaw, Cambridge triple Blue, Surrey batsman and captain of Bedfordshire, who had been killed while serving

with the RAF during the Second World War and who
remained the icon of what we all rejoiced in calling the
'RCC' (Rondels Cricket Club).

Surreptitiously, I would try on these caps, with their
flamboyant markings, and experience a strange frisson of
excitement. As I studied the yellowing scorecards, with
their lists of elaborately initialled gentlemen-cricketers, I
wished that my own initials, H. J., were not so humdrum
– if only my father had acceded to my mother's fancy to
call me Peregrine, I might have ended up as, say, P. H. L.
(Peregrine Hugh Langton). Such initials seemed key indi-
cators to the style and dash I romantically craved in the
world of amateur games in the 1950s. Our cousin Julian,
who played in the Winchester XI (and whose remarkably
furry legs fascinated my sister and myself), was listed as
'J. J. B. Rowe'; that double 'J' struck a particular chord
with me and, in homage, my fantasy alter ego, a brilliant
baronet called Bruce, whose attainments away from his
legendary deeds on the cricket pitch and football field
included the Victoria Cross, was styled 'Sir John Julian'.

This paragon of my daydreams took careful shape in
A. S. R. de W.'s den. Within its walls, the bumbling,
blushing figure of 'Lovey-Boy' (the hated pet-name
bestowed on me by our doting cook-housekeeper Florence,
herself nicknamed 'Biddo' by J. J. B. Rowe) would
metamorphose into Sir John Julian Bruce, Bart, MA,
OBE, VC, the great all-rounder, famed for his good looks,
modesty, charm and confidence, the hugely popular, all-
powerful president of RCC. (The undue prominence of
'MA' among the letters after his moniker must have been
inspired by the fact that my parents had first met as
Cambridge undergraduates.) Attended by his faithful
Boswell, J. R. Tegberry, a Surrey stalwart whose prose
style owed rather more, alas, to the sports journalese of
the day than to the magisterial cadences of the god-like

E. W. Swanton of the *Daily Telegraph*, Bruce would regale
his readers with tales of derring-do in a series of copiously
inscribed exercise books, annotated with laborious statistics and adorned with 'action' illustrations in pencil.

The only reader for whom they were intended was
myself: the plan being to use the books as a sort of
shooting script for my solo play-acting of Sir John Julian's
exploits. Standing at an imaginary wicket, wearing one of
A. S. R. de W.'s colourful caps, I would play phantom
shots, accompanied by loud clickings of the tongue to
simulate contact with the non-existent ball. Unfortunately the clickings would occasionally lead to discovery.

'Look, it's Walter Mitty *daydreaming* again,' my half-
brother Roger would mock as I was caught in mid-salute,
doffing my cap and waving my bat in acknowledgement of
yet another standing ovation. To employ one of Tegberry's
favourite formulae, 'Was my face red?'

It was even redder when, as was inevitable in the
rough and tumble of family life, Sir John Julian Bruce's
voluminous memoirs were accidentally exposed to a wider
readership.

'Hey,' Roger called out to the cast of dozens which
generally seemed in attendance at Rondels, 'listen to this
bit: "As England's opening bowler, I found that wickets
fell like apples from a tree . . ."'

After this, I tended not to commit Sir John Julian's
activities to paper, but would still act out various epic
innings on a more improvisational basis. Indeed, Sir John
Julian (or one of his slightly more sophisticated deriv-
atives) continued to smite the bowling hip and thigh,
tongue busily clicking, until well into my twenties.

As far as writing was concerned, I felt it safer to
switch from games fiction to more or less straightforward
reportage of real-life fixtures. A. S. R.'s somewhat erratic
performances for the village side (one made memorable

by a cousin yelling out '*Idle!*' when a corpulent fielder for
the Handlebar Club, so named on account of its members'
uniformly luxuriant moustaches, let the ball through his
legs), or the Berkshire Colts, were painstakingly chronicled. Having a notebook about one's person – as any
trainspotter would confirm – gives one a sense of purpose
and belonging, and I felt that I was beginning to fit in, at
last, as a reporter. Winlaw's chancy style of batting also
helped define a vital element in my concept of hero
worship: the combination of insouciant flair and agonizing
vulnerability. It was typical of him, for example, to be
bowled while essaying an exquisite late cut.

The highlight of my boyhood came when Winlaw, who
had hitherto languished in the depths of the school's dud
leagues, was suddenly propelled into the Harrow XI after
Boy's Own-type heroics in a house match. The Eton and
Harrow game of 1955, the 150th renewal of the oldest
fixture in the calendar at Lord's, provided me with my
first glimpse of cricket's 'Headquarters' (as Tegberry
unfailingly called it). At the age of eight I found it all
overwhelming; I still do, for that matter.

In the era when debutantes were still presented at
court, the Eton and Harrow match remained a significant
occasion in the 'season': there were carriages parked
around the boundary, gentlemen wore morning dress,
ladies wore hats and long dresses. Acutely self-conscious
in my grey flannel shorts, I imagined myself one of the
sans culottes as I negotiated my way nervously through
the fashionable promenade during the luncheon interval.
The French Revolution – which I was learning about at
my preparatory school near Reading – came strongly to
mind when faced with the alarming, behatted, white-
painted apparition of Mrs Hugh McCorquodale (otherwise
Barbara Cartland, who, much later, was to tell me of how
she saw the Jarrow Marchers invade the Ritz Hotel) and

her daughter, Mrs Gerald Legge (the already formidable Raine, who would later campaign to have me sacked from my post at the *Daily Telegraph* for writing disobligingly about her 'improvements' as châtelaine of Althorp).

Not, of course, that, like Lady Anne Stepney in Anthony Powell's *A Dance to the Music of Time*, I would have been 'on the side of the People'. As may be judged from my adopting a baronetcy for my alter ego, Sir John Julian (a title that could probably be traced to the one traditionally turned down, as the story went, by my father's grandfather, an Ulster senator), I was even then a howling snob. But that golden summer day at Lord's my snobbery took flight from the suburbs of Maidenhead and fluttered downriver to every snob's favourite four-letter word, Eton. Like that other denizen of the Thames Valley, Mr Toad (a figure who loomed large in my child-hood, as his creator, Kenneth Grahame, had lived in what became our kindergarten at Cookham Dean and set *The Wind in the Willows* in the surrounding neighbourhood), on first encountering a motor car, it was a case of oh, Bliss, oh Rapture – *Poop! Poop!* – when I set eyes on Eton blue.

Inchoately, I seemed to sense that the stripy dark blue Harrovian headgear was flashy and vulgar whereas the simple pale blue Etonian caps exuded aristocratic style and panache. Various languid luminaries from the Eton XI – Edward Lane-Fox, Simon Douglas-Pennant, the promising young wicket-keeper Henry Blofeld – were swiftly added to my private pantheon. My next cricket book was duly dedicated to 'Blofeld & Co.' and this scion of the Norfolk squirearchy acquired mythic status when he came back after a horrific collision with a bus at Eton to win a Cambridge Blue – though to this and other observers he was never the player he promised to be before the accident.

Awash with heady new material to absorb into my daydreams, I refused to return to Lord's the following day. Instead, I played out my own version of events in and out of the empty house, where the 'pavilion' steps down to the lawn served as a passable stage for the studiedly casual entrances and exits (bat aloft) of the Etonian batsmen. My guilt at being a 'traitor' in this fanatically loyal Harrovian household (the Winlaws' father, R. de W. K., had taught at Harrow before the war) added a piquancy to the proceedings. 'You can represent "Eton",' Roger used to say when we set up some games contest or other. Little did he know what pleasure such conceits afforded me.

Socially, if not geographically, Crosfields, my prep school, was a long way from Eton. In fact it was the junior school of Leighton Park, a Quaker establishment to which my leftward-leaning mother, a schoolmistress, had been drawn on account of its abhorrence of corporal punishment. My father had been emotionally scarred by the sadistic cruelty of the appropriately named Mr Evill at his own preparatory (or 'private', as they were known) school, Ashdown House, and she was determined the same thing was not going to happen to me. My father was fond of recalling the only question put to him by Rudyard Kipling, a friend of his field-marshal uncle, when they met during his public schooldays: 'Tell me, my boy, is there much *licking* at Wellington?'

Crosfields's claim to fame was that it was the alma mater of the current England cricket captain, P. B. H. May, whose impressive initials duly ensured him a place among my heroes. As a nobly classical batsman, he was certainly of heroic stature but, try as I might, I could not warm to Peter May's personality. The trouble probably was that he seemed rather too like me – shy, buttoned-up, prim and proper – to be the stuff of fantasy. My impression that he was rather 'pi', something of a prig, was borne out by the reminiscences of his Carthusian contemporary, Simon Raven, with whom, many years later, I took tea at the Charterhouse, the hallowed retreat for 'decaied gents' in the City of London, where I now dream of ending up myself. Sadly, the old scapegrace Raven, once a byword for gourmandizing, was clutching a pot of sandwich spread as he sought to escape from a limerick-spouting 'brother' resident.

Captain Raven himself – who had resigned, under pressure from his bookmakers, his commission in my second father-in-law's regiment, the King's Shropshire Light Infantry – could hardly be classified as a hero but some of his raffish tastes appeared to be shared by the two most dashing cricketers of that era, Denis Compton and Keith Miller. By the time I came to study the game closely for my RCC chronicles, these cheery rivals were both well past their prime, yet an aura of faded romance still clung to them and occasionally a flash of the old brilliance would – irresistibly – light up the sky. Attractive characteristics they shared were modesty and a blithe disregard for statistics and records. Meeting one's heroes can so often prove a withering disappointment, but when, not long before he died, I bumped into the batsman for whom there were no rations (to adapt Neville Cardus's phrase) in a club, he struggled to his feet and said simply 'Denis Compton' (with the Cockney hard 'o' still intact). As if I would not have known who he was.

Peter May was no less modest, though meeting him at a game in the old boys' knockout competition, which Winlaw invented in the 1960s, lacked the same magic.

'Oh, Mr May,' I gushed in the traditional manner of the mad fan, 'it's such a thrill and an honour to meet you. You were my boyhood hero. I had a *Peter May* bat when I was at Crosfields – your old school, of course . . .'

(Somehow one always believes one's heroes will be impressed by your telling them something obvious about themselves with which they are, naturally, only too familiar.)

'Crosfields, yes,' the great cricketer mused in an accent that would once have been considered decidedly 'common'. 'My family were from Reading, you know.'

We sat in painful silence. I thought of mentioning John Betjeman's frustration when he attended a lecture by Lord David Cecil advertised as 'The Pleasures of Reading' only to discover that Lord David was actually discussing the joys of *reading*, but decided against.

Not for the first, or the last, time, I considered that it might be better to watch one's heroes from the boundary and marvel, in all innocence and ignorance, at their feats from afar. How happy I had been – and, come to think of it, still am – to sit and watch Surrey play at the Oval (truly 'the People's Ground', and an infinitely less stuck-up place than Lord's), without the burdensome inside knowledge I was later to acquire about certain players' tendencies to 'sledge' (bad-mouth), whinge and moan. In my fantasy world, I liked to believe the Gentlemen were all devil-may-care cavaliers with patrician accents, and the Players cheerful, salt-of-the-earth worthies honoured to be engaged in the beautiful summer game.

Reality was kept at bay, with reams of Gradgrindian facts and statistics lovingly tabulated each season in my exercise books. To take refuge in daydreams on the one hand and first-class cricket averages on the other was more necessary than ever now that I had ceased to attend Crosfields as a day boy and had followed my half-brothers and cousins as a boarder at Port Regis in Dorset. My father's brother, Peter, a bachelor of artistic and social bent, who was paying for my education, had come to the conclusion that Crosfields was too *outré*, and my mother, encouraged by the fact that Port Regis ('PR') was patronized by various Labour and Liberal politicians, liked to believe that it also eschewed the slipper (it didn't).

The Winlaws' games-playing achievements at PR were recalled with genial warmth by the hearty masters with their pipes and leather-patched tweed jackets. On the verdant pitches beside the vast 'Jacobethan' pile built (and occupied all too briefly) by the Grosvenors, I yearned desperately to emulate my brothers, and failed abysmally. Assigned to guard the goal at soccer (I think we were supposed to call it 'Association'), I managed to let in six shots from the junior school of Millfield, whose team seemed largely composed of aggressive Orientals, doubtless already on professional terms. I was handicapped by the fact that the elastic in my shorts suddenly snapped slack before the game; consequently I tended to be hitching up the waistband when I needed my hands to be free to catch the ball.

'Monty,' the PR captain admonished me, alluding to the familiar diminutive of my surname, Montgomery. 'You're absolutely *spastic*.'

Sacked from the side (to be replaced, according to a rumour I was ready to believe, by the headmaster's godson), I rather lost interest in soccer. My dreams of becoming another Bert Trautmann – the Manchester City goalie who carried on playing in a Cup Final after breaking his neck – had faded. Trautmann's place in my dream team owed something to his being a former German prisoner of war; PR had housed a prison camp during the war years and the old huts still littered the grounds. I bored my dormitory mates with a fantasy about Gertrude, an erratic cow in the neighbouring field, heading an escape committee. Although the war had been over for more than ten years, my dreams were full of enemy aircraft flying overhead.

It was an aircraft which never properly took off that curtailed my own football fantasy. One fateful evening in February 1958, while I was making an ashtray for my mother (who not only didn't smoke but also offered handsome bribes for her children not to do so) in the woodwork 'hobby' hour, the tracksuited figure of George Willing, the gym master, took me to one side.

'Sonny,' he said, 'there's been a tragic accident. Most of the Manchester United side have been killed in a plane crash at Munich airport.'

Knowing of my particular support for Man U and hero worship of the so-called 'Busby Babes', the kindly Mr Willing had sought me out to break the shocking news. Those killed included my special favourite, the cheerful England centre forward Tommy Taylor, aged twenty-five. Soon, the dashing left half Duncan Edwards was to die too. With awed fascination, I scoured the *News Chronicle* (the newspaper favoured by the Liberal headmaster) for ghoulish details about Matt Busby's oxygen tent. It was a sobering business to see a whole wall of my pantheon crumble into dust.

From now on Sir John Julian's publishing wing of the RCC was to be devoted entirely to the summer game. Escape into the comforting arms of cricket was all the more urgent because of the unwelcome switch in RCC's headquarters. Following the deaths of my grandparents, the Edwardian 'rambler' up at Cookham Dean had had to be sold, and my parents were faced with the difficulty of squeezing themselves, their five children, the redoubtable Biddo (who, quite rightly, commandeered the best room) and assorted animals into an undignified and uncompromisingly suburban bungalow down in Cookham's least salubrious quarter. 'Do tell me, Marsali,' enquired one of my mother's brothers-in-law with earnest sincerity, 'how you were clever enough to get a *council house?*'

Seeing the new Rondels – an architectural curiosity, with its central feature a lavatory nicknamed 'Cliveden View' – for the first time on my return for the holidays from PR proved too great a shock to the system. This was, to say the least, hardly a suitable 'seat' for Sir John Julian. At the age of eleven I flipped for the first, if certainly not the last, time. That night, after dark, I packed my trusty Bakelite suitcase and jumped out of my bedroom window – it was, I am reluctant to repeat, a *bungalow* – before heading purposefully back towards old Rondels. I was making fair progress up the hill when lights and bells emanating from my mother's and half-sister's bicycles alerted me to imminent apprehension. 'There's nothing to go back *to* or *for*, Hughie,' it was patiently explained.

I consoled myself by sticking up pictures of my heroes, a gallery of graven images, on the walls of my tiny 'cell'. ('A room I would hesitate to put a pantry boy into,' as Lady Berners observed of her son's accommodation at Eton.) By this time they included the rising England star E. R. Dexter, an imperious batsman whose naturally attacking approach recalled the golden age of Edwardian amateurism (even if, as I harshly judged from eavesdropping much later outside the Radley old boys' dressing room on one occasion, his faintly suburban persona did not quite live up to his 'Lord Ted' image); and the authoritative E. W. Swanton, for whom A. S. R. was now working as a dogsbody.

'Jim' Swanton had been a friend of Winlaw's father before the war and took a benevolent view of the young shaver's scrapes, such as writing off the master's motor car. But 'Swanny', whose gruff, schoolmasterly tones were much imitated (particularly on the occasion when, while summarizing the day's play at the Oval on television, he had cause to remonstrate with a boy pulling faces at him from behind the camera), was less forgiving after one unfortunate telephone call to Rondels.

'Good evening to you,' he boomed at Biddo, who had picked up the instrument. 'This is Mr E. W. Swanton speaking. I was hoping to find Mr Antony Winlaw in. Please would you be good enough to put him on the line, or, failing that, tell me of his whereabouts?'

'Oh *no*, Antony,' bawled back Biddo, who was slightly deaf, in her broadest Wiltshire accent. 'I know it's only you, larking about as usual. You're always pretending to be that old twerp Swainson.' (Biddo was something of a Mrs Malaprop and had once told one of my bemused aunts that she had enjoyed 'a lovely time at the Crematorium' – she meant the Planetarium.) 'You can't fool me!'

'I *beg* your pardon . . .'

'Come off it! Pull the other one . . .'

'Now come, come, my good woman, I can *assure* you this is Mr *Swanton* speaking – and when Mr Winlaw comes to hear of this, as he indubitably will, he may have cause to regret his misplaced mimicry.'

Biddo, a staunch fan of 'Fearless Fred' Trueman, the Yorkshire fast bowler and tail-end hitter, had a place of honour among Sir John Julian's fulsome acknowledgements in the RCC publications. A peerless cook – who had begun her working life as a kitchenmaid of fourteen at Coleshill (Pratt's Carolean masterpiece) for the Pleydell-Bouveries shortly before the outbreak of the Kaiser's War, in which she was to lose her 'young man' to the unmentionable Germans – the benevolent Biddo bound me to her ample bosom not with hoops of steel but ambrosial dishes. I was her 'Lovey-Boy', the son she never had and the first born with whom she was allowed free rein following the death of my mother's old nanny, who had looked after my half-siblings.

Looking back, I exploited my privileged position next

to Biddo's kitchen stove shamelessly and doubtless fully deserved any robust treatment I may have received from my half-siblings outdoors. Nor did I properly appreciate Biddo's generosity of spirit in devoting her sole annual holiday to sitting beside me at Scarborough's seaside cricket ground for the duration of its festival, a regular feast of enjoyable cricket. This ingenious scheme to cheer me up had been hatched with my mother, who had happy memories of pre-war Scarborough festivals when her first husband, R. de W. K. Winlaw, played for the Gentlemen.

In those days they put up at the Grand, the *schloss*-like structure which dominates the still elegant resort's south coast, and Sir John Julian naturally hankered after a palatial suite here. But instead the spoilt little snob learned a valuable social lesson by accompanying Biddo to dear old 'Ma' Ferrington's spick-and-span boarding house in Trafalgar Square, which backed conveniently on to the cricket ground up on the brasher north coast. Ma (a nickname sparingly used) was a formidable Yorkshire-woman who expected strict punctuality in Nelson House's basement dining room, capaciously stocked with sauce bottles, and would issue no-nonsense edicts against tak-ing the stairs two at a time or using the lavatory at night. Yet in the front room of an evening, over the salty beef sandwiches served for late supper, she would relish, teeth out and grey hair askew, a 'good laff' with her assembled guests.

The other regulars at festival time included an impec-cably courteous miner, a very jolly family from Man-chester and a slightly snooty spinster of a certain age. 'Probably a ladies' maid,' observed Biddo, who (like Alan Bennett's mother on her hotel outings) took pleasure in pigeonholing the guests during her people-watching. Watching the cricket day after day must have been some-thing of a trial even for her good nature and from time to

time she would look up from her knitting and yell, to my
embarrassment: 'Come on, hit a six!' In keeping with the
festival spirit someone, usually Trueman, would oblige.

Yet, what with the odd outing to Peasholm Park
(where mock-battles were fought on the lake between
mini-fleets of model ships, manned by prostrate pilots),
The Merry Widow in the open-air theatre, the Fol-de-Rols
concert party at the Floral Hall and perhaps a guest spot
from Biddo's favourite pianist, Russ Conway (the mer-
chant seaman with the Steradent smile), I hope that she
was happy. For me, it was like one of my dreams coming
true: every morning I would take up my accustomed
place underneath the press box and begin my on-the-spot
report with a summary of the weather. Once my idyll
was interrupted by a patronizing journalist looking over
my shoulder and remarking: 'What's this, son, are you
after my job?' Blushing furiously, I snapped shut the
book.

During the intervals, as the band oompahed away, I
would stalk my heroes to and from the marquee. Although
I eagerly collected the daily rushes (or prints) from the
local photographer, I was too shy to thrust the pictures
forward to the blazered and flannelled figures for them to
autograph, and contented myself by eavesdropping on
such characters as Colin Ingleby-Mackenzie, the swash-
buckling Hampshire captain. The best I could dredge up
was merely a single word – '*Y-e-e-s*' – enunciated in
a moderately high-pitched Etonian drawl and endlessly
imitated to the boredom of my fellow cricket nuts back at
Port Regis.

'Ingleby' became an idol after his hilarious television
interview with a po-faced reporter for *Junior Sportsview*
which, as I recall, went something like this:

'Mr Ingleby-Mackenzie, now to what do you attribute
Hampshire's success?'

'Oh, wine, women and song, I should say.'

'Er . . . but don't you have certain rules, um, discipline, I mean – helpful hints for the *younger* viewer?'

'Well, everyone in bed in time for breakfast, I suppose.'

'Yes, thank you. Perhaps we could take a look in the dressing room?'

'Certainly, if you don't mind me wandering about in the nude . . .'

If only I could have injected some of Ingleby's joie de vivre into my own nerve-ridden efforts on the cricket pitch at PR. I did manage to scrape into the 1st XI after a breezy young temporary master had inculcated in me the basics of inswing, but I bowled in terror of delivering an interminable over of wide balls. By the end of my last season I had still not been awarded my colours, though one of my collaborators on the cricket books, which were now cascading consolingly from the RCC, told me that he had overheard an altercation between the master-in-charge and the headmaster on this very topic.

Not long before, the headmaster, a temperamental bachelor widely revered (if not by me) for his liberality, had accused me of 'eccentric behaviour' in a report, which was hotly challenged by my mother. Having apparently chosen to put a sinister interpretation on my innocently kissing a boisterous contemporary on the cheek, 'Uppers' chose to rebuke me in front of the whole school for consorting with younger boys in an inappropriate manner. Although two of my cricket-book collaborators were admittedly a year or so my junior, I was mystified by the old boy's attitude. Then he tore up my end-of-term mug-shot with the words: 'You don't need this – you're vain enough already.'

If Uppers hardly measured up to heroic status, Mr Trotman, the games master, proved my champion in the end. At the last gasp I did finally receive the much-

coveted white and red cap, similar to the one sported in
Winlaw's old den. It smelt delicious. The only trouble was
that it was now too late to wear it.

What I wore when I took my leave of PR that winter,
without any fond adieux, was a blanket over my head: the
school was in the grip of a jaundice epidemic. 'Is this
the way you're going to behave at *Eton*?' a sarcastic senior
master at PR had once sneered at me as I danced along
in a daydream, but, as things turned out, it was not, alas,
the 'Wat'ry Glade' for me. My glamorous uncle Peter
favoured Eton but my mother hated what she thought
was its snobbish ambience and she could invoke an
unlikely ally in her unconventional father-in-law, a major
general who had been unhappy there in the 1880s. She
wanted me to go to Bryanston, PR's senior school. Harrow
was the compromise solution.

Here again, as at PR, the Winlaws' athletic prowess
preceded me. Stuck in a boorishly 'keen' house (where it
was not done to pass into the school choir), I sought to be
as inconspicuous as possible. 'Most of the time,' observed
my form master in one report, 'he seems to be in a world
of his own.' How right he was. I had retreated to the
fantasy world of Sir John Julian (now supplemented by
P. G. Wodehouse's Psmith), wishing myself the toast of
'Pop' at Eton. Once, in an absent-minded moment, I
started combing my recalcitrant curls in class. 'Dear me,
Montgomery,' expostulated the anguished master, 'you'll
gain a *very* unsavoury reputation if you carry on like
that.'

My attempts to keep out of the way of my housemaster, a deceptively hearty Low Church rugby football international (one cap, anyway) were not always successful.
'D'you know, Monty,' he snarled at me as I crept behind
his bald head, 'I don't think you're shy at all. You're just
bloody rude!' Sometimes these ushers can be strangely

perceptive, don't you know, I murmured to Sir John Julian as I sloped off to extra maths. ('At his best he is incredibly bad, at his worst unbelievable.')

My only protests against the prevailing philistinism were to affect vaguely aesthetic attire and to eschew, in the best Brigade of Guards manner, the silly school slang – such as 'eccer' for exercise and 'tosh' for bath. But, to my shame, I went along with the Harrovian consensus that anyone bad at games (including, of course, myself) was simply not worth bothering with. Thus I missed out on making friends with such amusing, if unathletic, contemporaries as the budding comedian and novelist Andrew Barrow, the actor Simon Williams, the film-maker Andrew Birkin and the architectural historian Gervase Jackson-Stops. The pop singer Michael d'Abo (later of Manfred Mann) was in an entirely different category: as a talented games player he was up there among the gods as an unapproachable hero. He spoke to me once, during a cricket game, when he asked to borrow my duffer's cap to keep the sun out of his eyes. Flustered, I refused with bad grace.

Quite unjustifiably, on the whim of a strangely sympathetic beak (who later shot himself), I had been plucked from obscurity to a place in the Colts XI. It was the only time in my Harrow days that my daydreams collided with reality: I actually went with the side to Eton and relished a 'Strawberry Mess' in 'Tap' (now Etonian slang is quite another matter). But I proved pitifully out of my depth in both cricketing and social terms and landed up in the aptly named Outcasts XI, only just obtaining my stripy house cap from the grudging school captain. After I had celebrated with a few flashy shots outside the off stump, this charmless individual shouted out for all to hear: 'That's the first time Monty's ever smiled!'

Someone who did make me smile at Harrow, and

became one of my heroes, was the wonderfully snobbish
and eccentric history beak Charles Lillingston, who
would regale us with tales from his friend Barbara
Cartland's dinner table and mercilessly tease his class-
room neighbour, a pompous young 'educationalist' called
John Rae (who later tried to become a television pundit,
though it was said that his head proved too large for
the screen). On one memorable occasion Lillingston kid-
napped Rae's emissary, who had been sent to ask the
next-door class to be less uproarious, and bundled him
into a cupboard. 'Where's my boy, Charles?' demanded
Rae, when he eventually deigned to enter the Lillingston
stronghold.

'Your *boy*, John?' returned Lillingston, as his glasses
made their customarily comical descent from his bald
pate to the bridge of his beaky nose.

Somehow, Charles Lillingston, an Old Etonian dandy
himself, seemed to understand. 'Monty,' he would
announce in class, 'has ended up among the peasantry by
some hideous mistake.' One high summer evening we
stood together on the balcony of Lord's pavilion at the
close of play after a representative public schools' match,
watching the dying sun catch the golden tresses of Rupert
Daniels – then, as indeed now, the epitome of the Etonian
schoolboy star – as he gently rolled the ball, as if he were
playing bowls, towards some pesky pigeons in the out-
field. 'There,' said Charles admiringly, 'you see the difference between Etonians and Harrovians: the Etonian
remains for ever young at heart.'

By now I had made the earliest possible exit from
Harrow (though I remained at Eton in my daydreams),
much to Winlaw's fury. 'I'll never forgive you for missing
your chance of playing at Lord's,' he fumed. But he
chivvied me into turning out for the Harrow Wanderers.
It was the usual nervous nightmare of wides, ducks and

dropped catches. ('The Field Marshal could have caught that, Monty.')

Apart, that is, from one magical day on a village field in Hampshire. 'Tiger', the truly heroic, one-eyed Nawab of Pataudi, playing for the Old Wykehamists, had thrashed us for 144 when he unexpectedly skyed a drive off my bowling. 'Catch it!' the skipper, Winlaw, shrieked at me. I backed away in shock, mumbling: *'Yours.'* Whereupon Winlaw did the decent thing and threw himself forward, barking his forearms on the shaved pitch in making the catch. The Star of India was a princely scalp in which even Sir John Julian could take pride.

THREE

Standing By the Last

'YOU GO AND stand by the last, Hughie,' said my uncle Joe from underneath his jaunty pork-pie hat, as his alert, friendly eyes darted towards the sturdy birch hedge in the run-in at Wincanton Racecourse. 'I'll see you later,' he added before his tweeded figure vanished into the buzzing throng of ruddy-faced West Countrymen congregating around the bookmakers' boards. Although usually ill at ease and nervous in crowds, I soon overcame my fear of the general loudness, punctuated by urgent yells of the odds – 'Six-to-four the field' – and a strange, unfamiliar sensation of excitement flickered inside my head. It was the autumn half-term of 1954 and my first day at the races.

Purposefully I made my way through the scrum of punters – 'All right, sonny?' – down to the running rail beside the last fence of the steeplechase course, where I found my aunt Daisy, well wrapped up against the wind that whipped across the centre of the track above the Somerset marshes. 'Go on,' she said in her warm tones, 'get right to the front for a good view.' I insinuated myself as close to the side of the fence as I could – no safety barrier in those rugged days – so that I was virtually nuzzling the twigs of the birch.

Then, after a long wait, a pulsating vibration communicated itself to me. It was the thundering of hooves approaching the fence on the first circuit of the race. In a terrifying flash, the space immediately above my head was suddenly filled with an indistinguishable mass of giant horseflesh, flying horseshoes, gleaming boots, brightly coloured jerseys and caps, whirling whips and faces creased in concentration. The noise was overwhelming. The wooden frame of the fence banged with a loud report and cracked alarmingly; the birch buckled and flew; the whips cracked; and the frantic cries of the jockeys (*'Steady!' 'Go-aww-rrn!'* 'Stupid bugger') mingled with the exhortations of the crowd (*'C'mon*, my son!').

I stood in shock, unable to move, as the field galloped away on their second circuit of the course. It was as if I had positioned myself in the path of the Charge of the Light Brigade (which, as I had been assured by my friends at Crosfields, had 'got stuck in the marmalade'). The spectacle, so brief as to seem an illusion, had knocked me for six – a phrase I had picked up from watching my namesake 'Monty', the garrulous Field Marshal, on television. This, I thought, must be what war is like.

And then, as if in confirmation of these musings, another long, long wait before the final flurry of action as the fence – from which, to the amusement of my aunt, I was now keeping a respectful distance – came into its own as 'The Last'. By now, the jockeys' faces, the new focus of my rapt attention, were wild-eyed with determination and their whips were up. Their shouts were lost in the full-throated roar of the crowd. As the field, reduced to a ragged, and in some cases riderless, procession, raced away from us towards the winning post, I knew that I had experienced the thrill of a lifetime.

'Well,' said Uncle Joe, when we finally caught up with him beside the unsaddling enclosure. 'What about *that*, eh, Hughie? Want to come racing again, my son?' Sensing that this was not a moment to complain of the boredom attendant upon the yawning gaps between the races, slowly filled by the long drawn-out progress between paddock, bar and grandstand, I blurted out: 'Yes – if I can always be standing by the last.'

'That's the best place to be, all right,' said Uncle Joe, who had ridden in point-to-points himself in his younger days. Of solid Somerset farming stock, Joe Dinham was a passionate racing man and punter. When the gambling was going well – and he once proudly confessed that his *coups* had put his stepson, J. J. B. Rowe, my boyhood hero-cousin, through Winchester, where he was in the Cricket XI with 'Tiger' Pataudi – he even ran to owning a few racehorses in training. For some reason they all had names beginning with the letter 'Z' – Zivai, Zaytor, and so forth – and the Dinham colours were registered under the name of my aunt Daisy. Paintings of these revered animals, coats glistening, jockeys 'up', hung prominently on the walls of their comfortable stone farmhouse, Catcrow, near Somerton, which became the beloved holiday home-from-home of myself and my siblings.

The atmosphere there was distinctly different from the rather buttoned-up, po-faced and puritanical ethos which pertained at RCC. Words such as 'bum' and 'fart', never uttered at Rondels, would be common parlance at Catcrow. Aunt Daisy was my mother's youngest sister – known to my mother alone as 'Hermione' – and something of a rebel, who had studied at the Slade School of Art. She had met Joe Dinham during the Second World War when, as the estranged wife of a London stockbroker, she was staying in Somerton with her sister Daphne ('Aunt Daffa'), stationed nearby with the WRNS.

Much to my youthful embarrassment, Aunt Daisy and Uncle Joe slept in the nude (the bedroom door remained open) and would wander about in this state. They also had the distressing habit of openly 'grunting' (as they put it) on the lavatory in the bathroom while I was attempting to attend to my ablutions at the basin. Blushing furiously,

I would avoid eye contact. My shyness and self-consciousness was evidently out of place. I paid excruciatingly for
my prissiness one day on the beach down at Beer, across
the Devon border, when Uncle Joe spotted some modest
skid marks on my underpants which were airing among
the pebbles while I bathed. On my return from the sea, I
was regaled with a rousing chorus of *'Hughie's grunted in
his pants, doo-dah, doo-dah . . .'*

Mortified, confused and indignant, I submerged into a
long sulk. Only one of Uncle Joe's *'Zummerset'* stories on
the way back managed to break through my escapist
daydreams of faraway cricket matches. He recounted the
occasion when a farm labourer called Alfred Hartigan was
up before the beak. 'Your name?' enquired the magistrate.

'Alf 'Artigan, Your Honour.'

'What?'

'Alf-artigan, sir.'

'Good God, man, if you do, I'll clear the court.'

It was the funniest thing I had ever heard. Tears of
joy replaced the tears of shame I had been too pent-up to
shed earlier.

Laughter and doubtless good-natured fun were the
constant themes *chez* Dinham. Although most of the time
I felt like an alien in this relentlessly hearty household,
the raffishness of Uncle Joe's racing chums intrigued my
imagination. The dashing figures who came to stay with
the Dinhams in the late summer when the West Country
became the centre of National Hunt racing assumed a
heroic status – especially the trainer Captain Ryan Price,
a harsh-voiced ex-Commando who wore his trilby at a
rakish angle, and his stalwart jockey, the great Fred
Winter, a tightly coiled bundle of superhuman energy
who reminded me of Mr Punch in appearance. There was
also a colourful character called Stuart Pattemore, a
portly, fairish man who sold antiques in Somerton to

support his racing habit, as well as a full supporting cast
of jovial men of the Turf.

As an awkward boy, I thought that these glamorous,
confident grown-ups for ever cracking jokes and guffawing
helplessly somehow had the secret of enjoying life to the
full, one which seemed most unlikely ever to be vouchsafed to me. Off we would pile to the West Country tracks
– Wincanton, Taunton under the Quantocks, Haldon
('Devon & Exeter', as it was billed) high on its dramatic
hill, little Newton Abbot ('bit of a dog track, old boy') and
dear old Buckfastleigh, which then still held convivial
meetings under 'Rules'. A hectic dash across country –
'There goes Stuart in his Jag: he doesn't want to miss the
first' – would be followed by the traditional rounds of bar,
paddock, bar, grandstand, unsaddling enclosure, bar and
the no less traditional obloquy heaped on the hapless
stewards before the advent of the photo-finish camera and
the security video.

Mummerset mumblings about the unspotted 'bumping and boring around the bend' and how 'the blind judge
must have backed the second' would reverberate in my
ears as I headed off 'into the country' to stand by the last
or watch the start of the next race. My fantasies had by
now firmly fixed on the jockeys, those heroes who risked
life and limb in every race. Watching them intently as
they milled around at the start, I was struck by how
cheerful and smiling they invariably appeared. I learned
that the pre-race ritual was for them to trot up to the first
obstacle in order to show their mounts what they were
about to jump. I would loiter near the fence and eavesdrop
on the jockeys' badinage while the horses stuck their
heads over the jump, ears as eagerly pricked as my own.

'Your fellah's looking as big as my missus.'

'Now, lads, let's take it really steady first time round.'

'I'll take the inner, OK, and you make the running.'

This type of 'horse-trading' as to the plan of the race never seemed to have the slightest influence on the way it turned out, but it was all part of the routine. Gradually, I began to identify the jockeys' weatherbeaten features under their helmets – Johnny Gilbert, the hurdles specialist, whose wizened walnut of a face made him look like an old man; the sturdy Michael Scudamore (Peter's father); the wise-cracking Molony brothers, Pat and Tim; and Uncle Joe's legendary friend Fred Winter. Towards the end of the 1950s, when I was at Port Regis, not far from Wincanton, a boisterous blond teenager called Terry Biddlecombe particularly caught my eye. His ebullient manner and wide West Country grin came to epitomize National Hunt racing for me. 'Go on, Terry!' I would pipe up enthusiastically as he mixed sympathetic horsemanship with driving jockeyship – a rare combination – around my favourite Somerset course.

In between race meetings I would while away the long afternoons on Uncle Joe's farm by crouching astride bales of hay pretending to be old Fred or young Terry in a desperate finish. A stick would be put into vigorous service as a flourishing whip while I urged my mount home by a short head or a neck. Sometimes my half-brother Roger, already a budding agriculturalist who would eventually join Uncle Joe in a farming partnership, would break off from his milking or harvesting chores to disturb these daydreams. Thereafter he would imitate the fevered whip-waving he had witnessed whenever he was encouraging me to get a move on. Roger was also a keen student of form and drew my attention to the outstandingly smooth and stylish riding style of another jockey, Johnny Haine, who had begun his career on the Flat.

Style, dash, insouciance – these were the cavalier qualities I so admired in my heroes. At Port Regis I may have belonged biologically to the 'Cavaliers' (as the

uncircumcized boys were called) but I know that temper-
amentally, despite all my yearnings to the contrary, I was
stuck with a Roundhead manner. As snobbery seeped into
my system, growing ever more intense at Harrow, I
switched my daydreams from the tough existence of the
professional jockey to the more pampered life of the
gentleman-rider, as amateur jockeys used to be called.

Like my cricketing alter ego Sir John Julian Bruce,
Bt, my idealized hero was a baronet – Sir William Pigott-
Brown, who became champion amateur. In person, as I
discovered when I stalked him from the weighing room at
Wincanton, Sir William turned out to be a somewhat
unprepossessing, reddish man already showing signs of
chubbiness. Nor could I summon up much romantic
passion for his two aristocratic rivals, the Honourable
('Mr' on the race cards, quite properly) John Lawrence
(later Lord Oaksey), who wrote so eloquently about the
joys of jump-racing in the *Daily Telegraph*, and the
indomitable Mr Gay Kindersley. But the dapper Mr Nick
Gaselee exuded elegance and, ever a sucker for a card, I
was fascinated by the suave appearance at Wincanton of
Mr Michael Caborn-Waterfield, celebrated in the gossip
columns as the playboy 'Dandy Kim'.

Probably the nearest I ever came to a flesh-and-blood
ideal was Mr Edward Underdown, to whom A. S. R.
introduced me at a cricket match. Not only was the
courteous and charming 'Teddy' a gentleman-rider
(mainly on the Flat, alas) but a gentleman-actor with
ageing matinee idol looks. It was a magical combination
to fuel my fantasies.

Sir John Julian Bruce, Bt, suddenly found himself
required to ride in hunter chases on his way to a standing
ovation at the theatre. Elaborate timetables were worked
out on paper enabling my alter ego to be whisked from
Wincanton to the West End in time for curtain up. My

parents' Chesterfield sofa at Cookham began to creak from the frenetic if, I hoped, stylish 'riding' and beating to which it was regularly subjected by the fearless Baronet.

At Harrow there was actually a real-life 'Racing Baronet', Sir Mark Prescott (subsequently an indifferent amateur jockey but later a successful Newmarket trainer), among my acquaintance, but I was far too withdrawn, and my passionate Turf daydreams too deeply concealed, to strike up a friendship. Mark, a toothy, chatty enthusiast for the racing results in the evening paper perused at the tuck shop, was a particular chum of my housemate James Walker, whose family had a stud in Sussex and with whom I mildly indulged in a betting syndicate through the junior racquets 'pro'. Our greatest coup was in the Grand National of 1962 when my selection, Kilmore – trained by Ryan Price and heroically ridden by Fred Winter – obliged at gratifyingly long odds. 'Monty – you've made us rich,' exclaimed Walker, an engaging sybarite (later to be killed in a car crash). The excitement of that win, and the sensual, guilty pleasure of handling cash that I had done nothing to earn, afforded me a glimpse of Shangri-La.

Unfortunately my unaccustomed cheerfulness aroused the suspicions of an officious older boy in our house, but I was able to put him off the scent by resuming my morose demeanour. 'Somebody told me you had been keeping a book on the horses, Monty,' he announced portentously, 'but I wouldn't believe that your still waters could run that deep.' Today, I learn, he is a judge.

My own 'career' in the Law after leaving school came to grief at an early obstacle: the Land Law examinations. The racing results during three dreary years stuck in a solicitors' office in Lincoln's Inn proved one of the few distractions. Fortunately, the gnarled old messengers in the post room, where I spent much of my time, were all dedicated punters. One of them, equipped with a suitably equine set of teeth, claimed to have been apprenticed on the Flat. He tried to win me over to this code, but I would always persist in viewing the Flat as an uninspiring business tied up with bloodstock deals. The overpaid little jockeys on the level had no heroic glamour for me. Terry Biddlecombe – by now, according to the absurd sporting lingo, 'in his pomp' and ridiculously dubbed 'the Blond Beatle' – together with his friend and rival Josh Gifford were my pin-ups. Literally so, as their pictures were displayed in my bedroom at Cookham from where I commuted daily to my prematurely middle-aged employment in Lincoln's Inn.

At weekends I would often tag along to race meetings with A. S. R. who, like Roger, had also been infected with the Turf bug by Uncle Joe. A. S. R. was attending in an official capacity as, in the mid-1960s, he switched from games journalism to becoming a handicapper with the Jockey Club. In the traditional manner of a besotted fan I would hang around the weighing room and the unsaddling enclosure soaking up the aura of my idols. I never dared to ask for autographs, or presumed to buttonhole them – despite my uncle Joe's assurance that 'good old Terry has a smile and a word for everyone on the course'. The ample opportunities that racecourses afford for uncomplicated people-watching are unrivalled. You can settle down to a stare safe in the excuse that you are 'studying form'.

Never quite at home on the bigger, fashionable courses, I delighted in discovering the charms of the lesser-known tracks, such as Stratford, Worcester, Windsor (eccentrically ramshackle with a bewildering figure-of-eight course no longer, alas, used for jumping),

Towcester (on the Northamptonshire estate of the motor-racing peer Lord Hesketh, 'Mr Toad' in person), Wetherby and my co-favourite (with Wincanton), the cheerily intimate Market Rasen, on the edge of the Lincolnshire Wolds. It was at Rasen in 1967 that I enjoyed my biggest success as a punter with a fluke bet on a 33–1 outsider that paid 120–1 on the Tote, or the 'Nanny Goat' as it is known. Such a freakishly generous return convinced me that my preference for the kindly matrons in red uniforms behind the Tote windows over the crude and frightening bookies with their boards had some merit, after all – notwithstanding Roger's sneers at my spinsterishness. The dozen 'brown ones' pushed through the aperture by my 'Nanny' benefactress that winter afternoon at Rasen seemed untold riches. After racing I went on to evensong in Lincoln Cathedral to give thanks.

My regard for Terry Biddlecombe redoubled as the mange began to show on the ageing lion. His courage in the saddle, as he battled against increasing weight and injury, and his cheerfulness were inspiring. As Peter O'Sullevan observed in his television commentary after the jockey, controversially seeking better ground on the stands-side of the run-in to the Grand National, just failed to 'get up' on Gay Trip: 'You can't wipe the smile off Terry's face.' For my part, I was in tears. The combination of vulnerability and devil-may-care were irresistible.

With Biddlecombe there was always the possibility that he might still pull something spectacular out of the fire which many thought was extinguished. The last time I saw him in action, at Sandown, he treated his fans to a vintage ride on a horse called Potentate. From a long way out, down the closely bunched 'Railway Fences' on the other side of the park, Potentate looked beaten, but Terry Biddlecombe could be seen (and indeed heard) urging the horse on with dynamic force. As Potentate stormed up the hill to win, the cheers confirmed my hero's mythological status.

Such was my admiration for the professional jockeys, and the way they would ride often unfamiliar mounts five or six times an afternoon at 30mph over stiff fences for derisory amounts of money and then emerge, even after the inevitable crushing falls, in good spirits, that I was happy once more to believe in my daydreams I might be a pro myself. On Biddlecombe's retirement, I transferred my affections to his then brother-in-law, Bob Davies, a highly efficient and underrated rider with a studious look. He had a degree, something of a rarity for a professional jockey, which suited my particular fantasy of a gent beating the pros at their own game.

Later, I latched on to three characters more in the extrovert Biddlecombe mould – Jonjo O'Neill, the ginger-haired Irishman whose astonishing fightback on Dawn Run to complete the Champion Hurdle/Gold Cup double provided the biggest Cheltenham thrill of all; 'Gypsy Johnny' Francome, the tousle-haired Swindon lad for whom my beloved Biddo, herself a Swindon girl, also had a soft spot; and the rumbustious Steve Smith-Eccles, cavalier offspring of a northern miner. Latterly I nurtured a faithful, and frequently expensive, devotion for another northerner, Graham Bradley, a supremely stylish and cheeky rider whose chequered career and occasional brushes with authority only added to his appeal. His dramatic retirement, live on television after riding a winner at Haydock Park, when he took off his crash helmet and threw it into the crowd like a true showman, moistened my eye.

When I drifted into publishing and journalism the occasional opportunity arose for me to meet some of my jockey heroes in the flesh. I chatted briefly to the charming and exceptionally bright John Francome at a hacks' cricket match near Lambourn; he had retired with his good looks and youthful personality still intact. There was some suggestion that I might write a profile of Steve Smith-Eccles but, when it came to the crunch, I preferred to admire him from afar – or indeed from behind a tree at Sandown while my young son, Luke, having been appropriately bribed, asked the dashing ladies' man jockey for his autograph.

Back in the late 1970s, on hearing that Terry Biddlecombe, like so many ex-jockeys, was slightly down on his luck, I put together a publishing proposal for an authorized biography. The answer came back from the great man, who had apparently had a few, that he would expect 'ten grand minimum'. Later he took to the bottle in a bad way and disappeared Down Under. Wincanton, to my disgust, scrapped the Terry Biddlecombe Trophy and renamed the race after Desert Orchid. Yet the story has a happy ending: Biddlecombe bounced back, sober but cheery as ever, and married the trainer, Henrietta Knight, forming a fine partnership. It seems a shame, though, that she is still listed as Miss Knight on the racecards rather than Mrs T. W. Biddlecombe. I still stalk the now portly middle-aged gentleman around racecourses, and my admiration for him has not faded.

Over the years I have added numerous 'obscure' courses – 'gaff tracks', as the jocks call them – to my Turf trainspotter's portfolio, including the standless Bangor-on-Dee; Ludlow (so evocatively portrayed in the novels of Simon Raven); and the pocket-handkerchief Cartmel, on the Cavendish estate of Holker in North Lancashire. But Wincanton and Market Rasen have stayed the course as my special favourites, so much so that I briefly lived within easy reach of them. The sheer escapist pleasure of losing oneself, forgetting all worries and cares, in a day at the races cannot be overestimated.

Stuck in London, scratching a living in Grub Street, I frequently fantasized about becoming a professional punter who would peregrinate around the National Hunt racecourses of Britain, following that curious caravan of officials, vets, owners, trainers, jockeys, valets, bookmakers, stable lads and assorted hangers-on which form the Turf community in transit. To be anonymous, yet surrounded by familiar faces and stimulating sport – what could be more fun? Yet, as A. S. R., the racing professional, has pointed out: a hobby is one thing, a way of life quite another.

One afternoon in London in the late 1970s, slumped in a Soho pub after a 'misunderstanding' with a magazine over a vaguely briefed piece, I heard myself confiding in my neighbour, the boulevardier Ian Dunlop: 'I know where I would rather be today – Wincanton.' I had a sylvan vision of the horses silhouetted against the Somerset skyline on the back straight, which is partially obscured by an old barn.

'Ah,' responded Dunlop in sympathy. '*Wincanton!* Now there's a Republic of Friends.'

Not a day has gone by since that life-affirming moment without my wishing to be 'researching in the country', or in other words standing by the last at some far-flung National Hunt course. Sometimes I have been happily reunited with Uncle Joe and the Winlaw brothers at Haldon or Taunton. Joe Dinham has continued to joust and josh with the West Country bookies into his late eighties and still has the odd 'leg or tail' in racehorse-owning partnerships. At one stage, during a losing streak in the 1960s, he decided to follow the poacher-turned-gamekeeper path and become a turf accountant himself

in partnership with an amusing old rake called Rupert
Incledon-Webber, who went down with the cruise ship
Lakonia. 'Honest Joe' was popular with the local punters
at Millfield School, but too often bet against himself –
with disastrous results.

Aunt Daisy suffered a stroke in the 1980s, but spoke
highly of the viewing platforms provided for disabled
racegoers at the West Country tracks. When I was reminiscing to her not long before her death about the luscious
cream (and butter) we used to enjoy straight from the
Guernsey cows on the farm, she muttered poignantly:
'That's probably why I'm in this wheelchair now.'

Yet – aside from such occasions when I was sent to
bed for overdosing on blackberries and consequently failing to do justice to Aunt Daisy's steak and kidney pudding
– I have happy memories of my childhood stays in Somerset. The Dinhams demonstrated that life could be enjoyable and, above all, showed me to a well from which I
could continue to draw draughts of fantasy, fun and frolics
to the end of my days: the tonic of the Turf.

Without their example, I would not have savoured the
joyous experience of backing a couple of lucrative outsiders one afternoon at Wincanton in the early 1990s while
assorted aficionados, such as Geoffrey Wheatcroft and
Simon Courtauld, not to mention the late Sir Tobias
Rodgers, Bt, an antiquarian bookseller, looked on in
appalled amazement. 'Ludicrous fellah, that Massingberd,' observed one of my fellow fogeys, sucking his silver
pencil.

Nor would I have been able to relish a glorious victory
by Graham Bradley at Market Rasen on another extreme
long shot. 'You must be the only person who backed it,'
the Yorkshireman quipped as he acknowledged the fer-
vent cheers from my children and myself in the unsaddling enclosure afterwards. I then pressed my teenaged

daughter – another bribe – into accosting 'Brad' for his autograph. She made the approach.

'Come on, Bradley, take that fag out of your mouth in the presence of a pretty young lady,' admonished the chirpy Clerk of the Course, Major 'Charlie' Moore, as I listened in, agog.

'You rode brilliantly,' gushed my daughter, flashing her teeth and flicking her mane of hair as scripted by me.

'Ta, luv,' said the great man, grinning lasciviously.

Of such vignettes are daydreams made.

'He's very attractive, isn't he?' remarked my daughter on her return to the Tote window for the four-figure payout. This gave me pause for a moment. But I recovered enough to mumble: 'This wad is even more so.'

My attempts to foster a love of racing in my children cannot be said to have borne much fruit. They, too, found the gaps between the races boring. By contrast, when I go racing now so intense is my desire to drink in all the romance, colour and atmosphere that these intervals seem terribly brief. Sometimes it is a struggle to secure in time my cherished post standing by the last.

FOUR

Lots of Lords and Ladies

'JUST TO THINK,' mused Roger as we fished for pike in the middle of the deep, mysterious lake at Blessing-bourne in County Tyrone one sultry afternoon during the summer of 1959, 'one day all this will be yours.'

In fact, I had been so wrapped up in my daydreams about cricketers and jockeys that I had never thought of such a contingency. The sudden realization that Roger's novelettish cliché could be true crashed through my sand-castle fantasy like a tidal swell. Flushed with excitement, embarrassment and confusion, I stammered: 'Oh, I don't know about that.'

'Yes,' insisted Roger. 'You'll be the Master of Blessing-bourne all right.' He pointed out that my bachelor uncle Peter, with whom we were spending the summer holi-days, would eventually be succeeded in the estate by my father and then it would be my turn. The glow of pleasure that suffused my face as this startling intelligence sank in could not be disguised. 'Gosh,' said Roger. 'You are actually smiling for once.'

I gazed up from the lake at the romantic, pseudo-Elizabethan pile, built by my great-grandfather in the 1870s, with an overwhelming proprietorial pride. Although I had been to Blessingbourne before, as a child, this was the first time that I really took it all in: the grey stone relieved by reddish creeper; the finialled gables, curved and scrolled pediments, mullioned windows; and the swaggering coat-of-arms, fleurs-de-lis and rings, crested by an armoured hand grasping a sword and adorned with the motto *Honneur Sans Repos*. This was heady stuff for a shy little boy from the suburbs.

My earliest memories of the place flickered into focus. It was a winter evening in the late 1940s and I was lying in a darkened, peat-scented bedroom with the measles. Paddy, the gentle, kindly and largely silent butler, came in to cheer 'Master Hughie' up by showing me a brace of pheasants he had shot. The son of the gamekeeper on the estate, Paddy was prone to interrupt serving the potatoes in the William Morris-papered dining room by popping out and potting birds he had spotted through the great picture windows. I could remember the exotic colouring of the pheasants glowing in the half light.

Another fragment of memory from that first childhood visit to Blessingbourne was the presence – no more than that – of my grandfather in a dark, double-breasted suit coming down the wide wooden staircase, presumably on his way to Belfast for a meeting of the Irish Association, which he had founded to bring North and South closer together socially, culturally, economically, but not, of course, politically. 'The General', as he was known, had retired from the Army as a major general in the 1920s to devote himself to fighting bigotry in Northern Ireland through such schemes as Boy Scouts drawn from both Protestant and Roman Catholic communities. Similarly his own father, a senior senator at Stormont, had built one of Ulster's first interdenominational schools on the Blessingbourne estate.

After Roger's revelation, the family history took on a new interest for me. Much to the surprise of my father – who tended to remain rather detached from everyday affairs thanks to his employment of waxed earplugs – I pumped him for information. Two items that particularly

intrigued me were the news that some of the Montgo-
merys had been to Eton and that my great-grandfather
had been offered a baronetcy. Perhaps, I tried to convince
myself, my daydreams were not so far removed from
reality after all.

'But, Dadda,' I protested shrilly. 'Why on earth did he
turn the title down?'

'Well, erm, that's a bit awkward, really,' mumbled my
father. 'You see the problem was, when the offer came, he
had only just heard that his eldest grandson – your uncle
Hugh – had become a Catholic.'

'Surely he was a liberal, as you explained, in favour of
fair treatment for the "left-footers"?'

'Ah, yes, indeed he was. But he felt that once it was
known his eventual heir was *a Catholic* his public pleas
for toleration would be compromised. Do you understand?'

'I still don't see why he couldn't have become a baronet. It seems a rotten swiz to me.'

Although I failed to grasp the labyrinthine com-
plexities of Northern Irish politico-religious dialectics at
the age of twelve, the dynastic repercussions of my great-
grandfather's quixotic refusal became painfully clear to
me as I perused *The Landed Gentry of Ireland* in the snug
library at Blessingbourne, with its Morris paper and
chimneypiece niches for logs and peat. Like Sir Walter
Elliot in *Persuasion*, I found that 'the page at which the
favourite volume always opened' was for my own genealogy – *Montgomery of Blessingbourne*.

And there, like Sir Walter, I found 'occupation for an
idle hour, and consolation for a distressed one'. Yet the
distress was caused by the bare bones of the narrative
pedigree set out before me: that if my great-grandfather
had accepted that blasted baronetcy it would have been
inherited first by my grandfather, then by my uncle Hugh

(who had left the Diplomatic Service to become a Catholic priest), then by my bachelor uncle Peter, then by my father – and then, of course, by me!

The only consolation that occurred to me was that Uncle Peter might be offered a baronetcy himself. Henceforth I decided to concentrate my fantasies upon this glamorous figure – he was to be my new hero. Surely he richly deserved a title? After all, he was the proprietor of Blessingbourne and its (to my eyes) vast estate stretching up to the surrounding mountains. He seemed to sit on many important committees to do with the arts, prisons and the National Trust – and he was always dashing off to Government House at Hillsborough to help entertain visiting royalty.

I listened eagerly to his anecdotes about the eccentric, not to say half-witted, Duke of Gloucester, or 'Uncle Potty' as he was known.

'So, your father was the Field Marshal,' barked the Duke when Uncle Peter was presented to him by the Governor of Northern Ireland, Lord Wakehurst. 'Knew him well.'

'Er, no, Sir,' ventured Uncle Peter.

'*Eh*? Don't tell me who I did or didn't know! Course I damn well knew the fellah.'

'I'm sorry, Sir, um – what I *meant* to say was that the Field Marshal was actually my *uncle*, not my father – who was only a general.'

'No, no, no,' countered the Duke. 'I'm not talking about that blighter Monty. I mean *Montgomery-Massingberd*. He was your father, dammit!'

'I'm afraid not, Sir . . .'

'What! Don't you know who your bloody father was, man?'

'If I could just explain, Your Royal Highness,' said Uncle Peter in his most charming manner. 'My father was called Major General Hugh Montgomery and his brother, my uncle, was Field Marshal Sir Archibald Montgomery-Massingberd.'

'Are you sure?'

'Yes, Sir. I'm so sorry.'

'Well, I'll be damned.' Then, turning on the Governor, the Duke roared: 'Wakehurst, you *bwiefed* me *wwong!*'

On another occasion at Government House, Uncle Peter, who was an honorary aide-de-camp to the Governor (a role he had earlier filled in India for the Viceroy, Field Marshal Earl Wavell), found himself escorting the Duke of Gloucester to the gentlemen's lavatories. His Royal Highness managed to break the chain in his cubicle, whereupon Uncle Peter – far from the most practical of men – climbed on the seat to investigate the cistern. He then slipped and fell into the bowl.

'You've *fallen in!*' shrieked the Duke in tones of hysteria. 'Fallen between two stools, you might say,' he sobbed as his laughter took on the timbre of a demented horse's whinny. '*Tee-hee-hee-hee-HEE! Tee-hee-hee-HEE-HEE-HEE!*'

Uncle Peter's repertoire of Gloucester stories also included the one of HRH spotting a lady-in-waiting engrossed in *Jane Eyre*. 'Oh yes, that one,' he enthused. 'Bloody funny, what?'

And then there was the time in the Second World War when a belly dancer who had been giving a royal command performance in a nightclub in Cairo joined the Duke at his table. Stuck for small talk, HRH eventually came out with the enquiry: 'Ever been to Tidworth?'

Although Uncle Peter himself had indeed been to Tidworth, the military settlement on Salisbury Plain where his father, a gunner, had been stationed for a spell, and was invariably referred to as 'the Cap'n' in the traditional Ulster manner, his natural leanings were towards the aesthetic rather than the military. While still an undergraduate at Cambridge, he had formed his own choral society in Fivemiletown on the family estate and he went on to conduct the BBC Northern Ireland Symphony Orchestra in Belfast and, as first president of the Northern Ireland Arts Council, to found the Ulster Orchestra.

When not studying *The Landed Gentry of Ireland* in the library at Blessingbourne, I would immerse myself in Uncle Peter's photograph albums in a room, overlooking the lake, known as the billiard room, though, to my disappointment, there was no billiard table in it. I particularly liked the album devoted to his days at Trinity, Cambridge, where as an evidently handsome undergraduate he dazzled the dons. The old Bloomsburyite 'Dadie' Rylands cast him alongside Michael Redgrave in Shakespeare plays, and among his most intimate friends was the young research fellow Anthony Blunt.

When the art historian was eventually unmasked as a Stalinist spy, what shocked my father even more than Blunt's treason was the 'revelation' of the nature of Uncle Peter's friendship with Blunt when up at Cambridge. As ignorant as my father on such matters, I frequently met Sir Anthony (as he then was) with Uncle Peter, whether at his club, Blunt's flat above the Courtauld Institute (in what is now the Home House Club in Portman Square) or at curious drinks parties – plenty of Oriental young men in attendance, as I recall – in Bayswater.

My most vivid memory of the usually rather chilly and forbidding Blunt was when I went round to the Courtauld one warm July evening in 1965 for a drink. Uncle Peter, who, as usual, was staying with his old friend when visiting London from Northern Ireland, had just returned, in full morning dress, from a garden party at Buckingham Palace. Sir Anthony cut a skeletal figure, clad in nothing but a skimpy pair of blue briefs.

'My dear,' he trilled. 'You find us at a disadvantage. Peter is absurdly *overdressed* and I, as you can see, am a little underdressed. Do have a glass of sherry.'

In my innocence, even then I still did not twig Uncle Peter's proclivities. The veil was finally ripped aside at a cricket match later in the 1960s. One of my team mates in a Butterflies match against the Eton XXII ('2nd XI' to those not steeped in the lingo of 'the old Light Blue', as 'The Eton Boating Song' has it), an amiable Etonian thespian turned motor-trade publisher, interrupted my reverie about the romance of the 'Wat'ry Glade' by saying: 'I've just realized you must be the nephew of my former brother-in-arms, Peter Montgomery. How is the old round-the-wicketer?'

'Erm . . . sorry, what do you mean exactly?'

'Oh dear, surely you *knew* he was homosexual.'

'Of course,' I lied unconvincingly, blushing uncontrollably.

My cricketing chum went on to explain how he and his fellow officer cadets had called Peter 'Uncle Monty' in the Army – or sometimes 'Marmalade Monty', on account of his answering the question as to why he wanted to be commissioned: 'Because I would like to have marmalade for breakfast.' Uncle Peter had apparently approached this Old Etonian cadet on suspicion that he was 'a bit prissy'. 'Frankie Howerd made the same mistake when we were in panto together in Liverpool after the war . . .' continued the former actor, by now in full anecdotage.

From this raconteur's monologue on Upper Club that afternoon Uncle Peter emerged as a camp, Cowardian figure. At Blessingbourne I was assured by this treader on dreams, Peter used to say that Paddy, the butler, was 'very understanding about finding strange young men in

the morning'. A more sympathetic story that rang truer
was the recollection of Peter coming down to breakfast
at Blessingbourne in his dressing gown at about 11 a.m.
to find his old Army friend and his family apparently
well installed in the dining room, though they had only
surfaced about quarter of an hour before.

'Ah,' Uncle Peter said, with exquisite theatrical
timing. '*Early birds.*'

I listened to these disclosures with a burning sense of
shame, for only a short while before I had been pouring
out my troubles to Uncle Peter over an uneasy work
relationship with a colleague.

'By the sound of it,' Uncle Peter had said in his gentle,
soft murmur, 'he isn't of the marrying kind, is he?'

'Good Lord, no,' I blurted out with the unthinking
callousness of youth. 'He's an obvious pansy.'

Sitting in the Upper Club pavilion, I could now envisage Uncle Peter's pained expression that evening in the
panelled hall at Blessingbourne. How could I have been
so crass and insensitive? I also felt I was somehow betray-
ing my erstwhile hero by allowing this friend to bang on
about the double life poor Peter had had to endure.

Certainly the 'straight' side of the Ulster public figure
had seemed convincing enough: Deputy Lieutenant, then
Vice-Lord-Lieutenant of the county, High Sheriff, magistrate – all duties carried off with consummate style. 'But
then,' as Uncle Peter used to say, 'unpaid jobs are awfully
easy to come by, aren't they?' Such were his good looks
and vague, absent-minded charm that several local dowagers, doubtless as innocent as my father and myself
regarding his sexuality, were plainly in pursuit of Uncle
Peter.

Back at Rondels I had been quite unused to any sort
of social life. Everything revolved around the family and
its athletic pursuits. Outsiders did not call for drinks (an

unheard of practice) or dinner. Cousins might come by for informal family lunches or high teas, but that was about the extent of any formal entertaining. Our annual holidays at Blessingbourne introduced me to an unfamiliar world of country-house parties and continual chit-chat for which I was hopelessly ill-equipped.

My mother also found Uncle Peter's relentlessly packed social calendar a constant strain. 'Do you live nearby?' was her unappreciated opening gambit to the local bigwig, Lady Brookeborough, formerly a pillar of the ATS and the wife of the Prime Minister of Northern Ireland (a firm believer in Walpole's maxim of 'Let sleeping dogs lie'). Sometimes the conversational burden could safely be left to another house guest, such as the hardy perennial Sir Steven Runciman, an old Trinity friend of Uncle Peter's. As Uncle Peter used to say behind his back, and sometimes to his face: 'You would never guess from Steven's scabrous stories that he had written so many scholarly – not to say, unreadable – tomes about the Crusades, and so forth.' Looking like an ancient Chinese mandarin, Sir Steven would deliver his party pieces with an elaborately feline diction; sometimes he seemed to be literally purring during the dramatic pauses. Most of his stories tended to involve royalty or cannibalism, frequently both.

The eminent Sir Steven's donnish appearance was a trap for the unwary. At one Blessingbourne dinner party Lady Brookeborough's obstreperous son John, a hearty horseman (later a minister at Stormont), set about teasing what he supposed to be Sir Steven's old-maidish tendencies with a series of schoolboyishly smutty stories. As Roger subsequently reported to me – I had been obliged to leave the table with the ladies owing to my tender years – Sir Steven had his revenge as the port passed round. Finally, during one peculiarly horrific and revolting yarn, doubtless impeccably sourced in the annals of ancient history, John Brooke was reduced to protest: 'I say, steady on, old boy. I'm as broad-minded as the next chap [a claim that might well be questioned by students of Ulster politics] but there is a *limit*, you know . . .'

What struck me forcibly about Uncle Peter's friends and neighbours was that they all appeared to have titles. Every estate in the vicinity could boast its own earl, viscount, baron or baronet. I was mightily impressed and one morning, with supreme suburban lack of sophist-ication, I scribbled on a picture postcard to a prep-school friend, the son of a doctor in Enfield, North London: 'Lots of lords and ladies here.'

The postcard was put on the copper salver in the hall for the outgoing post (my great-grandmother had been a pioneer in Arts & Crafts copper work), and I thought no more about it. Then my parents accosted me as I was transporting myself back to the days of the Raj in Uncle Peter's albums of his time as ADC to the Viceroy. (One evening as he was dressing for dinner at the Viceregal Lodge in Simla, he used to recall, a face popped up at the window and shouted: '*Quit India!*' In his usual mild way, Uncle Peter replied: 'I'm quitting it as soon as I can – in fact, I leave next week.')

'I'm sorry, Hughie,' began my father, 'but you really *can't* send this postcard.'

'Why not? I went to stay with the Simpsons in Enfield, you know, and they were very nice.'

'Of course,' said my mother. 'But you must write another out – *without* this bit about "Lots of lords and ladies".'

'What's wrong with that? It's true, isn't it? Why, we've met the Earls of Erne, Enniskillen, Belmore, the Duke of

Abercorn . . . Lord Robert Grosvenor – Uncle Peter said he's going to inherit the Dukedom of Westminster . . .'

'Shush, shush,' said my father. 'Oh dear, oh dear . . .'

My mother had to spell it out in her most patient, schoolmistressy voice: 'The point is, Hughie, that it is simply not done to mention such things. It looks silly and snobbish.'

'And think of the embarrassment it will cause at the Fivemiletown Post Office – not to mention the appalling impression it will make on poor Dr Simpson and his nice family in Enfield.'

The postcard was solemnly returned to me for revision. After lunch, I sneaked off through the woods circling the lake and popped it, unaltered, in the postbox by the church. I could not see what all the fuss was about.

At the time I had recently taken to reading P. G. Wodehouse, whose stories were chock-a-block with lords and ladies of a most comical variety, and the sighting of so many real-life specimens, many of them emulating the Master's depictions of aristocratic eccentricity, was like a dream come true. The old Duke of Abercorn, for example, a delightful old buffer, perfectly embodied my idea of the endearing Earl of Emsworth.

Several of Uncle Peter's neighbours seemed to have strayed from the pages of fiction. There was a redoubtable old bearded spinster, Florence Peebles, still insisting on travelling by pony and trap, who relished Uncle Peter's mischievous teasing. A running joke at Blessingbourne was that Miss Peebles would eat only beef. When, as usually happened, lamb was served up by Paddy, we would all dutifully chorus: 'Isn't this *beef* delicious, Miss Peebles?'

'Capital!' growled Miss Peebles through her luxuriant whiskers. 'There is nothing like beef . . .'

'And this *is* nothing like beef,' murmured Uncle Peter
sotto voce.

'. . . Nothing like beef,' continued Miss Peebles, who
was hard of hearing, 'to keep you young. I swear by it . . .'

'*Bloody* beef,' interjected Uncle Peter in a stage
whisper.

'. . . And will never eat anything else. Yes, Peter, this
is most *excellent* beef, the best I've ever tasted. Please
give my compliments to Mrs Coulter.'

'You can compliment her yourself, Florence,' said
Uncle Peter. 'You also wanted to find out the source of
her marvellous coffee, you may remember.'

Later, in the kitchen, the secret was vouchsafed. 'I jus'
boils it, ma'am,' shouted the worthy Mrs Coulter.

'Quite right!' pronounced Miss Peebles, before summoning her carriage.

It was not a pony and trap but a magnificent and
venerable Rolls-Royce, with expansive running boards,
which swept up to the front door of Blessingbourne one
afternoon, containing some singular guests for a memorable tea party. Emerging from the back, where he had
been swathed in fur rugs, was the chief among them, a
fantastic Edwardian figure in a broad fedora hat, an
elaborate three-piece suiting in white Donegal tweed and
dove-grey spats above crocodile boots.

'So *that's* where that tweed I wanted in Enniskillen
had all gone,' hissed my half-sister Juliet to my mother,
as we all stood in amazement at this apparition.

'May I present Mr Raymond Charles Savile de Mont-
morency Lecky-Browne-Lecky of Ecclesville,' announced
Uncle Peter. 'Or may we all call you "Tibby"?'

The heavily rouged face creased into a smile. 'Tibby,
naturally, my dears.'

Compared with their exotic leader, the eccentric
troupe accompanying Tibby were of decidedly dowdy

plumage. After tea, the musical entertainment began in the drawing room, with Uncle Peter at the piano. Two of the colourless old ladies warbled an excruciating duet of Irish folk songs.

'Rather *amateurish*, don't you think?' observed Tibby to no one in particular in a whisper that reverberated round the room.

Then another of the old ladies took the floor and, in a *coup de théâtre* that discomfited Tibby, flourished a tricorn hat which she proceeded to place on her wispy black-dyed locks. 'I am Miss Bonaparte Wyse,' she declared as she buried one hand in her blouse, 'and this poem celebrates the glory of my great kinsman, the Emperor Napoleon!' There then followed stanza after stanza of dreadful doggerel about the 'Rudolph of his Race' and his triumphant conquest of Europe. Miss Bonaparte Wyse's delivery was somewhat handicapped by the lack of teeth, and apparently even a roof, in her mouth. Unfortunately I happened to be sitting in her direct line of fire and was showered with her spittle.

'*Very amateurish*, I'm afraid,' simpered Tibby as Miss Bonaparte Wyse droned on, and on.

Finally, Tibby rose majestically, if unsteadily, to his feet and with a theatrical gesture that brooked no refusal, brought Miss Bonaparte Wyse's recital to an abrupt close. 'You have delighted us long enough,' he said, echoing Mr Bennet in *Pride and Prejudice*.

'And now, my dears,' he intoned. 'Just one song – and then we must regretfully take our leave.' Having displaced Uncle Peter at the piano, Tibby draped his bejewelled old hands elaborately across the keyboard and gave tongue to a high-pitched falsetto – a sound, doubtless, of eerie beauty but which reduced my twelve-year-old self to stuffing a handkerchief into my mouth to suppress a fit of howling guffaws.

Tibby, it transpired, had been a legendary female impersonator and the toast of Ascendancy amateur actors. After the Rolls-Royce bearing him and his supporting cast back across the mountains to Ecclesville had departed, Uncle Peter showed us a yellowing newspaper cutting in one of the albums. It was a review of a production of *The Second Mrs Tanqueray* by Sir Arthur Wing Pinero, in which Tibby had played the title role. 'Mr Lecky-Browne-Lecky,' noted the critic, 'queened it bravely . . .'

These heady impressions were being projected on an inchoate introvert, still largely wrapped up in reveries about cricket and racing. Yet as my fantasy world began to expand in the 1960s through immersion not only in the works of P. G. Wodehouse but those of Evelyn Waugh, Anthony Powell and John Betjeman, the romantic possibilities of Blessingbourne and the country-house life it offered increasingly preoccupied my imagination. If Blessingbourne was no Brideshead, at least it appeared to approximate to the loopily Gothic Hetton Abbey in *A Handful of Dust*. And I fell in love with it just as passionately as Tony Last did with Hetton in Evelyn Waugh's best novel. One day, I kept repeating to myself on our annual summer visits, all this will be mine . . .

Every time a new Honours List was published, I would scrutinize the names to see whether Uncle Peter had yet received the baronetcy he so manifestly deserved. I was not yet sufficiently well versed in correct form to realize that even if he was so honoured – an extremely unlikely event in view of his complete lack of involvement with politics – I would not have been 'in remainder' to the title, which would have died with him.

The trouble remained that while in my daydreams I cut a suave, dandified figure with insouciant charm, sparkling wit and effortless style, the reality was a blushing, self-conscious wimp and 'wet', as the prep-school slang put it. I read how John Betjeman in *Summoned by Bells* took his

> *First steps in learning how to be a guest,*
> *First wood-smoke scented luxury of life*
> *In the large ambience of a country house.*

But the painful truth is that I never did learn. Unlike Betjeman, I did not have the confidence (or, of course, the talent) to fit in with *la vie de château*. Betjeman, as his daughter Candida Lycett Green has pointed out, managed to do so 'by not pretending to be one of them but by playing up his middle-class background and making what he decided was its comedy into a virtue'.

For me, the middle-class elements of my background were something to suppress. As a schoolboy, I was relieved to find that Cyril Connolly's classic study of 'The Importance of Being Etonian', *Enemies of Promise*, shared my embarrassing obsession with class. I identified with the author to the extent that one of his parents was regarded as middle class, the other upper class on account of a landed Ascendancy pedigree. And I knew exactly what Connolly meant when he confessed to feeling 'middle class in England, aristocratic in Ireland'.

Or at least I hoped to feel that. Yet, going round with Uncle Peter to savour 'the large ambience of a country house', much as I longed to revel in its intoxicating, carelessly elegant, shabbily grand comfort, I would usually freeze into a ghastly parody of middle-class self-consciousness. I would become all pinched politeness and filled with terror of committing some shaming faux pas or social solecism. Once, while staying with Uncle Peter at the lavishly sybaritic Glenveagh Castle in County Donegal, a fairy-tale creation (in, as I was later to learn, more ways than one), our munificent host, the American art connoisseur Henry McIlhenny, asked what I would like to drink. Trying to sound grown-up, I said: 'A Bloody Mary, please.'

'Not before *dinner*, please,' said Mr McIlhenny. 'Far too *weighty*.'

Time and again, I would dodge once-in-a-lifetime opportunities of seeing squires and country houses in their heyday – such as, for instance, Sir Shane Leslie, Bt, the legendary saffron-kilted storyteller, at Glaslough, County Monaghan, or my father's old Trinity friend, Lord Talbot de Malahide, at Malahide Castle, County Dublin, then still the oldest inhabited castle in Ireland and boasting a great botanical garden. I would plead carsickness, but it was just sheer social funk. Instead, I scored imaginary centuries beside the lake, progressing to and from the terrace (Blessingbourne, I fancied, bore a certain resemblance to the pavilion at Lord's) with my bat held aloft.

Knowing my love of cricket, Uncle Peter kindly insinuated me one summer into a fancy-dress Georgian 'Match at Cricket' to be held at Castle Coole, the Belmores' serene Hellenic palace nearby, which was now in the care of the National Trust. I was appropriately kitted out in a vintage military uniform from the dressing-up trunk in the top-floor nursery at Blessingbourne, and felt the same rush of sensual excitement I had experienced when being made up to play Demetrius in *A Midsummer Night's Dream* at Port Regis. My pleasure was complete when Desmond Guinness, the mythically glamorous president of the Irish Georgian Society, greeted me with a compliment on my appearance when we arrived at Castle Coole.

'I say, what *wonderful* boots,' he said as I blushed under the gaze of his 'brilliant Mitford-blue eyes' (a phrase I had picked up from Godfrey Winn's gushing

profile of the architectural conservationist in Biddo's copy
of *Woman's Own*). 'Where *did* you find them? You're *so*
clever.'

I mumbled, inaudibly, that they were really only a
very ordinary pair of Chelsea boots I had bought in Baker
Street on the way back to school, but my dashing new
hero had imperceptibly moved on. I was assigned to the
'North of Ireland' XI, captained by Henry Clark, a genial
scion of a County Londonderry family who had been in
the Colonial Service before becoming MP for North
Antrim (later unseated by Ian Paisley). I was attempting
to make conversation with a long-haired gentleman called
Mr Forde of Seaforde ('Are you a poet?' 'No, a farmer'),
when he cut my gaucheries short: 'Do look – Mariga is
about to make her entrance.'

There, framed in the doorway, was the dramatic
vision of Princess Hermione Marie-Gabriella Petronella
Sophia Devota Florestine of Urach, otherwise the Honourable Mrs Desmond Guinness, with a towering wig and a
plunging décolletage. The assembled company gasped
appreciatively. 'Mr Montgomery,' she addressed me with
bewitching formality, and I was agog, eagerly hanging on
to such pronouncements as 'The Pakenhams – they have
left Ireland for reasons of *literature*, I believe.'

I swiftly signed up for the great conservationist cause
which Mariga and Desmond Guinness led with such inspirational elan. Within a few years they had transformed
the Irish gentry's traditional enthusiasm for point-to-
points into the joys of tramping off in pursuit of a ruinous
obelisk buried in the depths of a soggy field in County
Roscommon. The deputy president of the Irish Georgian
Society, I learned, was a dashing young scholar called the
Knight of Glin. What could be more romantic? The title
seemed to come from *Alice in Wonderland*. I had found a

new alter ego. I murmured the appellation under my
breath: 'The Knight of Glin . . . The Knight of Glin . . . of
Glin Castle.'

The 'Match at Cricket' soon degenerated into a
drunken fiasco, much to the disgust of the cricket-loving
local Bishop, a kindly soul with whom I had enjoyed
several earnest talks about the summer game. But I was
too carried away on a daydream of aristocratic Georgian
glamour to worry overmuch about the Laws being so
outrageously flouted by the berobed figure of Eoin 'the
Pope' O'Mahony, the umpire, who was liberally dispen-
sing claret from behind the stumps. By the time they
were drawn, I had shed not a few of my naive suburban
inhibitions.

'Well, what did you make of all that?' asked the tall
figure of Marcus McCausland (later to be murdered by
the IRA). 'Don't you feel absolutely *rogered*?'

I leered politely, not being quite sure what being
'rogered' meant. In a manner of speaking, I was soon to
find out.

Back from Blessingbourne in the dwarfish, jerry-built
bungalow we now called home, my father beckoned me
one morning into the cramped bedroom he shared with
my mother. On his desk were various papers, to which he
cast his eyes as he gave me the news.

'Er, Hughie, there has been a . . . well, *development*
about the future of Blessingbourne. As I think you know,
in the normal course of events it would pass on Uncle
Peter's death, which naturally will be a long time in the
future, to me – that is assuming I'm still alive – and then
on to you. Quite, yes, well . . . But unfortunately the farm
there is in a frightful mess. Uncle P., who is not of course
agriculturally minded, has had a series of hopeless farm
managers and something has to be done to put things
right, without delay. So it's been decided that your cousin

Rob, who is keen to get out of the Army and start farming anyway, should take on the running of Blessingbourne straight away – and become Uncle Peter's heir to the estate.'

'Oh,' I said, not quite comprehending what was going on. 'I thought Rob was going to live at Gunby.' This was my father's maternal family home in Lincolnshire which his uncle and aunt, Field Marshal Sir Archibald and Lady Montgomery-Massingberd (otherwise 'Uncle Archie' and 'Aunt Da') had made over to the National Trust during the Second World War when it was threatened with demolition to make way for an aerodrome.

'That *was* the plan, yes,' said my father patiently, 'but you see there's no land for Rob to farm up at Gunby. Everything now belongs to the National Trust.

'So what's going to happen at Gunby when Aunt Da dies?' I piped up, playing for time, not wanting to hear any more about the final game plan for the future of Blessingbourne.

'Well, when the time comes, *we're* going to live there.'

'But I've never even seen it,' I said impulsively.

'You will soon, I promise you. We'll go up and stay with Aunt Da.'

It was time to face up to the worst. 'And what about Blessingbourne, then?' I said, trying to remain calm and grown-up.

My father coughed nervously. 'Uncle Peter thought that you would not really be very keen on the farming side, which is so vital to keep Blessingbourne going, and that, in any event, the crisis needs to be dealt with urgently . . . So he thought the best course would be for Rob to get cracking as soon as possible – and the fairest solution would be for you and Rob, so to speak, to swap your birthrights.'

From my Scripture studies at school I vaguely recalled

something about birthrights and 'a mess of pottage', but thought it safer to let this pass. In fact, I was dumbstruck.

'I hope,' continued my father quickly, 'that this is not too painful a blow for you, as I know you like Blessing-bourne, as indeed I do – I was brought up there, after all. But everyone feels it is the only sensible, practical solution in the circumstances, and that it is all for the best. Actually, given the always volatile political situation in Northern Ireland, we might well be better off in Lincoln-shire when the time comes. Who knows? Anyway, I trust you understand.'

'Yes, Dadda,' I said automatically. My inner self was musing that it was unfortunate I had not been considered old enough to be included in the 'everyone' who had made this decision. That afternoon Sir John Julian scored a notably savage double century before going on to an evening race meeting where he booted home the winner of the last in spectacular style.

FIVE

Rather Above the Law

MY FIRST IMPRESSIONS of Gunby, on a chill September weekend in 1962, were not inspiring. Still in a sulk over my banishment from Blessingbourne (though that did not stop me from dreaming of my residence there), I was simply not prepared to like it. Having fallen passionately in love with the craggy romance of the Victorian pile beside the lakes and mountains of County Tyrone, how could I be expected to transfer my affections to the austere Puritan primness of this dreary doll's house in Lincolnshire, the pointlessly vast county dismissed by George III as 'all flats, fogs and fens'?

For a start, Gunby did not smell right. Having always fancied being a dog (an illuminated inscription in the dining room at Gunby bearing the legend 'The More I Know Men ... The More I Like Dogs' at least struck a chord), I set great store by scent. The smell of my prep school, for instance (unwashed boys, greasy bacon, disinfectant failing to disguise the sickly stench of sewage), was lodged in my nostrils with unhappy associations; the peaty perfume of Blessingbourne remained rich in nostalgia. Gunby seemed to have a whiff of death about it. (I learned later that the late-eighteenth-century diarist John Byng wrote of 'a most melancholy place; suicide in every room'.) I was ready to believe that it might indeed have a curse along the lines my father had explained on the way up in the train from King's Cross direct, eventually, to Firsby (in those pre-Beeching Cuts days).

'The story goes,' my father said as we crunched our British Railways crisps, 'that a Miss Massingberd eloped with a groom, a "buttoncap" as they were known, and her father, the Squire, chased after them. He shot the buttoncap who, with his dying breath, put a curse on the Massingberds and Gunby.'

'What was the curse?' I piped up. This was the first item of intelligence about our possible future home that had intrigued me.

'That,' intoned my father with unaccustomed relish, 'no Massingberd should ever succeed his father at Gunby.'

'Rather a complicated curse to come up with when you have a bullet lodged inside you,' commented my mother, who had recently taken up a teaching post helping backward readers ('remedial classes' they were soon to be called) at a secondary modern school in Marlow – where her pupils included Steven Redgrave, the Olympic oarsman.

'And did the curse come true, Dadda?' I asked, with a view to my own prospects of succession.

'Well,' he mused. 'Curiously enough it did, more or less. You see, the Massingberd baronetcy died out almost immediately—'

'I didn't know there was *another* baronetcy in the family,' I whined. To my acutely snobbish young mind, my ancestors seemed to have made a thorough hash of passing on to me the status I craved.

'Yes, actually it was originally created by Oliver Cromwell.'

'Cromwell? I thought he was against titles and so forth.'

'Not for his friends like the Massingberds, who were staunch Roundheads.'

'I would have been a Cavalier.' At my prep school, after all, I had belonged, not very convincingly, to the

non-circumcized Cavaliers as opposed to the circumcized
Roundheads (or 'Knobheads', as they were more vulgarly
known), though I had always carefully avoided the crude
competitive fights involving towel-flicking and fearless
exposure. Quoting *1066 And All That*, I said aloud:
'Wrong but Wromantic.'

'Right but Repulsive,' countered my mother.

'After the Restoration of Charles II,' continued my
father in uncharacteristically garrulous flow, 'the Massingberds managed, even though they had been had up
for High Treason under Charles I, to have the baronetcy
recreated. The Patent of Creation even claimed that they
had "maintained an inviolable allegiance to their lawfull
Sovereign".'

'So much for principle,' sniffed my mother, 'like the
Vicar of Bray.' I let go this allusion to the Thames-side
village where her elder sister, Daphne, lived with a medical man whose delight in serving as honorary medical
officer to the Household Brigade Polo Club at Smith's
Lawn was liable to be interrupted by harsh Guardee
drawls of '*Doctor!*', whereupon he had to hurry on to the
field bearing his black bag. He had his own daydreams of
grandeur; I had mine to pursue.

'Yet the baronetcy still died out?' It was vital to get
this point absolutely clear.

'Yes, I'm afraid so,' said my father. 'But then you've
got to remember it would never have come to us anyway.
Gunby kept on passing through the female line – and
each time the heiress's husband had to change his name
to Massingberd in order to keep the traditional association going.'

'So you really think there might be something in this
curse?' I persisted.

'Could be. There's still a field on the estate called
Buttoncap Lane.'

'Perhaps it has turned out to be a blessing rather than a curse,' chipped in my mother. 'Some strong women have inherited the place for generation after generation instead of weak men.'

'Aunt Da certainly comes into that category,' pondered my father of our hostess for the forthcoming weekend. 'And so did her mother – my grandmother – who was a pioneer feminist and the first woman county councillor. She was a fierce teetotaller and used to buy up pubs and turn them into temperance hostels, including the Massingberd Arms on the estate.'

'*What*, isn't there a pub called the Massingberd Arms any longer?' Gunby was proving a serious disappointment even before I had clapped eyes on the place.

'Not at Gunby, but there *is* one up in the Wolds at Ormsby where the Massingberd-Mundys, the branch of the family descended from Sir Drayner Massingberd, live.'

'*Sir Drayner*,' I mused aloud. 'That's more like it.' I had been reading *Lorna Doone*. Fantasies formed of quaffing flagons of cider (ale never attracted me), clad in Cavalier togs and surrounded by adoring tenantry in the Massingberd Arms. The beauty of daydreaming is that inconvenient facts can be tidily rearranged.

My reveries were interrupted by my mother, at her most beady.

'Didn't your grandmother,' she asked my father with mock-innocence, 'used to dress as a man?'

'I really don't think we need to go into that now, darling,' said my father, suddenly irritable. 'Besides, I'm feeling unaccountably unwell.'

'It must have been that *beer* you drank at the station,' my mother said in her most disapproving tone.

'Probably just indigestion,' my father ventured in a manner carefully coded to convey that he was fast approaching death's door.

'Perhaps it's the curse,' I volunteered helpfully.

'If it is,' snapped my father, by now thoroughly out of sorts, 'you'll never inherit Gunby anyway.'

Resuming my customary gloom, I murmured under my breath: 'I am not all that keen to do so.' My antipathy was far from overcome by the unwelcoming atmosphere about the place when we finally arrived. A bossy house-keeper earned my undying enmity with the greeting: 'Well now, Master Hughie, coming as you do from the suburbs, I don't expect you've ever stayed in such a large house before, have you?'

This person behaved as if it were she who was the proprietrix of Gunby in collaboration with the National Trust rather than the now blind, nonagenarian Aunt Da. Uncle Archie had died soon after I was born and Aunt Da was no longer the domineering chatelaine she had once been. Gunby struck me as an old lady's house. There was a stuffy air of stultification and gloom; a general sense of unopened, even shuttered windows, dust sheets and a somnolent sea of sage-green painted panels. The interior had evidently been done over in the 1920s when Aunt Da had come into Gunby following the death of her childless brother Stephen (the curse, of course) and not touched since. I had the feeling I had wandered on to the set of an Agatha Christie play in the local rep – an impression enhanced by the unfortunate way in which the original library had been run into the entrance hall to create a sort of hotel-style through-lounge.

Theatrical analogies also occurred to me when I was taken by the housekeeper the next morning (my father had been rushed to hospital during the night to have his appendix removed) to be presented to Aunt Da. 'HERE'S YOUR GREAT-NEPHEW HUGHIE COME TO SAY HELLO, LADY M.,' the housekeeper shouted with unnecessarily loud volume in the nearer ear of the old lady propped up in bed. (Surely she was not deaf as well as blind?) 'Go on! Cat got your tongue, Master Hughie?' the housekeeper hissed in my direction.

'You can leave us,' enunciated Aunt Da precisely, summoning up an echo of her former authority. She looked, and spoke, like a Dame of the Theatre. A scene from *Arsenic and Old Lace* (or 'Lace-Knick and Old Arse', as one of my school friends had called it) came to mind.

'Give me your hand, Hugh,' she commanded imperiously. At least it was a relief, as a teenager, not to be addressed as 'Hughie'. I placed my habitually sweaty palm in her cold, firm claw.

'I hope you haven't been *drinking*,' Aunt Da said archly. 'I can *always* tell, my dear, even if I am now as blind as a bat. My mother made us all sign the pledge, you know. No alcohol has ever passed my lips, I'm proud to say.' What a waste of the wine cellar I had spotted on my explorations of the basement, I thought, but could think of no suitable rejoinder.

Later, Aunt Da came down to 'luncheon', as she called it, in the dining room adorned with carved maxims such as 'Love Thyself Last' and 'There's a divinity that shapes our ends, / Rough-hew them how we will'. Standing startlingly erect, albeit with the help of sticks, Aunt Da seemed set on defying, or literally embodying, the former of these truisms. 'I trust that you have noticed my straightness, dear,' she trilled in her embarrasingly flirtatious manner. 'Only the other day, don't you know, I was *whistled at* by some American airmen who happened to be in the park here. Yes, they *whistled*, my dear. I had to go and remonstrate with their CO. "Colonel," I said, "will you kindly inform your men that I may look *eighteen* from the back but I am *eighty* at the front."'

I sat mute, blushing unseen. Fortunately no response seemed to be required as Aunt Da stressed the importance of good posture and elocution, before launching into reminiscences of her musical youth in the 1880s. As I had developed an allergy to what I dismissed as '*Hey-nonny-no*' (a big no-no) warbling, I am afraid I shut my ears to her gush about 'dear, sweet Sir Hubert [Parry] – he was up at Oxford, of course, with your, let me see, your *great*-grandfather . . . darling Gervase [Elwes], who actually decided to become a *professional* singer right here, in the music room at Gunby'; and, of course, 'dearest Cousin Ralph [Vaughan Williams], one of whose pieces is beautifully and so appropriately entitled *Happy Days at Gunby* . . .'

Looking back, I was the truly blind one at that table for not appreciating then that happiness and Gunby could indeed be linked. Instead, I drifted off into a daydream about emulating my Harrovian hero Michael d'Abo with his pop group A Band of Angels. Eventually Aunt Da, doubtless bemused by my lack of response and almost total inarticulacy (if the truth be told, I barely gave tongue at all until I was in my twenties, and then not very often), lapsed into silence. Her eyes tightly shut, she concentrated on vigorous mastication, as precise as her diction. The only sounds were the clicking of Aunt Da's false teeth and the ticking of the marquetry long-case clock ('by Matthew Bunce, circa 1690', I had noted in my trainspotterish way).

Afterwards I wandered aimlessly about the place, half hoping, half dreading that I might find the magic which had captivated me at Blessingbourne. But something was lacking. Life, I suppose. Gunby seemed stuck in a time warp. There was a picture of Winston Churchill (whom I had seen in the flesh on his last visits to Harrow) in the back hall, hung with the same unappealingly patterned paper which decorated some of the corridors in my house at school. These associations were off-putting, to say the

least. The walled gardens had the lifeless look of a muni-
cipal 'amenity'. The east wind whipped across the dank
parkland from the Fens (and, it seemed, the Urals).

Seeking warmth, I gravitated towards the kitchen,
with its coal-fired old Aga. This was unwise. Seeing her
quarry isolated (my mother was at my father's hospital
bedside), the housekeeper went in for the kill.

'I suppose you *know*, Master Hughie,' she began in
her conspiratorial manner, 'that you are not really the
true heir to Gunby?'

'Er, well, you see, my cousin Rob who *was* going to
come here when Aunt Da – I mean, Lady Montgomery-
Massingberd, um—'

'"Lady M.", I call her . . .'

'But now Rob's going to inherit Blessingbourne from
my uncle Peter, er, Captain Montgomery, and I'm, um,
well . . . I *believe* the idea is for my father to succeed to
Gunby.'

'Oh, no, that's not really right, you see. The rightful
heirs to Gunby are the Leith-Hay-Clarks.'

'Who?'

'Lady M.'s aunt, Miss Alice Langton, married a Mr
Percy Leith-Hay-Clark, and their issue, Mr Norman
Leith-Hay-Clark and Mrs Freda Massingberd-Campbell,
both still alive, are named as the ultimate beneficiaries in
the will of Lady M.'s mother, Mrs Massingberd, who died
in 1897.'

'I don't understand. Surely Mrs Massingberd wanted
Gunby to go to her own children?'

'*Three* of those children have already resided here, in
turn: Major Stephen Massingberd, Mrs Leonard Darwin
(who declined to change her name to Massingberd, and
then departed) and now Lady M. None of them had issue,
so upon her death Gunby Hall – or rather the right to live
there as a tenant of the National Trust for Places of

Historic Interest or Natural Beauty – will be vested in her cousins, the Leith-Hay-Clarks.'

'But, hold on, what about *my grandmother*, my father's mother – she was the second sister, in fact Aunt Da's – Lady M.'s – senior?' I was floundering out of my genealogical depth here, but I was damned if this busybody was going to put a spoke in my wheel of fortune.

'She was not mentioned in her mother's will.'

'*What?* Why on earth not?' My blood was up and I seemed to have discovered my tongue.

'I really couldn't venture an opinion. The terrible tragedy is that Mr Norman's two boys were both killed in the war – within a few months of each other,' the housekeeper said with a croak in her harsh voice. 'If they had lived, *your lot* would never have had a look-in!'

The tone was now of unrestrained hostility. An image of Judith Anderson as Mrs Danvers in the film of *Rebecca* flashed across my mind: was I the second Mrs de Winter?

I must have looked bewildered. 'If you don't believe me,' said the housekeeper, 'go and look at the memorial in the church! There it is in black and white: *the rightful heirs of Gunby*.'

'Notwithstanding their early demise,' she continued in her barrack-room legalese, 'the succession still rests with their father, Mr Norman Leith-Hay-Clark, and his sister. I can show you the documentation in order to make the position perfectly clear.'

'Er, no thank you very much. I believe someone is kindly going to take me to see my parents in Louth.'

'That will be Mansey. He's Lady M.'s chauffeur, you know – almost as blind as the old girl if you ask me and quite unfit to be behind the wheel. But never mind, Master Hughie: won't it be an experience for you being driven by a chauffeur!'

As the ancient Rover chugged out of the gates slap

into a hideous new roundabout on the main road to
Skegness (the geographical re-arrangement necessary for
any daydreaming in this direction would have to be
radical indeed), I thought I would be content never to
pass through them again. Gunby had become the stuff
of nightmares, with the housekeeper assuming a role
similar to the sneering voices heard by Gilbert Pinfold
in the novel by Evelyn Waugh which I was then reading.

I was not to know then that the high road across the
top of the Wolds, so erratically navigated by Mansey in
his alarmingly thick pebble-glasses, was to become my
favourite highway in the world, leading to the perfect
small market town of Louth, with its Georgian redbrick
and glorious church spire pointing like a finger to Heaven.
My mother, who had taken rooms in an uncompromisingly 'commercial' hotel, the Masons Arms in the
marketplace, was less enamoured of Louth's charms and
complained of the pub's alehouse pong. On one of our
perambulations about the town between hospital visits
we happened to pause outside a handsome eighteenth-
century building housing a firm of solicitors.

'Have you given any thought to your career, Hughie?'
asked my mother, as if on cue beside the gleaming brass
plaque with its promise (amply fulfilled in my own case)
of 'oaths' being sworn within.

'I want to be a writer, Mummy, you know that.' My
head was full of notions about becoming an amalgam of
P. G. Wodehouse and Evelyn Waugh. She forbore to ask
me the dread question fired at me by Sir Tyrone Guthrie,
one of Uncle Peter's more frightening neighbours in Ireland. After Uncle Peter had intimated to 'Tony' Guthrie
that I had literary longings, the lofty theatre director
barked at me: 'What have you written?'

'Erm, um . . . nothing really.'

'Well, you can't be a writer, then,' he snapped and strode away, as I turned scarlet with suppressed fury.

'But writing isn't a *profession*,' said my mother, for ever haunted by the Crash that had devastated her hitherto prosperous stock-jobber father in 1929. 'And if you were to end up living at Gunby, you would need to have an occupation. You are not a farmer, and in any event there isn't the land available – all the estate now belongs to the National Trust.'

'Yes, that's why Rob didn't want Gunby and preferred Blessingbourne. Sensible fellow.'

'You know Dadda really didn't have any choice in the matter.'

'Yes, Mater.'

'Now being a solicitor is a proper job that you could do from a place like Gunby. Such as here, for example,' she said, eyeing the plaque.

'Talking of solicitors,' I said in an attempt to steer the subject elsewhere, 'why was Dadda's mother cut out of her mother's will and excluded from the succession to Gunby?'

'I believe it was because her mother thought she was a sickly child and unlikely to survive. Of course, as it turned out she had six children, including Dadda, when she was well into her forties. Or it may have been because her mother thought she had married a Montgomery of Blessingbourne and so would not need to come into the reckoning of Gunby as her siblings would be bound to have children – which, in the event, none of them did.'

'It seems very rum to me.'

'If you were a solicitor you could sort out such muddles. But please don't go bothering Dadda in hospital with all these Leith-Hay-Clark machinations. It will only get him upset, and he needs to recuperate.'

Back at school, a year or so later, my parents paid me
an unexpected visit. Aunt Da had died – too soon for the
purposes of avoiding death duties – and the Leith-Hay-
Clarks, doubtless encouraged by the housekeeper, were
questioning the succession to the Gunby tenancy. My poor
father was faced with a dilemma: should he take it on,
change his name and move to Gunby, even though there
was not enough cash, with a view to taking some admin-
istrative job locally; or should he let his eccentric cousin
Norman, an inventor, have a free run in contravention of
Aunt Da's wishes. For when Gunby was given to the
National Trust in 1944, her sister Mary Montgomery's
children – save for my uncle Hugh, a Roman Catholic, but
including my father – had been formally restored to the
succession under an agreement, to which the Leith-Hay-
Clarks were party, that effectively superseded Mrs Massingberd's strange will.

My parents were asking for my views on the situation.
Did I envisage my own future at Gunby? At a stage in life
when I was increasingly keeping reality at bay with
fantasy – a process which continued to accelerate rather
than to decrease – I could not grasp the practicalities.
Sometimes my daydreams encompassed Gunby as a setting for my own pop music studio, private rehearsal
theatre, cricket ground or racing stables and stud; other
times it did not. A particular fantasy then prevalent was
of me as the Great Novelist, far from young (in fact more
or less Evelyn Waugh, born 1903), living in a luxury
retreat on a Caribbean island attired in stripy shirtings
and creamy linen trouserings. With such exotica filling
my mind – 'most of the time', as one of my school reports
accurately noted, 'it seems that Montgomery is somewhere far, far away in his own thoughts' – I failed to latch
on to the consequences involved in this conversation on a

cold winter's day 'on the top of Harrow Hill', as one of the school songs put it.

'Whatever you decide, Dadda,' I heard myself saying in the pompous manner of Little Lord Fauntleroy (it was tempting to substitute 'Pater' for Dadda), 'you can count on my full support and understanding.' As the whole saga appeared to have strayed out of a Victorian novel – country houses, contested wills, scheming servants, changes of names and coats of arms – I thought I should play my part with suitable gravitas.

In the event, my father played for time. Cousin Norman, a stringy, querulous old boffin who basically just enjoyed being a nuisance and making trouble, was to be given enough rope with which to hang himself. After months of mischief-making – during which he outlined such projects as turning Gunby into a theme park complete with a menagerie of Longleat-style creatures – it was the National Trust official he dealt with who seemed most likely to string himself up. The wretched man was reduced to a nervous breakdown. Having had his fun, Norman finally relented – though his sister Freda, otherwise 'Cousin Vinegar', continued to transmit poisoned barbs from the South of France – and in the summer of 1964 the path was open, if far from clear, for my father to become the new Squire of Gunby.

When the deed poll arrived for the change of name (it should, of course, have been a royal licence involving the coat of arms, but we could not afford this), I was in my last term at Harrow, having decided to leave a year early as I could not stand the oppressive heartiness of my House. I was no longer on speaking terms with my housemaster – a state of affairs exacerbated by my having to sit opposite him at lunch every day. I had perfected the art of avoiding his eye in my constant quest for invisibility.

Yet somehow the news of my new moniker leaked out before I left. This led to an absurd, and embarrassing, incident at House Bill (roll-call) one evening after lock-up.

'Mont-gomery—' mispronounced the Head of House, an old enemy of mine who had tried to block my cricket colours.

'Here,' I muttered in my customary sotto voce mono-tone.

'Massing*berg*,' he continued as if he had heard nothing.

'Still *here*,' I blurted out, blushing furiously, amid bemused laughter from the whole house. This drowned out my attempted correction of the mispronunciation, though not the parting shot of another peculiarly unpleasant sixth-former.

'Surely old Monty hasn't the personality to sustain *one name*, let alone two?'

Notwithstanding the deliberate hash made of it by the Head of House (who later scraped a Cambridge cricket Blue), it was the first time I had heard my new style. Privately, I felt as if I had finally achieved the last laugh over 'the peasantry', as Charles Lillingston, my history beak, categorized my housemates. 'Montgomery-Massing-berd': it had a certain ring to it, a nicely alliterative quality, don't you know. It conferred on me a new identity at a convenient moment as I ran happily down the Hill to the station for the last time.

I was heading not for Cambridge, as my mother had hoped (she met both her husbands while up at Newn-ham), but for Lincoln's Inn and articles with a firm of solicitors, as she had arranged. By now I was addicted to Anthony Powell, constantly rereading the *Music of Time* sequence, though this was not a case, I liked to think, of emulating Widmerpool by cutting out the Varsity in order to get on with life but rather of getting *out* of life. I had

had a bellyful of being cooped up with my contemporaries in hothouse conditions: the thought of university terrified me.

Naturally, in my dreams, I had variously relished rooms in Tom Quad or Peckwater at 'the House', and in the Great Court at Trinity; ridden in the Grind or the Cottenham point-to-point; dazzled the Footlights; scored double centuries at Fenners and in the Parks; and dined with John Fothergill at the Spread Eagle in Thame or Kim de la Taste Tickell at the Tickell Arms at Whittlesford. But the reality of modern university life in the mid-1960s held no appeal whatsoever. Each group I conjured up in my misanthropic imagination – student radicals, rugger buggers, *Brideshead* poseurs clutching teddy bears, northern chemists – seemed as unattractive as each other.

In short, I funked it. I refused to play. Above all, I did not want to be young any more: I wanted to be middle-aged, even old – a quiet, comfortable recluse with my books and my pipe dreams. I would commute from Gunby to my legal practice in Louth and become a pillar of provincial respectability. No pain, no problem, no risk, no worries.

In the meantime, I was obliged to commute from Cookham to Lincoln's Inn as my parents had decided to delay moving up to Gunby until my sister Mary had done her time at a rather downmarket day school at Beaconsfield (where her ambitious contemporary Tina Brown was already making her presence felt). Curiously, as it now seems to me, I was in no desperate rush to establish myself up there as the Squire's son and heir.

Another weekend at Gunby had done little to deepen my affections for the place. It now seemed more than ever like a morgue, and the bolshie head gardener went out of his way to be disagreeable. After my mother had picked some herbs, there came forth an invoice on National Trust paper bearing the inscription 'To One Sprig of Parsley, 6*d*'.

The housekeeper had decamped to Skegness, having pushed the central heating system to breaking point with disastrous consequences not only for the boiler but also for the old furniture which had cracked in the greenhouse climate. She apparently received an excessively warm reception in the seaside hotel she managed: an exasperated chef threw a pan of scalding water at her. In her place as caretaker my father installed his father's former chauffeur, Bob Rogers ('Just call me "Rogers", Mister Hugh,' he would say, 'that was always good enough for the General') and his wife Alice, daughter of Carrie Eveleigh, Mrs Coulter's redoubtable predecessor as cook at Blessingbourne.

Latterly Rogers had worked in the Prison Service, as a warder in the Crumlin Road Jail in Belfast, and on our annual summer pilgrimages to Ireland we would pay a ritualistic call *chez* Rogers where the bumptious Bob, who loved the sound of his own voice, would regale us with excruciating renditions of such ballads as 'Just A' Wearyin' for You', 'The Road to Mandalay' and a tearful 'Bless This House'. The highlight for my sister Mary and myself, though, was to provide the most inappropriate cue possible for Alice's nervous laugh.

'So sorry to hear of Carrie's death, Alice,' one of us would gush.

'Ah, yes, Miss Mary, it was very sad *aha-ha-ha-ha-ha*.'

The jackpot was on offer when Uncle Graham, a retired Naval Commander, came to collect us from the Rogerses for our sojourn in the Mountains of Mourne en route for Blessingbourne. The trick then was to orchestrate Uncle Graham's long drawn-out ward-room guffaw as counterpoint to Alice's high-pitched giggle.

'Can we have one more song from Rogers?' we would ask.

'I think we've really had enough, Bob – *aha-ha-ha-ha-ha—*'

'Yes, pipe down, Rogers – *ho-ho-ho-ho-ho-aaah.*'

The two laughs would merge most satisfactorily until Uncle Graham's closing, and always surprising, falsetto note expired like the wheeze from a bellows. The Rogerses' spinster daughter, Dorrie, would beam with special warmth during this annual pantomime.

Poor Dorrie, supposedly 'backward' but with saintly cheerfulness and forbearance of her father's dictatorial ways ('Fetch Daddy his slippers, there's a good girl,' he would bark at her when she was well into her thirties), was obliged to accompany her parents to their new billet in the staff wing at Gunby. Sadly for her, this meant giving up her job in a cafe near the repertory theatre in Belfast, which must have been a jolly refuge from domestic drudgery. She was particularly proud of a signed photograph from the Irish actor J. G. Devlin.

Rogers arrived armed with a mass of doormats stitched in the prison ('That one was made by Alfie Hinds, the great escaper, Mister Hugh') and especially relished the security aspects offered by his new role as the janitor of Gunby Hall. He longed to parade about the premises with an Alsatian on a leash, but my mother put her foot down over this plan, much to his chagrin. Every conceivable door was scrupulously locked and bolted at all times which made it difficult to move about at all. Visitors on open days – and here Rogers was in his element showing them round with his rodomontade about the (almost entirely invented) history of the Montgomery-Massingberds of Gunby – were liable to be referred to as 'Cons' and frequently upbraided for shifty behaviour. 'I've got my eye on you, *feller-me-lad*,' I once heard him admonish a blameless National Trust punter who was making a close study of the Stuart miniatures in the music room.

On the same occasion, when I was tagging along incognito on one of Rogers's tours de force, another visitor dared to interrupt his flow of verbiage with a question.

'Do any of the family still live here?'

'Why, bless me down, madam, you are looking at a fine young sprig of the great family tree just over there now,' said Rogers, with a roguish wink in my direction. As so often, my vascular motors duly went into overdrive.

Yet the truth – never a natural part of Rogers's armoury – was that we were very much absentee tenants. My father was still working at the BBC (increasingly unhappily, as he felt Hugh Carleton Greene was busy destroying the Reithian principles of public-service broadcasting); my mother was teaching; Mary was at school. As for my half-siblings, who had all fled the nest, Antony was reporting on cricket and racquets for the *Daily Telegraph*; Juliet was a married physiotherapist in Bristol; and Roger was farming in Somerset with Uncle Joe. I had the benefits of dear Biddo's incomparable cooking as well as my cosy cabin at Cookham containing my gallery of heroes – cricketers, jockeys, novelists, conservationists – and my well-thumbed paperbacks.

From this hermitage, at the age of seventeen going on seventy, I ventured out to catch the 8.12 a.m. train from Cookham Station attired in a stiff collar, my Old Harrovian tie and my new blue suit (from Montague Burton, Maidenhead). On the platform I noticed a boy hardly older than myself wearing a bowler hat. Perhaps, I mused, I should do the same? But he looked such a prat that I decided against.

'First day at work, eh?' volunteered a doubtless well-intentioned acquaintance of my parents. 'Welcome to the

rat run. It only gets worse from now on, let me assure you
– *ha-ha-ha*.'

I vowed to take evasive action in future, as I buried
myself in Peter Simple's 'Way of the World' column in the
Daily Telegraph. From Paddington I progressed in slow
stages to Chancery Lane on the Underground and then
slipped through the hole in the wall into the enchanted,
enclosed world of Lincoln's Inn towards the leafy New
Square, where the firm of solicitors to which I was articled
could be found. The square seemed to be chock-a-block
with parked Aston Martins, Jensens, Bristols, Alvises and
other sleek motor cars. Was this all a dream?

I suppose I had an interview here before I was offered
my articles, but I have no clear recollection of it. I believe
I had a vague notion of life in Lincoln's Inn being like the
jolly picture conveyed in the Boulting Brothers' film of
Brothers-in-Law. I sleep walked, all unknowing and innocent, into the august chambers of an old-fashioned firm of
solicitors.

By now feeling as if I were on another planet, I was
installed in a book-lined waiting room where two impossibly grand and languid young gentlemen – probably only
a couple of years older than myself but appearing to
belong to an infinitely more suave and sophisticated
milieu than I could ever aspire to – were reading out,
with fine contempt, two copies of a document to each
other. ('Examining,' I soon learned, was the technical
term.)

'The party of the first part do hereby irrev – *irrever-
ently*? – irrevo—'

'*Fuck*-ably, as far as I'm concerned, old cock. Talking
of parties of the first part, are you going to that hop of
Suki Twice-Nightly's next week?'

'Don't think I'm on the right list. What's the time?' –

consults elaborate fob watch – 'I've had enough of this tedious mumbo-jumbo. Let's take it as read.'

'What about buggering off for a spot of brekker?'

'Capital idea, old bean.'

They duly buggered off, having studiously ignored my presence throughout the proceedings. After an extremely brief introduction to my bemused 'principal' – who seemed surprised to see me and at a loss as to what should be done with such a young shaver – I was placed in the care of the senior clerk, a bald, bewhiskered figure who seemed to have strayed from an illustration by Boz.

'The Countess of Mountjoy,' he pronounced in sepulchral tones, 'is, I regret to inform you, my good sir, *deceased.*'

'Oh dear.'

'Oh dear indeed, young man, for your task is to calculate the probate value of the good lady's securities at the time of her demise.'

I was then taken to an airless, windowless cell containing a table, a chair and a gigantic calculating machine resembling an old-fashioned cash register. Here I was left alone to struggle with the assessment of the late Lady Mountjoy's portfolio of stocks and shares. I stared unavailingly at first the list given to me, then the Stock Exchange prices and finally the fearsome contraption. Before long, I had fallen into a state of catalepsy.

In an attempt to shake myself out of my trance, I wandered to and from the lavatory in the basement courtyard – a perambulation which remains my chief memory of my sentence as an articled clerk, the clarity of the recollection doubtless being accentuated by the musty odours associated with the sanctum. At lunchtime I took my three-shilling luncheon voucher to an even sniffier cellar in an alley off Fleet Street where the senior clerk had assured me that a nice salad could be obtained for half a crown. As I munched my way through this depressing repast, the grim reality of my situation at last began to dawn on my numbed senses.

What on earth was I doing in this Dickensian drudgery? How had I drifted into this slough of despond? Was I to spend my working life wrestling hopelessly with ledger sheets of figures after failing my mathematics O level on countless occasions? What sort of madness could this be?

Back in the cell, I could no longer bear to look at the calculating machine, let alone try to operate it. I sat in the dark with my head in my hands. Before long I was shaking with silent sobs.

Hours passed. Then suddenly a shaft of light burst into the room. A *deus ex machina* arrived on the scene in the elegant form of the dandy with the fob watch upon whom I had gazed in awe in the waiting room at the start of this fateful day.

'Sleeping it off, eh,' said this apparition. 'I didn't see you in the Stars during the luncheon interval.'

'The Stars?' I blinked through my tears.

'Public house at the back of these premises, my dear fellow – the Seven Stars. It's where the boys of the Yard Club foregather.'

'Yard?'

'Yes, yes, *Yard of Ale*, don't you see,' he said, flourishing his necktie, a vivid pink affair adorned with an embossed, elongated white glass. 'We all have to quaff a bumper of beer at luncheon.'

'I'm afraid I don't like beer,' I heard myself saying prissily. 'And I've never really been in a pub. My mother's a teetotaller.'

'Steady the Buffs! I'd keep *Harry-Mummers* about that if I were you. I say, you're not one of these Red-Brickies,

are you? We don't approve of Polytechnic pseudo-intellectuals around here: we like proper Townsmen. This is still
a gentlemen's establishment, I'm glad to say.'

'I've only just left school,' I pleaded.

'Oh,' he said, glancing nonchalantly at my neckwear.
'Isn't that a Monkton Combe tie?'

'No,' I said indignantly, before wondering whether he
might be pulling my leg. 'Harrow, actually.' I inwardly
vowed never to wear the bloody thing again.

''Fraid my old man dragged me off to a ruddy cram-
mer's halfway through my schooldays. But at least I was
Twelfth Man at Lord's before the axe fell.'

This elliptical allusion seemed to imply that he must
be referring to Eton. I was put in mind of Psmith in the
Wodehouse stories who had made a similarly early exit
from Agar's Plough. Only later did it emerge that the
reference was to the Clifton–Tonbridge fixture and that
Richard Conynghame (as I learned he was called when
we finally effected a formal introduction) had attended
the celebrated sports academy of Kent, alma mater of
Colin Cowdrey – a great England batsman, if never a
special hero of mine.

Conynghame promptly joined the pantheon, though,
when he breezily dispatched the late Lady Mountjoy's
valuations on my behalf with an admirably cavalier performance on the calculating machine. My tears turned to
laughter as we cackled together over the absurdities of
articled clerkdom.

Richard continued to cheer me up through the two
and a half years (half the intended sentence) I managed
to endure of my articles. With his film-star good looks and
raffish charm, he cut a swathe through the bureaucratic
uniformity of office life. When he deigned to put in appearance on the premises between late nights on the tiles,
lengthy 'luncheon' breaks, early departures in order to

dandify himself for deb dances, or even unexplained 'days off', the crustiest of senior partners would greet him in rapturous terms.

'Ah, my dear Richard. How very decent of you to drop in.'

Whereas if I returned a few minutes late from my lunch hour (too often spent on solitary, furtive visits to striptease clubs in Soho) or extended a blissfully mindless errand with a call at the local Wimpy Bar (where I once disgraced myself by unwisely electing to tuck into the 'Kingsway Grill' at the window table in full view of a passing partner at 4.30 p.m.) fearful wiggings would ensue.

'Really, Massingberd, your conduct is unbecoming to an articled clerk. We are going to a great deal of trouble and expense to train you for a learned profession and you appear to behave as if you are in a holiday camp.'

As Richard spelt it out: 'It's simply a case of starting as you intend to carry on. They had you down as a conscientious swot, so if you later stray from the path, you'll be noticed. They've always regarded me as a play-boy, so I get away with it.'

Richard was also the toast of the typing pool and flirted incessantly with the sexy young women who slavered over him. I was assigned the secretarial services of an elderly spinster called Miss Kenning, a kindly person almost as shy as myself with whom I maintained a scrupulously formal relationship.

'My mother says your trouble, Hugh, is that you are lacking in *charm*,' Richard obligingly informed me after I had spent a night or two at his parents' flat in South Kensington. Mrs Conynghame, with whom I fondly imagined I had got on rather well, was not the first mother of a friend to make such an observation. 'Mumsie told me,' a school room-mate of mine thoughtfully passed on, 'that you'll never get on in life unless you learn how to flirt. You've got to gush, *gush*.'

Years later, I learned that the ferocious Barbara Skelton (supposed model for Pamela Flitton in *A Dance to the Music of Time*) was given identical advice by her second husband, George Weidenfeld. At the publisher's relentless dinner parties (where I was to make a single sullen and silent appearance in the distant future), Weidenfeld would whisper in Skelton's ear: 'Gush, *gush*!'

Richard did his best to transform his charmless, non-gushing young colleague into 'a proper Townsman', though it was a case of taking a twit out of the suburbs but not being able to take the suburbs out of the twit. I never took to pubs, whether in the City or Chelsea, and I shied away from the suggestion that my name should be put on 'a list' for dances. I was not the stuff of which 'debs' delights' are made.

'Massingberd's a confirmed bachelor, I'm afraid,' Conynghame announced to his hearty comrades-in-arms over the succulent mulberry pie in the Sutling Room at the Honourable Artillery Company on the City Road during one of our long luncheon escapes from the dreaded office.

'Good God! Is the feller a pooftah?'

'Certainly not,' I protested, probably rather too hotly. 'I happen to be a regular club cricketer.'

'Ah yes, we *all* know that membership of cricket clubs rocketed around the country after dear old Oscar was sent down,' said Conynghame, who shared my fascination with the Wilde tragedy and also with Oxonian aesthetes such as Harold Acton and Brian Howard, joint models for Anthony Blanche in our bible, *Brideshead Revisited*. Such interests, as Conynghame found to his consternation, were liable to send out confusing signals to certain elderly bachelors of his acquaintance. ('I thought you'd given me the green light, dear boy,' one had remonstrated with him. 'All I'm asking for is a cock stand.')

After we had polished off a decanter of the HAC's port, and I had risen unsteadily to my feet, I could not understand why the carpet was suddenly hitting me in the face.

'That feller can't take his poison like a man,' I heard a voice saying from somewhere seemingly far away, as if in a dream. 'We don't want *him* in the Regiment.'

My unpardonable exhibition in the Sutling Room had inadvertently solved a tricky problem. Although Conynghame was encouraging me to join this venerable Territorial unit – and I had been tempted after seeing him firing a salute at the Tower of London during the television coverage of Churchill's funeral – the CO reminded me all too resistibly of Edward Heath who, to my horror, had recently replaced the erstwhile Earl of Home as Tory leader. Indeed, Ted himself was an old HAC hand. I was relieved of any further responsibility in the matter.

Contentedly, I continued to keep real life firmly at bay as I daydreamed my way through the regular ritual of perusing Peter Simple and the *Telegraph*'s racing and cricket coverage on the 8.12; proceeding to and from the lavatory in Lincoln's Inn; lapping up library books on the 6.15 back to Cookham. Then, an evening invariably spent on Biddo's cosy sofa in front of the television with a casserole dish reminiscent of a dog's bowl overflowing with her scrumptious food. We would happily sit through terminally trivial rubbish, interspersed with the 'Trotslot' drama of the day ('The *language!*' Biddo would occasionally protest. 'And you can see her *form*') until my father arrived to decree lights out. And so to bed, spinning fantasies of epic innings, heroic rides, brilliant books, plays and performances.

Such was the rhythm of the suburban groove that I

had carefully climbed into ('Semi-Detached Suburban Mr James', as my school hero Michael d'Abo sang on *Top of the Pops* with my new favourite group, Manfred Mann), the squirearchical possibilities offered by Gunby seemed somehow unsettling. My father suggested that I might like to escape there for the occasional weekend – doubtless he needed a break from the tensions of lights out as much as I did – but I was in no particular rush to do so after one attempt in which I found it impossible to escape from Rogers's crackerbarrel philosophizing.

'An erect penis is no sign of a man's conscience, Mister Hugh,' he once suddenly announced, apropos of nothing, while I was addressing my breakfast fry-up in the kitchen. He always waited until he knew I was installed there before bursting in, sweating copiously and theatrically mopping his brow, with a heavy load of coal for the Aga. His damp chest hair bristled alarmingly through his vest as he flexed his biceps.

'They also serve who stand and wait, Mister Hugh,' he would say in his strange mixture of Hampshire burr and Belfast brogue.

His favourite topics were his days in the 12th Lancers ('The cream of the Cavalry, Mister Hugh – surely you should be going for a soldier yourself?'); the idiosyncratic rages of my grandfather ('The General had a terrible temper, Mister Hugh, terrible – but I respected him for it'); and the peerless charms of my uncle Peter, his beloved 'Cap'n'.

'Cap'n Peter honoured me by coming to my farewell concert at the Crumlin Jail, Mister Hugh,' he loved to recall. 'He came on straight from Government House, where he had been entertaining royalty, in all his finery – white tie, tails, the full fig. As he walked towards the piano – he was accompanying *Rogers*, you see, Mister Hugh – he looked so, *so* . . .' Here Rogers would break into convulsive sobs, the tears rolling down his babyish face. 'So *beautiful*, Mister Hugh.' Big sniff; deep breath. 'A fine figure of a man.'

While Conynghame wanted me to join the HAC, Rogers was convinced that the answer to all my problems lay with the Freemasons. 'Nothing like the sensation of cold steel against the chest, Mister Hugh,' he claimed, 'and as for the useful connections you make – well, wait till I tell you, they own *half the county* in my new Lodge.'

There was no escape from his buttonholding and blandishments. One afternoon I threw him off the scent by locking myself away in a remote lavatory on the southern extremity of the largely unused third floor. I was comfortably ensconced on the polished mahogany bench, daydreaming about the revival of the Massingberd baronetcy and the expulsion of the National Trust from my rightful acres when I heard the ominous tread of footsteps in a nearby corridor. Then came a vigorous shaking of the door handle.

'Are you within, Mister Hugh? Is that you in there?'

'Er, yes, Rogers, what do you want?'

'Please will you accept my Masonic sponsorship, Mister Hugh? It would be a privilege to propose one of the family to my Lodge. The "Blood Royal", as it were. When I think of Cap'n Peter standing there, that vision of beauty . . .'

It was fantasies about family baronetcies which indirectly led to a sea change concerning my view of Gunby. To keep his end up during my unguarded ramblings about the Massingberd title, Richard Conynghame pointed out that an uncle-by-marriage of his mother's, a Nottingham businessman and politician, had been created a baronet but unfortunately the title had died with him. Conynghame seemed to be under the curious impression that it could be revived in his favour.

'Nottingham is not all that far from Gunby, actually,'
I said. 'Perhaps we should investigate – and the striptease
clubs there are famous.'

On one of our joint forays to Soho, Conynghame and I
had unwisely ventured down some steps to a cavernous
basement where we were set upon by a gaggle of blowsy
blondes demanding that we buy them drinks.

'Not at those prices, my dear girl,' said Conynghame.
Then, in an aside to me, he whispered: 'This is a clip joint.
Let's leg it.'

As we retreated hurriedly up the stairs we were
pursued by the harpies and their sarcastic shouts of 'Jolly
hockey sticks!' and 'Keep a straight bat!'

Not long after that unsavoury incident, an old prep-
school friend told me that he had been wedged in a
crowded tube one rush hour when a fluting voice ('that of
a stuck-up ponce, I thought') sang out for the edification
of the passengers.

'. . . And the weekend after *that*, I shall be putting up
at Gunby in Lincolnshire – you know, the Montgomery-
Massingberds' place. William and Mary . . . No, no, that's
the *period* of the pile. My chum is *Hugh* Montgomery-
Massingberd. ["Never has a moniker sounded more
absurd," murmured my prep-school friend] I'll probably
take my gun. The shooting is supposed to be rather good
in those parts.'

On hearing of this surreal incident, secret pride out-
weighed the all too visible embarrassment I felt. The
experience of hearing, at second hand, that one's name
was being dropped in public places, albeit the Underground, gave me a rare frisson. Suddenly the prospect of
entertaining Conynghame at 'my place in the country'
took on the flavour of an adventure.

We bunked off early from our increasingly neglected
duties in New Square and sped up the Great North Road

in Conynghame's souped-up Mini. The journey was broken with a robust dinner, and lordly selection of wines (Conynghame's sophistication coming into its own with the smirking sommelier), at the George, Stamford's old coaching inn. In the hall we admired the Georgian portrait of Daniel Lambert, a gaoler like Rogers and, according to the *Dictionary of National Biography* 'the most corpulent man of whom authentic record exists'. As two slim young things we could afford to mock poor Daniel; today, although Conynghame had retained his youthful slenderness the last time I saw him, in my own case the approximation to Lambertian girth is close enough for me to adopt his name as a pseudonym on occasion.

A glimpse of Gunby's entrance facade in the ghostly headlights when we eventually arrived late that night gave me an unexpected thrill. It whetted the appetite for the excitements to be revealed in the light of day. Seeing the place through my real-life hero's eyes gave Gunby a new perspective for me. Conynghame, no mean fantasist himself, showed the way this particular fantasy – spacious, squirearchical, scholarly – could be savoured to the full. Calf-bound volumes were taken down from the shelves and even read; crested wine glasses filled and drained; the 'show' dining room actually used, as opposed to camping out in the kitchen; rabbits and hares pursued in the park.

Soon the two of us were weekending regularly at Gunby. The entertainments were expanded to include racing at Market Rasen the other side of the Wolds and explorations of the largely hidden glories of Lincolnshire, such as the box-pewed Georgian church in the hamlet of Langton. Emboldened by Conynghame, I contacted my kinsmen and 'neighbours', John Langton of Langton and Adrian Massingberd-Mundy of Ormsby (later to make Turf history by suing the Jockey Club). Squire Langton

kindly arranged a special tour of the treasure-filled
Burghley, where he acted as agent to the Marquess of
Exeter, the Olympic gold medallist (not silver, as depicted
in that travesty *Chariots of Fire*). Burghley became the
first great house I got to know.

Conynghame, who commandeered the best bedroom
at Gunby as his personal fiefdom, appeared to have the
enviable confidence to carry off the squire's role with
infinitely more panache than my own bumbling, self-
conscious and suburban essay. A stylish cook, methodical
gardener, hawk-eyed shot and studious bibliophile, he
seemed to embody the Renaissance ideal of the *uomo
universale – con sprezzatura* ('with the emphasis on the
con', as some of the less sympathetic articled clerks might
have appended). Attired in his well-cut tweeds and
cavalry twills ('Simply a question of a standing order
to Billings & Edmonds, my dear fellow'), Conynghame
enchanted Rogers. 'Mister Richard' reminded him of an
officer in the halcyon days of the 12th Lancers. Nothing
would be too much trouble for the young master.

'Can I give those boots of yours the benefit of a good
spit and polish, Mister Richard?'

'Capital, Rogers. Much obliged.'

'Now what about that motor of yours, sir? I'm sure the
young ladies will want to admire their new hats in your
gleaming bonnet, eh, Mister Richard?'

'Absolutely, Rogers. Carry on.' (Then, in an aside to
me: 'Can I touch you for a ten-bob note? Got to keep
the old josser sweet. Salt of the earth. Backbone of
England . . .')

Soon a young lady, or, in fact, a woman of rather more
mature years known as 'Sue-Sue', was added to the
strength, in a room adjoining 'Ricardo', as she called him.
Sue-Sue, too, knew how to butter up Rogers. Even having
to clean up after her incontinent King Charles spaniel did

not diminish his devotion to this mistress of the flirting arts.

Other guests, generally but not always of my own invitation, to what Conynghame was now referring to as 'house-parties' did not quite come up to scratch. Of one amiable, if admittedly oafish, articled clerk I had asked along for the ride, Rogers observed: 'You'll forgive me saying this, Mister Hugh, but Mister Pinker has no figure of speech. I'm used to serving the gentry.'

Sometimes my reveries in the dream world of Gunby would be rudely, and crudely, interrupted by Rogers's insistence on sparing me no details. 'I'm sorry to say, Mister Hugh, that the toilet was blocked with sanitary towels.' Or 'Can you guess what I found today, Mister Hugh? A used french letter.'

'It was nothing to do with me, I assure you, Rogers.'

'I don't doubt it, sir,' he said with ill-disguised scorn, 'but I thought you ought to know what is going on under your own roof.'

By this stage, I was tending to think of Gunby more as *Château* Conynghame, not that this upset me unduly. It was a relief to be free of almost all responsibility – save for indulging Rogers in his prurient pomposity – and to have time to work on my daydreams. More and more these came to revolve around Gunby itself, to which I was now passionately attached. Thanks to Conynghame, it was humming with life. The atmosphere of 'Lace-Knick and Old Arse' had been replaced by joie de vivre and laughter. The dust sheets had disappeared; the bedrooms were in use – if not always (and, alas, never by me) in a manner that my absentee parents would have approved.

Gunby's comfortable, unpretentious panelling and well-managed proportions seemed to enchant almost everyone. It was generally agreed that anybody could project their imagination into regarding this quintessentially English

late seventeenth-century country house as home. The only
exception was an American girl, whom Sue-Sue had
kindly invited as a potential date for me. After moaning
miserably about the cold (the central heating had never
recovered from the housekeeper's last blast), the American apparently sent herself a telegram requiring her
immediate departure for warmer climes.

Sometimes the house-parties were not models of harmony. A German girl refused to help with the washing-up
and her breezy boyfriend (another articled clerk) upset
Conynghame and Sue-Sue's culinary pretensions by suggesting we sent out for fish and chips. I was on the side of
the breezy one, but feebly kept my own counsel. (Any
dream will do – as yet another articled clerk of my era,
Tim Rice, put it.)

Conynghame's broad success as a host encouraged
him to organize a more ambitious series of 'reading-
parties' – some of them of several weeks' duration – for
our so-called 'study leave' for the Law Society's examinations. Conynghame was by now sitting his Finals; I was
still struggling with the incomprehensible arcana of Part
I, along with a fellow commuter from the Thames Valley,
Harry Morris, an amiable, red-faced Tonbridgian (though
the would-be Etonian Conynghame was never keen to
have this connection mentioned). Not a single law book
was ever opened, though the three of us immersed ourselves in the war books of my great-uncle, the Field
Marshal. Morris subsequently 'went for a soldier', much
to Rogers's delight, and I was tempted to join him. As
my latest alter ego Captain Sir Peregrine Montgomery-
Massingberd, Bt, of the Irish Guards, I cut a dashing
figure in my bearskin and scarlet tunic.

Dressing up became a favourite pastime once we had
discovered a well-stocked old fancy-dress trunk in the
attic. An opportunity to take this exhibitionistic activity a

stage further arose one Bank Holiday weekend when the under-gardener, an awkward character who ran his superior a close second in bolshieness, gave a garrulous, probably inebriated interview to the local paper about the ghost-ridden horrors of Gunby. On the day of the Bank Holiday Conynghame, Sue-Sue, Morris and myself duly dressed up as figures from Gunby's past, deploying a suit of armour (dismantled from its customary position half-way up the main staircase) and all manner of cloaks and ruffs, frills and furbelows. We then advanced down the drive, rehearsing our 'mugging' and 'gurning' gesticulations, and proceeded to march round the grassy island on the roundabout in full view of the cars leading in and out of Skegness. We soon brought the traffic to a standstill.

This self-indulgent performance – we liked to think it was a protest against the under-gardener's shabby behaviour – went on for most of the afternoon. Between 'shows' we recuperated in the Lodge, where 'Nobby' Clark, the Field Marshal's chirpy former batman, and his redoubtable nonagenarian mother-in-law, Mrs Padley, generously fed and watered the strolling players. They thought it all a great laugh.

Rogers, unfortunately, took a less tolerant view of the fun. On our return to the main house, flushed with triumph, we found ourselves comprehensively locked out. I rang the back-door bell.

'Is that you, Mister Hugh?' he shouted through the still unopened portcullis. 'I'VE CALLED THE POLICE, MISTER HUGH. There's been a robbery here – and you're responsible! I mean, *I'm* responsible. I've also telephoned your father, Mister John, Mister Hugh. You've got it coming, I do promise you that, Mister Hugh. And as for *you*, Mister Richard, and Miss Sue-Sue and Mister Harry – well, I'm ashamed of you. You've let me down badly. You've led Mister Hugh astray . . .'

'Come on, Rogers,' we chorused. 'Let us in, for God's sake.'

'Oh no,' he yelled hysterically. 'It's more than my job's worth. My duty is to Mister John. You lot of jackanapes can cool your heels outside till my Freemason police friends arrive. I hope they throw you in the glasshouse.'

'It was just a *joke*, Rogers. You can't stand that gardener any more than we can.'

'I'm not laughing, Mister Hugh. And nor is Mister John.'

In fact, once we had finally been allowed inside, my father had difficulty in suppressing his amusement on the telephone from Cookham, though he went through the motions of admonishing me for upsetting Rogers who, after all, had been set in a position of representative authority, and so forth.

'But Dadda,' I pleaded. 'He still thinks he's running the Crumlin Road Jail.'

My father, an experienced administrator of personnel, preferred to pursue an analogy from Rogers's Army days. 'I'm going to try to persuade him to look at it as a case of an exuberant young subaltern overstepping the mark and needing the wise guidance of an experienced sergeant major, tough but fair – and with a heart of gold.'

This flannel did the trick, though my relations with Rogers never really recovered. The examinations held at Alexandra Palace in a cavernous great chamber – in which a disembodied voice would boom out at the serried ranks of law students: 'YOU MAY START NOW' – were a fiasco. I walked out of one pointless paper and dropped in for a drink next door with my eccentric uncle Esmond (my mother's only brother), who was a film editor with BBC Television News and kept cool in the studios by wearing shorts and sandals. All three of us were ignominiously ploughed and decided to jump the Law before we were

pushed. Conynghame, like many a dandy before him, fled
to the Continent; Morris headed for Sandhurst; and I,
ever indecisive, returned to Lincoln's Inn for a while to
ponder my future.

I ostentatiously read *The Happy Hypocrite* during a
conveyancing 'completion' with my bemused principal. I
informed the new senior clerk (who used to ask one to
make a telephone call with the unvarying injunction:
'Give him a *Bwavington*, old cock') that I wanted 'to be an
artist, not someone's "man of business"'. My father's wise
old lawyer in Lincolnshire, Major 'Left-Right' Haddon
Owen, a veteran of the Royal Flying Corps, had confirmed
that I was on the wrong tracks when he remarked: 'The
key point about being a solicitor is that you need a good
head for business.'

The inevitable conclusion was hastened by the day of
the senior clerk's return from a caravan holiday in Scotland. 'We had thwee *glowious* days,' he recited intermi-
nably during each and every 'Bwavington', 'two weal
shockews and the west was typical *Scotch* weathew.' The
last straw was being shouted at by a client from Camberley, a puce-faced major angry at the admittedly unconscionable delay in his mother-in-law's probate. I cancelled
my articles and went to say goodbye to the faithful Miss
Kenning.

Unlike some of the outraged partners of the firm, Miss
Kenning did not seem in the least surprised at my
decision. 'I always thought, Hugh,' she said gently, using
my Christian name for the first time in our pleasant
association, 'that you were rather *above* the Law.'

I walked out of Lincoln's Inn with my head held
uncharacteristically high after such a vote of confidence.
But the morning after this show of bravado I woke up on
the Embankment – after a night spent wandering aimlessly around London – without any clear idea of where I

was headed next. The Gunby dream was over. The curse of the Massingberds had come true: I was not to succeed my father as squire.

'I'm afraid, Hughie,' he had patiently explained, not long after the Roundabout Revels, 'that I simply can't afford to maintain Gunby as a weekend retreat and holiday jaunt for you and your friends any longer. The plain facts are that the financial requirements of a National Trust tenant are proving way, way beyond my means. Fortunately, however, I have managed to find the very nice Mr and Mrs Wrisdale, who are from Lincolnshire, to take on the responsibility of Gunby.'

'Coming as you do from the *farming* community, Mister Jack, I don't expect you to be used to the standards of the gentry,' was the wretched Rogers's welcome to his new masters. Fortunately for Gunby, Rogers did not stay long, and the Wrisdales, the place's great benefactors, did.

Now in my twenty-first year, I needed a new dream in which to believe, a new hero to look up to and, more pressingly, a new occupation. I needed somewhere to run, somewhere to hide. Where was I to find it?

SIX

Travels with My Uncle

EVENTUALLY AN UNEXPECTED hero emerged in the ursine shape of my uncle Hugh, by now a Monsignor of the Roman Catholic Church. Perhaps this had something to do with the fact that both my grandfathers – Rogers's feared 'General' and my mother's father, Frank Seal, the stock-jobber who had taken a tumble in the Crash – had died before I formed little more than a hazy memory of their presence. Uncle Hugh, born in 1895, was a generation older than my father and his bossy, even bullying, treatment of his youngest sibling (a word he introduced me to) became a family joke.

'I've told you before, John,' he would say in a startlingly peremptory manner. 'You're far too indulgent of those step-children you so rashly took under your inadequate wing. All this nonsense about *cricket*, that absurd pastime for philistines. It's the only subject that appears to interest them – and it's infecting young Hughie too. You should be broadening their minds with travel, architecture, literature, music, philosophy and, yes, *faith* . . .'

'I think I know rather more about music than you do, Hugh,' my father would protest. 'Travel is expensive. And may I remind you that I am now nearly fifty years old, not fifteen.'

The infamous occasion when Uncle Hugh physically restrained my half-brother Antony from fleeing a church crawl in order to listen to Donald Bradman's last Test at the Oval in 1948 passed into legend. Each time he came to stay with us another anecdote would be added to the apocrypha. Doors would be slammed so hard that they fell off their hinges. Voices would be raised with a thrilling frisson of violence.

'Poor Uncle Hugh,' my father would attempt to explain after such outbursts. 'He was never the same after the Somme.'

Uncle Hugh's chronic absent-mindedness required constant vigilance. On more than one visit he flooded the house by turning on the taps full blast into a plugged basin and then wandering off without having turned them off. Another regular idiosyncrasy was to mistake the door of the cupboard in his bedroom for the exit. This would result in his locking himself into the cupboard until his angry bellows secured release.

As a boy who had equated food with love from an early age thanks to my beloved Biddo's ministrations, I was especially drawn to Uncle Hugh's Bunterish greed. Particular treats, including otherwise unseen vintage wine, would be laid on to satisfy his delight in the 'pleasures of the table' – one of Jeeves's expressions, as he pointed out. Our shared passion for the works of P. G. Wodehouse was another bond that drew us together. Uncle Hugh liked to claim the credit for persuading the Master, through persistent correspondence, to persevere with his greatest creation, 'Uncle Fred', the enchanting Earl of Ickenham, 'a sort of elderly Psmith' (as P. G. W. himself put it) who spreads sweetness and light with such stylish insouciance.

The scene when we went up to Warwickshire one summer's day for tea with Uncle Hugh seemed to have echoes of Wodehouse. We were seated around the dining-room table in his snug presbytery (a relic of recusant days with the chapel hidden in the rafters above), and Miss

Harte, Uncle Hugh's housekeeper, one of those wiry Irish-women the fragility of whose appearance belies their steely temperament, brought in an enormous bowl brim-ful of strawberries. My gluttonous eyes lit up at this then rare and strictly seasonal prospect. My parents and my sister Mary also focused their close attention on this climax of Uncle Hugh's hospitality. Supremely oblivious to our anguished gaze, Uncle Hugh proceeded to address the bowl of strawberries with undisguised relish.

'I say, Miss Harte has done us proud,' he exclaimed. 'These must come from the Squire's garden – rather a bogus gent, in my view, but never mind. His strawberries are succulent enough. Yes, indeed. Mmm, *mmm . . .*'

And on he munched, in an ecstasy of greed, until he had polished off the entire contents of the bowl intended for the five of us.

This incident crystallized Uncle Hugh in my mind as an endearing eccentric. Formerly I had found him rather frightening but I increasingly came to revere him as a great comic figure. His cries of alarm when a cow or sheep announced their presence in a neighbouring field – 'The trouble with the country is that it's so *noisy*' – were straight out of my favourite Beatrix Potter story, *The Tale of Johnny Town-Mouse*.

Uncle Hugh, a true cosmopolitan who had spent twenty years in the Diplomatic Service (though anyone less qualified for the silken arts of diplomacy would have been hard to find) before pursuing a 'late vocation' in the Church, was certainly a town-mouse by inclination. After he had run his scooter into the back of a bus in Birming-ham, an accident that left him with a badly broken leg and a lasting limp, the Catholic hierarchy had found him this seemingly idyllic rural billet. In theory it should have suited him well: the recusant tradition of the hidden chapel appealed to his strong sense of history and he was taken up by the local gentry, who were entranced by his humour and greed.

One of his neighbours, a herald at the College of Arms, was able to fuel Uncle Hugh's peculiar passion for royalty and the aristocracy. Years later this herald told me that Uncle Hugh had taken him to one side and said ('in a manner both conspiratorial and strangely innocent'): 'I think I can claim to know *a dozen earls* by their Christian names.'

Every Christmas Uncle Hugh would give me a book about some member of the Royal Family which, out of politeness, I would pretend to have read when we next met. I was puzzled, though, by his own ambivalent attitude to royalty. While feasting on trivia and anecdotes about these august personages he did not trouble to disguise that he found them inherently absurd and ridiculous. The frozen stiffness of Her late Majesty Queen Mary, and her formidable bust, stimulated a scornful fascination.

'Those *bosoms*,' he would chortle as he made exaggerated gestures to indicate the capacity of Her Majesty's mammaries, 'and that po-face!' He would then usually apologize for this vulgar lapse into 'indelicacy', but on one occasion he mumbled on, as if to himself: 'My father always warned me against women and their breasts. All that soft flesh . . .'

Uncle Hugh's yearning to return to the dreary urban squalor of 'dear old Brum' seemed difficult to reconcile with his old-fashioned romantic snobbery. ('After all,' he liked to muse, 'my Maude grandmother was herself the granddaughter of a viscount.') Then a possible clue came to me when reading Evelyn Waugh's novel *Put Out More Flags*, set in the early days of the Second World War. One of the aristocratic characters, Sir Alastair Digby-Vane-

Trumpington, Bt, is asked why he prefers to serve in the ranks of the yeomanry regiment. Sir Alastair replies to the effect that he does not care to mix with the officers on social terms.

Once Uncle Hugh was happily reinstated back in Brum, surrounded by the humble parishioners of Handsworth (later to be the setting for so-called inner city riots) rather than the 'bogus gents' of the Cotswolds, Sir Alastair's observation rang true. For should not 'good old Monty', as his loving flock called him, have been a baronet himself, like Waugh's character? Sadly, as he frequently mused, the honour was denied him because his Ulster Unionist grandfather had declined the title on learning, coincidentally, that his grandson and eventual heir – himself – had converted to the Church of Rome.

Uncle Hugh's religious beliefs had cost him not only the baronetcy and the Blessingbourne estate but also the Gunby inheritance as well. The chart of succession drawn up when the Massingberd seat was presented to the National Trust in 1944 featured parentheses beside the senior heir's name bearing the legend '*RC*'. Like my uncle and namesake I had now lost out on both places.

Yet it was not consciously any shared sense of loss or disinheritance that drew me to Uncle Hugh in the late 1960s. His new heroic status in my besotted eyes owed almost everything to the fact that he had first-hand knowledge of a world which then absorbed my most passionate daydreams: 1920s Oxford. He had even known Evelyn Waugh, whose death in 1966 had given me a particularly nasty jolt.

Uncle Hugh, it turned out, had been a friend-in-common of Waugh's Catholic mentors, Monsignor Ronald Knox and Douglas Woodruff, editor of the *Tablet*, both names familiar to me from my devout Wavian studies. This Damascene-scale revelation made itself plain to me

when Uncle Hugh – doubtless sensing that I was at a
loose end after abandoning my training as a solicitor –
took me on a tour of Oxford. He had gone up to Christ
Church from Winchester just before the Great War and
then returned after the Armistice, when he was received
into the Catholic Church with encouragement from
Ronnie Knox.

As we wandered around 'the House', as I learned to
call it, with Uncle Hugh waving his stick to indicate the
glories of Tom Quad, Peckwater and Meadow Buildings
(from which Anthony Blanche regaled the oarsmen), I
dared to translate my daydream of Varsity life into
reality. It was not too late: I could make a fresh start as a
(supposedly) mature undergraduate – rather like Paul
Pennyfeather in Waugh's *Decline and Fall*. As my head
filled with Wavian visions, Uncle Hugh attempted to
explain the vast difference in pre- and post-1914 Oxford.

'You have to remember, my dear Hughie, that I was
of an older generation than this brittle, clever, sophisticated – and, if I may say so, often tiresomely affected –
'20s crowd with which you seem to be rather unheathily
obsessed. The boys I came up with in 1914 were fresh,
innocent, open, full of simple enthusiasm and essentially
unsophisticated. All that was changed for ever by the
Western Front. Not many of us came back up in 1919 and
we took life pretty seriously after all the terrible things
we had seen. The silliness and frivolity came later.'

Sir Maurice Bowra, then still Warden of Wadham
College, had been one of Uncle Hugh's Oxonian contemporaries (as well, of course, as being a mentor of Evelyn
Waugh) and it was thought a sound move to consult the
great man as to my university prospects. Contact with
such a legend gave me a special thrill as one of the more
self-satisfied lecturers at the Law Society's College of Law
loved to adorn his tedious talks on tort with 'a Bowra

story from my Oxford days'. Two recurring chestnuts were the occasion someone disparaged Bowra's fiancée ('Buggers can't be choosers') and the time some boating ladies disturbed the all-male nude bathers at Parsons' Pleasure. While the other dons hurriedly clasped their towels to their midriffs, Bowra covered his head. 'In Oxford,' he announced, 'I am known for my face.' Many years later, Anthony Powell, who really did know Bowra, put me right about this hoary old Oxonian story, which must have gone back to a generation before Bowra was born. In this original version, one of the ladies observes of the towel-headed figure: 'I had not appreciated before that the Dean has red hair.'

Sir Maurice considered that one of the newer universities might hold out the most hope and recommended me to one of his former pupils then in some senior position at the University of East Anglia. Ever suggestible, I set off for Norwich wearing my stiff collar and pin-striped suiting in the spring of what came to be known as the Summer of Love. I was shown round the curious concrete campus full of strangely attired students by a bemused young chap, probably only a year my junior, who addressed me as 'sir'. An ageing trendy with an American accent claiming to be a professor wondered whether I might care to take a degree course in 'European Studies, majoring in Russia' for which there happened to be a vacancy that fall. As I had recently embarked on reading Tolstoy, this seemed a reasonable scheme. The other alternative on offer was a place the following autumn at Selwyn College, Cambridge, to read history, but my matriculation would be dependent upon my passing O level maths or science – neither an easy option in my case.

Hedging my bets, and egged on by Uncle Hugh and Jonathan ('J. G.') Pearce, a schoolfriend who had made a similar decision to give up estate agency and belatedly pursue the Varsity dream, I enlisted at an Oxford crammers in order to study both Russian and biology. I presented myself to St Bernard's College, as it was grandiloquently called, complete with a dubious coat of arms and Latin motto, even though it was housed in a single poky room off the Woodstock Road from where 'the principal' (and sole member of staff) would farm out his students to 'tutorials' with impecunious postgraduates all over Oxford. I was assigned to a charming, chain-smoking Russian lady married to a don at St Antony's (who, I later discovered, translated Solzhenitsyn) and a muscular medical type down in Iffley whose exposition of biology invariably embraced 'the paradoxical'.

I would pedal my faithful ex-bobby's bicycle, with my books in the basket, to lessons from my lodgings in the Banbury Road. These were shared with Pearce, whose keen sense of business economics had been honed by his experiences in the property market. For a time we subsisted on meagre commons until he returned in triumph from the Summertown supermarket bearing 'an unbelievably cheap' tin of 'Chunky Meat in Rich, Nourishing Gravy'. I emptied the contents into my trusty electric frying pan.

'Blimey, what a filthy pong,' I said.

'Never mind, think of how much cash we're going to save if we can live on this stuff.'

A preliminary tasting confirmed my worst suspicions. 'Didn't it occur to you, J. G., you clot, that "Chunky Meat" might mean it was *dog food*?'

Wanting to be a dog was one thing, wolfing down tins of Chum, whether Pedigree or not, was quite another. In more sybaritic mode, we would venture out in search of the watering holes mentioned by Waugh, including the Spread Eagle made famous by John Fothergill at Thame, though the magic attached to these places had long since departed. Pearce shared something of my *Brideshead* obsession, though I was not prepared to accept his dogmatically homosexualist reading of the Oxford sequence.

'Of course he bloody well *must* have been a queer to write like that. Charles Ryder is quite obviously madly in love with Sebastian – and who can blame him, I say.'

'No, no, J. G. Why do all pansies assume *everyone* is a pooftah at heart? Waugh was writing about romantic friendship, beauty, patrician values . . .'

'Balls. It's a hymn to buggery.'

I preferred to look at the works of Waugh and the remnants of the Oxford he had so elegiacally written about through rose-tinted spectacles. I would while away largely solitary days watching cricket in the Parks or wandering, in Lord Sebastian's footsteps, through the Botanical Gardens and the enchanted grounds of Magdalen, alma mater of Oscar Wilde. ('You'll be claiming *he* wasn't an uphill gardener next!' jeered Jonathan.) These few months were to be my only approximation of Varsity life as in the event I did not – for the usual reason, sheer funk – take up either of my university places.

The joy of it all from the daydreaming viewpoint (the only viewpoint that actually counted as far as I was concerned) was that I could weave my fantasies from the fringes of the university world without ever remotely being part of it. Attending an open-air performance of *Charley's Aunt* (so much better, as it was here, when performed by amateurs), I could imagine myself as having just slipped out of my rooms in Peckwater for the evening. Watching Rupert Daniels go out to bat in his Harlequin cap beside the lake at Worcester College, it was all too easy to indulge in a touch of transference. Peering through the arcades of All Souls, it was the work of a moment to project myself into the brilliant young prize fellow already acclaimed for his literary prowess.

Even reality became bathed in golden light when the kindly Mrs Willetts, my Russian tutor, encouraged me to have a bash at writing short stories in Russian, a logical language perfectly designed for pithy irony. This enjoyable exercise and the thrill of reading Tolstoy and Turgenev in their original language were the high points of my time at dear old St Bernard's. I was profoundly touched by my tutor's mischievously tongue-in-cheek report for the principal: 'Sure to do rather well' was her conclusion.

Her well-meant attempts to overcome my fierce shyness were less happy. A blind date with a foreign student to see Olivier's absurd film of *Othello* led to our being asked to leave the cinema after the wretched girl, for ever chewing an unsavoury matchstick, growled for the umpteenth time: '*Vot* did ee say? *Explain*, pliss.'

My Russian tutor was no more successful with her introduction of a frighteningly precocious pupil of a 'progressive' girls' school not far from Oxford, where, she informed me, the matron (a Miss Jennifer Paterson) plied her charges with copious supplies of gin. For some reason – perhaps on account of my ill-disguised love of cricket – this hoyden affected to assume I was an Australian.

'The trouble with all the Oz types I have met – you know, Barry Humphries, Germaine Greer, Clive James and that crew,' she pronounced loftily (or at least way above my head), 'is that they are all so terribly *provincial*, so cravenly *desperate* to make a name for themselves in the mother country. It's absolutely pathetic.'

It was a relief to escape from such '60s sophistication on jaunts with Uncle Hugh to the nineteenth-century gloom of Disraeli's Hughenden or to the eighteenth-century robustness of Lichfield, birthplace of our ancestor Erasmus Darwin – as well, of course, as Dr Johnson. Uncle Hugh loved to talk about 'the Great Cham', to whom he seemed, to me, to bear a remarkable resemblance. Christopher Sykes, Evelyn Waugh's biographer who was en poste in the Berlin Embassy with Uncle Hugh in the 1930s, once described Monsignor Hugh Montgomery in print as 'a large, benevolent man'. This description struck me as being apt for both the good doctor and my hero.

Talk of hero worship discomfited Uncle Hugh. 'Unused to wine' (as the newspaper headline of Sebastian's unfortunate court case in *Brideshead* has it), I blurted out after our lunch at the George in Lichfield how much I admired him.

'I sit at your feet,' I gushed.

'What utter nonsense,' he said. 'I am an all-too-fallible sinner, very far from a wise or clever philosopher.'

'But you have experienced so much. You have known so many famous people. You are like a hero to me—'

'TOMMY-ROT!' he roared, suddenly furious, his complexion taking on a hue sympathetic to the purple of his monsignorial shirt front. 'How dare you say such a thing. HOW DARE YOU!'

'But Uncle Hugh, I didn't mean to offend you—'

'Offend *me*? You are offending God, you young fool! Don't you realize how shamefully unchristian all this talk of hero worship is? Haven't you heard of the evils of idolatry, graven images? There is nothing more unhealthy than placing mere human beings, with their feet of clay, on pedestals.'

'But what about Bennet Langton, our ancestor, and Dr Johnson?'

'*What* about them?'

'Well,' I floundered, trying to retrieve the situation. 'You were telling me at Dr Johnson's birthplace round the corner that Bennet wrote the much older man a fan letter while he was still an undergraduate at Oxford – and then they became friends.'

'Exactly,' said Uncle Hugh, who had by now regained his benevolence. 'They became *friends*, and friendship is based on mutual respect and a healthy feeling of equality – not on one person idolizing another.'

Later, on the way home, he said gently: 'You must understand, my dear Hughie, that I don't care to be looked up to as if I were an old sage. I may be over seventy but inside I am still seventeen.'

I thought of Aunt Da's crack about looking eighteen at the back but eighty at the front, and also of volunteering that I was nearer seventeen but longed to be seventy. Not wishing to provoke another avuncular explosion, I steered the conversation back to the eccentricities of the Darwins.

'Poor Cousin Charles looked rather like an ape,' mused Uncle Hugh, 'which might explain why he was so drawn to his disastrous theory. It made him miserable, of course, for essentially he was a man of religious faith.'

Thanks to Uncle Hugh, septuagenarians soon became the only substantial human company (as opposed to the ghostly figures of my daydreams) I could tolerate. On trips to London he would entertain me in comfortable masculine style at his club in Pall Mall, which he had joined as a young diplomatist in the Foreign Office, across St James's Park. I thrilled to the palatial grandeur of Barry's building, with its exhilarating feeling of 'wasted space', and felt deliciously overawed by its bufferish atmosphere – capacious dark brown leather armchairs and squashy sofas, cigar fumes, champagne cocktails in the cosy basement bar, barley water on the dining-room tables. ('It's properly known as the *coffee room* in club-land, my dear,' Robin McDouall, the splendidly camp club secretary pointed out.)

Uncle Hugh's fellow members made me feel extraordinarily welcome. His old Oxford and Foreign Office friend,

Sir Gilbert Laithwaite, the club chairman, an immaculately turned-out panjandrum invariably sporting a red carnation, gave my elbow an affectionate squeeze. 'You come from decent people,' he joked in a stage-Oirish accent (after a spell as the Viceroy of India's right-hand man Sir Gilbert had become Britain's first Ambassador to Éire). 'In the old country your family are the cat's whiskers.' This was accompanied by a broad wink.

A devout bachelor, Sir Gilbert adorned the club until his death, latterly commuting in to lunch from his old folks' home, never without the carnation. At the end, when Sir Gilbert could no longer manage the journey, his fellow clubman, Monsignor Gilbey, visited 'the dear old boy' at the home. 'He still looked so immaculate that I expected to see the carnation in the buttonhole of his pyjamas,' Gilbey told me. 'I believe he thought he was back in the club. At one juncture he said, with his distinctive wink: "I used to be chairman here, you know." I replied: "I don't doubt it."'

Although they were inevitably bracketed in the club as 'the two *Monsignori*', Uncle Hugh and Alfred Gilbey could hardly have been more different in manner and appearance. Whereas Hugh was bumbling, portly, untidy and often unshaven, the consummately sleek Alfred always cut a supremely elegant figure in his archaic accoutrements. His wardrobe of stylish priestly garb seemed straight out of Evelyn Waugh's novels, and it was tempting to think of him as Father Rothschild, the worldly priest in *Vile Bodies*. Yet underneath the exquisite exterior and the continental courtesy ('Alfred was fortunate enough to have a Spanish mother,' Uncle Hugh explained, 'whereas *our* only Spanish ancestress, Señorita Maria Dolores Plink from Malaga, was a few generations back') could be found a surprisingly humble and sympathetic priest far removed from the misogynistic snob of mythology.

It was, I learned during my increasingly frequent guest appearances at the club, that mythology which had led to Monsignor Gilbey taking up residence in the club after more than thirty years as Chaplain to the Roman Catholic undergraduates of Cambridge. The club became his home and the former boot room, a tiny eyrie at the top of some perilous stairs, was converted into an oratory for the Monsignor and his flock. Alfred always used the word 'flock' in the broadest sense to embrace non-Catholic friends ('even Black Orangemen such as yourself, dear Hugh') as well as co-religionists.

'I am only sorry that I will not be up at Cambridge myself in order to welcome you to the flock, dear boy,' Monsignor Gilbey said. He harboured no bitterness at his shabby treatment by the university authorities and urged me to take up my place in 'the sweet old missionaries' college' of Selwyn. A Trinity man ('As the old Master, Dr Henry Montagu Butler – Rab's uncle – used to say: God "was in some sense a Trinity man himself"'), Alfred Gilbey still went out with the Trinity Foot Beagles and attended various university dining clubs.

One evening he took me along as his guest but the experience left me feeling uneasy and out of my depth. Things started badly in the taxi from Cambridge Station when I found myself, in a crammed car, awkwardly perched on the Monsignor's knee.

This did not put me in the right mood for Alfred's tease of the night, which was to bait a snobbish left-wing don at the dinner by pretending I was called 'Viscount Gunby' in order to see how much he would toady to me. In theory, such aristocratic play-acting should have been a fantasist's dream come true. In practice, I found the charade acutely embarrassing and came to feel sorry for the wretched butt, who duly crawled to my exalted rank.

Like many practical jokes it went on too long. Out of

boredom, and a longing to be far away from Cambridge in a fantasy world of my own devising, I kept missing my cues.

'What d'you say, Gunby?' the Monsignor would say in his best Edwardian hunting-field manner.

I would be gazing up at the college portraits, lost in a reverie.

'What ho! *Gunby!* My LORD GUNBY! Keep up, Sir, keep up.'

'Eh? Oh, sorry . . .'

If I was to believe in daydreams, they had to be scripted by me. None the less, I remained on friendly terms with Alfred Gilbey and listened with genuine interest to his 'little talks' about faith. He recommended the novels of Robert Hugh Benson, which impressed me with their passionate, intense Catholicism, but I never felt I was being particularly 'proselytized'. The idea that there was some sort of Papist plot within the club organized by the *Monsignori* struck me as ludicrous, though one choleric colonel was heard to complain in the smoking room: 'This club is full of Roman Catholics. You can hear them talking and laughing together.'

For me, the two Monsignors' most enjoyable talk revolved not around religion but their recollections of life before the Great War. Alfred Gilbey still employed such archaisms as 'omnibus', 'the play' (for the theatre) and 'the moving pictures' (cinema), and would put on a glove, only to take it off at the crucial moment, when shaking hands in a formal introduction.

'If you were invited to luncheon,' he would recall of his youth in the then rural environs of Harlow in Essex, 'you arrived promptly at one o'clock, accepted a glass of sherry and then went straight in at ten past.'

Kingsley Amis, slumped in a nearby armchair during his brief membership of the club (which came to an end

on account of his distressing tendency to take off his
jacket in order to write letters), eyed the Monsignor
warily. 'Shall we go straight in?' ranked with the novelist
as the most dreaded phrase in clubland.

Uncle Hugh would work his way through his repertoire of anecdotes about earls – ranging from 'our
esteemed Maude kinsman', the first and last Earl de
Montalt, who according to Tipperary tradition was said to
have had his coat tailored to accommodate his forked tail,
and the fourth Earl of Lucan (son of the Crimean commander), whom Uncle Hugh had met as a boy.

'So you see,' he used to explain, 'that links me with
the Charge of the Light Brigade. The third Earl, of
Balaclava fame, is on record as saying in the Crimea:
"Bingham [his son, who took part in the Charge] is lousy."
And the Lousy Bingham is the one I met before he died in
the summer of 1914.'

This connection prompted me to take Uncle Hugh one
evening after an early supper at the club to see Tony
Richardson's tiresome film of *The Charge of the Light
Brigade*. Rather like the match-chewing foreign student
at Oxford, he kept up a running commentary more or less
throughout – 'Is that supposed to be Lousy Bingham?' –
and crowned my embarrassment by attempting to lower
my eyes when Trevor Howard (as the bristling Earl of
Cardigan) settled down to give Jill Bennett (Mrs Duberly)
a sound spanking.

'There is no need to show us physical evidence of the
cad's adultery, surely?' protested Uncle Hugh, fingering
his dog collar. 'I wonder whether I should have obtained
ecclesiastical permission to view this pornography.'

Undaunted, I also took him to see the film version of
Oh! What a Lovely War. I was disappointed by the strange
lack of an aristocratic young officer in the story with
whom I could identify and translate into my occasional

alter ego Sir Peregrine Montgomery-Massingberd, Bt, of the Irish Guards – though I did spot a former Etonian racquets player in the shape of Jeremy Child jump the queue to kiss the painted harridan of the recruiting drive (Maggie Smith). This, though, was not the place for day-dreams. To Uncle Hugh the ghastly memories the film brought back were all too real.

His customary running commentary developed into something little short of hysteria. The former subaltern's sobs and shouts were interspersed with snatches of the sentimental songs that held the film together. When Haig (played by little Johnny Mills) leapfrogged into view, Uncle Hugh shook his fist at the screen and bellowed: 'THE BUTCHER OF THE SOMME!'

Embarrassment in the face of such raw emotion seemed an impertinence. Infused, for once, with moral courage, I glared back at the insensitive clods in the cinema who dared to hiss and 'Shush' my hero as he relived his hellish experiences on the Western Front. I longed to shout out 'Don't you realize this old man won the Military Cross in this terrible war, which destroyed his generation?'

Eventually, as Uncle Hugh sang, in a faltering voice, 'It's a Long Way to Tipperary' (Lord de Montalt's tail temporarily forgotten), the hissing stopped as if by telepathy. Humbled by Uncle Hugh's heroism, we hummed along with him as the tears rolled down his face.

Subsequent attempts to draw him out on the horrors he had somehow survived in the Great War were met only with snuffles and grunts. But one night when I was staying with him and Miss Harte at the presbytery ('Edwardian Baroque', according to Uncle Hugh) in Hands-worth, the dam broke. Early that morning, after staying in Kensington with Conynghame (now returned from the Continent and supposedly working at a rare book auctioneers in Chancery Lane), I chanced upon a horrific, obscene road accident in the Cromwell Road. A young woman, naked under a leopardskin coat, had swayed unsteadily into the path of an articulated lorry which knocked her flying and charged on westwards. Her decapitated corpse was lying towards the side of the road. A pool – even, it seemed, a lake – of translucent blood, glistening in the sunlight, was seeping into the gutter.

I stood in shock, transfixed by the sight of the blood and the ghostly, slow-motion stillness of the scene. Suddenly I heard, as if from a long way away, the calm yet urgent voice of a uniformed nurse standing beside me (presumably she had just finished a night shift at the then flourishing St Mary Abbot's nearby). We appeared to be the only living people on an eerily silent planet.

'Please will you call the police and an ambulance?' she said. 'There's nothing more we can do. She is dead, I'm afraid.'

Having not confided in anyone all day – I could not concentrate on the various career-planning tasks in hand – I blurted out my inescapable waking nightmare to Uncle Hugh.

'It was all the blood. Such a strange, luminous colour. I never realized there could be so – so *much* of it.' I slumped sobbing into his arms.

'I know, I know. I understand,' said Uncle Hugh as he enfolded me in a bear-like hug. 'I was your age when I held dear friends close – like this – when they died on the Somme. I was drenched in their blood. Heads, limbs, torsos, insides – all blown to bits. The blood flowed like a tidal wave. You can never understand that vision of horror unless you have seen it.'

He talked on of the terrible things he had witnessed while serving with the North Irish Horse – the senseless waste of life, the nerve-shattering din, the filth of the mud and the rats, the blind obedience of those caught up in the military machine. What particularly impressed him was the way the Catholic priests stayed up with the men, whereas their Protestant counterparts remained safely behind the lines.

'The priests were always with us,' he recalled. 'They kept the men cheerful with their jokes and sympathy. And they would be there with them at the end, to comfort them and give absolution.' He paused. 'In fact, *that* was what really made me become a Catholic myself – not because of the clever "proselytizing" of the Oxford Jesuits, as my father and grandfather liked to pretend.'

The scene in *Oh! What a Lovely War* which had upset him most, he said, was the Christmas fraternization of 1914 in No Man's Land. 'It showed how tragically unnecessary the whole bloody conflict was,' he roared above his tears. 'The Germans were our friends, our cousins. We sang the same beautiful hymns.'

Uncle Hugh went on to reminisce about his good friendship with Adam von Trott, the German diplomatist, whom he had known while serving in the Berlin Embassy in the last years of the Weimar Republic. Another old friend of Uncle Hugh's, Patrick Barrington (known as 'the Vanishing Viscount' because of his mysterious absences), had told me that when he was sent out to Berlin as an honorary attaché under the fearsome regime of 'that pompous ass' Sir Horace Rumbold, he expected to be met at the station by an 'impeccable young dandy'. There was no one fitting that description on the platform: 'Just a shambolic figure in a filthy black plastic mackintosh wearing an incongruous beret and smoking a cigarette. This, of course, was your Uncle Hugh.'

Trott, as Uncle Hugh told me, was later one of the

July Plotters and Hitler ordered his execution – slow hanging by piano wire on a meat hook – to be filmed for his delectation.

Uncle Hugh spent much of the ensuing weekend praising the European ideal and emphasizing the vital need for me to travel in order to broaden my understanding of continental civilization.

'Why, you haven't even crossed the Channel!' he exclaimed contemptuously. 'And your French accent is like Mr Heath's.'

'Or Sir Winston Churchill's, for that matter,' I countered. 'I don't think my French master at Harrow had ever actually crossed the Channel either. Besides, I don't think I'd like "abroad".'

'What philistine rubbish! And how do you suppose you will ever be qualified to join the club, to which you have become so fondly attached?'

Uncle Hugh's ace left me floundering. A scheme was accordingly hatched at the club with my proposer, Sir Gilbert Laithwaite, and my seconder, Monsignor Gilbey, for Uncle Hugh to take me on a Grand Tour that would give me the required mileage to satisfy the club's election committee. I felt like Phileas Fogg in *Around the World in Eighty Days* but, much to my disappointment, our Grand Tour did not begin, as Fogg's had done, at a club, after a familiar lunch of kipper pâté, grouse and steak pie and Welsh rarebit. Instead, Uncle Hugh ordered me, in his most peremptory tones, to meet him at the barrier of the Victoria boat train.

This, I felt, was not a good omen, and so it proved. When he arrived, late and flustered, with underwear bursting out of his badly packed traps, I realized, as if for the first time, that he was an old man. It suddenly became painfully clear that he could not manage the practicalities of the daydream he had lovingly woven for our ambitious tour.

Relations were already strained by the time we reached Folkestone. The more neurotic and bad-tempered Uncle Hugh was, the sulkier I became. My seasickness on the ferry crossing earned his withering contempt.

'You'll never be elected to the club if you can't even cope with a Channel crossing,' he snorted, humour markedly absent from his voice.

Once installed on the train at Calais, Uncle Hugh donned his disreputable beret (which looked as if it might well be the same one he had sported in Berlin in 1929) and proceeded to jabber to our fellow passengers in fluent French. As I had not been introduced to these persons, I remained silent. I felt, and doubtless looked, ill at ease.

When we crossed the Italian frontier, Uncle Hugh enthusiastically switched tongues and wallowed in the warm respect due to his priestly status. In the dining car, by now feeling distinctly queasy, I declined the *vino rosso* in favour of the San Pellegrino water.

'Are you following the teetotal precepts of that schoolmistress mother of yours?' he sneered with a shrug to the galley's gallery. *'Puritano inglese!'*

'What about your own grandmother – the old dyke who turned pubs into temperance hostels?'

'How *dare* you insult my beloved Munny! You know nothing about her. I am devoted to her memory.' He crossed himself with elaborate flamboyance for the benefit of our delighted table companions. Seething with frustration and jealousy, I could have slapped his slobbering chops.

My frustration came to a head in Venice after an exhausting, neck-straining marathon of sight-seeing, led by Uncle Hugh limping manically along like a rogue

elephant. Over dinner in our pensione near the Arsenale,
I unwisely ventured the view – possibly prompted by
Uncle Hugh's exuberant table manners – that eating, like
other natural functions, might best be conducted in solitary confinement in a cubicle.

'What an OUTRAGEOUS idea!' he thundered. 'Eating
together at table is the foundation of this Christian
religion. Haven't you heard of the Last Supper? Your
eccentric mother, I suppose.'

'Leave my mother out of this. She was left a war
widow with three young children—'

'Which your wretched father – much against my own
advice, I may say – nobly took on.'

'Anyway,' I said, switching tack like the boats we
could see out of the pensione windows, 'What's wrong
with being eccentric? At least it means you are an individual. Come to think of it, wasn't Jesus Christ a bit of an
eccentric?'

'BLASPHEMY! Leave the table now. I am not sharing
it with you any longer, you impudent puppy.'

I stormed off into the night, and relieved my frustrations with a diminutive prostitute (who called me Ugolino
– 'Little Hughie' – for reasons I could not fathom) picked
up in the Piazzo San Marco. The next morning at breakfast, Uncle Hugh said: 'I trust your walk last night did
not lead you from the path of righteousness?'

I blushed. Could he have followed me to the seedy
hotel where the brief transaction had taken place?

'If so,' he continued, with an all-knowing look in his
eye, 'it could have damaged both your wallet and your
morals – remember the lazar of Venice.'

I did remember it. The lazar haunted my guilt-ridden
thoughts to such an extent – even though there were no
obvious symptoms of infection – that on our return to
London I duly presented myself at the 'Special Clinic' of

St Mary's, Paddington. I was convinced that the bells of
St Mary's, as in the odious Bing Crosby film, would be
tolling for me. As I waited my turn in the crowded
reception area, the voice of the chirpy clerk, who had
manifestly seen it all in his time, rang out – far too loudly
for my taste – 'MISTER MONTGOMERY-MASSING-
BERD. Now that's a moniker to conjure with. Wasn't
there a field marshal of that name in the '30s? I like to
study military history.'

Inside the cubicle, a breezy medic (who, for a moment,
I thought was my biology tutor from St Bernard's) said:
'Now let's have a shufti at your old man . . . Nothing to
worry about there . . . Look, quite frankly, you are far
more likely to catch the clap from an enthusiastic young
amateur – of which there seem to be a good crop around
in the nineteen-sexies – than an experienced old pro.'

Back in Rome a week or so earlier, the only whiff of
sex in the air seemed to be of the pederastic variety. One
of Uncle Hugh's old friends in Vatican circles, a bachelor
expatriate, lovingly displayed an explicit nude study in
bronze of the messenger boy in his offices overlooking the
Spanish Steps.

'Is *that* permitted now?' croaked a shocked Uncle
Hugh as we made our embarrassed excuses en route for a
public audience with the Pope. He had worked himself
into a state of self-righteous umbrage at being denied a
private audience with His Holiness, whom he had known
well as Cardinal Montini during his time as a diplomatist
with the British Mission to the Holy See.

'When I think that I was once Chargé d'Affaires for
His late Majesty's envoy to the Supreme Pontiff of the
Holy Roman Church, and a *personal friend* of the present
Pope, I feel I deserve better than this shabby treatment,'
he moaned.

At it turned out, we had the best of both worlds: the

high drama of the Pope's public arrival in St Peter's and then the intimacy of the electric moment when Paul VI spotted Uncle Hugh's beaming face in the front row. With hands held in prayer, His Holiness rushed forward past his aides and grasped his bear-like old friend's eager paws. Uncle Hugh then presented me. I stuck out my hand in my best English country-house manner (as if Cousin Jasper in *Brideshead* were telling me to treat the Pope just like the vicar at home) before Uncle Hugh thrust me violently to the floor by the neck. '*Get down!*' he hissed. 'Kiss St Peter's ring.'

Quite overcome by the thrilling theatricality of it all, I would happily have signed up for the Church of Rome there and then, proselytizing or no proselytizing. It was undoubtedly the highlight of our Grand Tour. After the Vatican, it was downhill all the way.

In Perugia I upset Uncle Hugh by asking an ancient principessa what 'those wasps' were doing on our plates. '*Wasps!*' shrieked Uncle Hugh, who had been busy crawling to the old crone. 'They are the Barberini bees, the proud armorial symbol of this great dynasty which has given us three popes. My profuse apologies, Principessa, for the shameful ignorance of my nephew – *Puritano inglese.*'

In Florence this by now well-worn insult was trotted out again when I was stupid enough to express surprise at the uproarious way an angel was depicted laughing in a fresco in one of the Medici chapels. 'Don't you Protestant killjoys understand,' Uncle Hugh admonished me, 'that laughter is a vital part of holiness?'

It was also in Florence, though, that Uncle Hugh's policy of 'my dog collar makes me welcome everywhere' finally came unstuck.

'This looks like an amusing trattoria,' he announced outside a grim-looking dive that even my modest linguistic skills could decipher was some sort of Communist Party Workers' Canteen.

'I don't think so, Uncle Hugh.'

'Nonsense – where's your spirit of adventure? I'm going in.'

A few minutes later he was back on the pavement, clutching his beret and muttering unpriestly oaths.

We stopped speaking altogether in Paris after I had unwittingly encouraged a dirty-postcard seller by the Arc de Triomphe. When I sought Uncle Hugh's help to disentangle me from my predicament, he snapped: 'Don't keep whining. Act like a man and get rid of the pest.'

'I thought Catholic priests were supposed to be sympathetic. All I want is sympathy.'

'Look it up in the *Oxford English Dictionary* – it comes between simpering and syphilis. I am absolutely fed up with your childish moaning. I'll have you know that I went to a great deal of trouble to organize this educational and expensive Grand Tour for your benefit – and I feel utterly exhausted by your ingratitude and insolence.'

Foreign soil is the graveyard of many a friendship, I had read, and my hero worship of Uncle Hugh certainly did not make it back across the Channel. The next time I saw him he was in a bad way at the Calvary Nursing Home ('I insist on calling it the *Cavalry*,' quipped Monsignor Gilbey, a faithful visitor) at, of all places, Harrow-on-the-Hill. Shaking and sobbing silently, he held my hands into which he thrust a copious collection of decaying toothbrushes, their urgent disposal obviously preying on his mind. I thought back to the pensione in Venice, where he had solemnly presented a pile of used underpants, which he had been unable to force into his suitcase, into the hands of a bemused waiter.

Apparently Uncle Hugh had bolted from his unhappy retirement billet in Banbury, with its younger priests talking only of football, and been found wandering on the beach at Grange-over-Sands in North Lancashire (as it still was, before the odious county of Cumbria was established). From there he had been taken across the Pennines to Ampleforth – where he had made an unsuccessful attempt to be both a monk and schoolmaster in middle age – and thence down south again to Calvary. One midsummer day in 1971 he died of a heart attack there while engaged in writing his umpteenth draft of a letter to Pope Paul VI. The purpose of the letter was to apologize, yet again, for the appalling solecism perpetrated by a former parishioner who had presumed – without his permission – to pester the Supreme Pontiff with the intelligence that his dear old friend, Monsignor Hugh Montgomery, had suffered a *'crise de nerf'*. Uncle Hugh's body was found with his fingers tightly clasped around his fountain pen.

He was buried in the Warwickshire countryside he had viewed so ambivalently (presumably it had been an out of date will). As I hesitated awkwardly over sprinkling holy water into the grave, I thought I could hear him whispering once more *'Puritano inglese'*. The gravestone is still lovingly tended by 'good old Monty's' parishioners from Brum.

Uncle Hugh left me his engraved gold cufflinks. In a profligate life they are the only prized possession that I have managed to hang on to. I keep them in a now faded leather box bought in Florence – a souvenir of travels with my uncle.

SEVEN

Your Lot and My Lot

AT THE TIME of Uncle Hugh's death in the summer of 1971 I was supposedly undergoing something of a *'crise de nerf'* myself. 'Nervous and physical debility' was how my Chelsea landlady's doctor put it on the medical certificate that persuaded my employers to give me a couple of months off to rest and recuperate. I retreated to a pub on the River Wye noted for its peace and cooking, and spent solitary days wandering the lush, roadless riverbank in order to work up an appetite for the evening's blowout. The only entertainment on offer was the mynah bird in the bar who mimicked the barmaid's coarse cackle to perfection. Time passed in a haze of fantasy as I daydreamed about escaping – with one bound, as the adventure yarns used to have it – from the messy reality which was troubling me.

After my stint at St Bernard's in Oxford I had decided not to take up my place at the University of East Anglia – 'All that *concrete*, my dear,' as Jonathan Pearce said, 'and those revolting students' – and to follow Pearce to Cambridge. My mother, whose old college of Newnham adjoined my proposed alma mater of Selwyn, was delighted with this prospect. My father seemed less enthusiastic.

'You would be nearly twenty-five when you came down from the university,' he pointed out in his most Micawberish manner, 'and I had rather hoped that you might have been supporting yourself by that comparatively advanced

age. I fear the necessary grants may not be forthcoming.
Still, if Cambridge is what you've set your heart on, we'll
have to do what we can ... Though how much longer I
can stand working for the BBC when – and Mrs White-
house is the only person brave enough to say so – the
Corporation is peddling such filth, I really don't know.'

In the circumstances my vague notion of idling away
the months before matriculating at Cambridge by daydreaming in front of the television in Biddo's room at
Cookham, while tucking into copiously filled dog bowls of
her matchless food, was evidently not the most tactful
scheme. With my head full of Evelyn Waugh and John
Betjeman's adventures as prep-schoolmasters, I wrote off
to my old headmaster at Port Regis asking for some sort
of temporary job. He seemed surprised to hear from me
again – understandably, in view of the strange way he
had behaved towards me during my time in his care.
Somehow my Betjemanian fantasies of larks with the
assistant matrons (one of whom was actually called Miss
Hunter-Dunn) after lights-out and jolly japes by the
cricket pav had wiped out the disagreeable realities from
my memory bank.

'I can't think why you want to come back here,' the
headmaster said when I went down to Dorset to see him.
'You were never especially happy at PR, I seem to remember.' He appeared agitated, as if I were about to denounce
him on the eve of his (long overdue) retirement.

I was not capable of explaining that in my capacity
as a daydream believer a spell of schoolmastering in
the Waugh–Betjeman tradition seemed, well, par for the
course (the headmaster was himself an ardent golfer).
Above all, it promised an enclosed world in which I could
escape into fantasy. The ritualized structures of the ped-
agogic order inside a rambling country house struck me
as the ideal cover for my headlong rush from reality.

In the event, this turned out to be one daydream that never hit the buffers of actuality. Consequently it remained a fairly regular number in my repertoire, liable to recur at particularly stressful times when the closeted cosiness of the usher's life appeared like Shangri-La. It was fuelled by visits to prep schools in my occasional role as scorer for E. W. Swanton's wandering Arabs Cricket Club (when hordes of enthusiastic boys would help me work 'the tellywag' for the scoreboard), and also by constant viewings of such nostalgic films as *Goodbye Mr Chips*, *The Browning Version* and *The Happiest Days of Your Life*. To this day I rather regret not having been a teacher. Perhaps, as the son of a schoolmistress, it is in my blood.

These educational musings were interrupted by Conynghame, in his *deus ex machina* role, who came to chivvy me out of my burrow in the Banbury Road, where I was still struggling with the biology O level required for my Cambridge matriculation.

'My dear old bean,' he pronounced. 'Ushering is no occupation for a gentleman. As it happens, I've got just the job for you. You remember jolly old Peter Townend, who keeps "the list" for deb parties?'

'If you recall, Richard,' I responded in my most prissy manner, 'I was never on the blessed "list". I don't go to parties – I loathe any form of social life.'

'Never mind about that,' continued Conynghame, whose ability to ignore points made against him robbed the Bar of a formidable advocate. 'The thing is he badly needs an assistant to help him on those big red stud books of his.'

I blushed with surprise. A trapdoor had suddenly been opened. The light of day flooded into one of my hitherto dark, secret fantasies.

Years before, just at the time I was leaving Harrow,

my aunt Daisy had spotted a personal advertisement in
The Times for 'a young man interested in history and
keen to work on genealogical reference books'. She had
sent it to me with a postcard saying: 'This looks rather
your type of thing.' Although I had not applied, as
requested, to the editor at an unpromising address south
of the river, I kept the cutting and during my years
as an articled clerk would often imagine myself to be
surrounded by the great scarlet tomes recording the
pedigrees of the aristocracy. What better escape than to
wallow in what Oscar Wilde had rightly called 'the best
thing in fiction the English have ever done'?

My passionate reverie about the intense pleasures of
The Peerage and *The Landed Gentry* fortunately went
unnoticed by Conynghame, who was by now preoccupied
with the ordering of 'a proper Raj-style curry' from the
bemused waiter in the Taj Mahal on the Turl.

'Now look here, my dear fellow,' he addressed the
waiter genially, 'I was brought up in India myself and I
know about curry. So don't go palming me off with the
sort of bland muck you dish up for the students (whatever
happened to undergraduates?). I want something really
hot, you understand? Yes – HOT! HOT! HOTTIE-HOT!'

The waiter, by now all smiles, retreated briskly to the
kitchens, from where sounds of muffled laughter could be
heard.

'Are you sure this is wise, Richard?' I asked nervously.
'I thought you told me that you had recently had your
tonsils out?'

'Yes, picked up a Harry-Throaters in Zermatt. But
these dives are incapable of producing anything too spicy
– don't worry, I can handle it. I just wanted to put 'em on
their mettle.'

When the waiter returned with an alarmingly steaming dish the entire kitchen staff hovered in his wake. 'We hope this is to your liking, sir.'

'Hot enough, is it?' said Conynghame, beaming.

A preliminary tasting reduced him to chokes and gasps.

'More *chilli*?' asked the waiter with mock-solicitude as his companions burst into unrestrained guffaws.

'I should think anything *chilly* would be welcome, eh, Richard?' I quipped, relishing a rare moment of advantage over my worldly companion. He shot me a look of watery loathing through his tears as he struggled, unavailingly it has to be said, to maintain his battered dignity.

The lunch with Peter Townend which Conynghame subsequently organized back in London was a more decorous, and resolutely non-ethnic, affair in an old-fashioned Fleet Street pub. Townend, a twinkling, dolphin-faced figure not far short of his fifties ('He only admits to thirty-seven,' Conynghame had told me), had the endearingly camp manner of a northern comic pretending to be a Mayfair toff.

'And so how is dear old *Gunby*?' he said with a roguish emphasis that recalled the delivery of Kenneth Williams. His eyes darted between Conynghame and myself as he enjoyed the effect his feat of memory had achieved. 'You see, I know *all* about you and your family. It's all in here.' He tapped the side of his head as if he were the music-hall turn 'Mister Memory' in the film of *The Thirty-Nine Steps*.

'That's what you say to all the boys, eh, Peter?' Conynghame grinned. He had warned me that 'Towners' loved 'to joust'.

'Now don't be cheeky, Richard. You *know* I'm *not* an old *Q*.'

'In fact,' said Townend, his eyes darting back in my

direction, 'we had a curious missive from some busybody who took it upon herself to inform us that your father should *not* be listed in *The Landed Gentry*—'

'*Stranded Bentry*, more like,' interjected Conynghame.

'As,' Townend carried on blithely, 'he was *not* the rightful tenant of Gunby. That honour, she claims, belongs to her *patroness*, Mrs Massingberd Campbell, now resident on the Riviera.'

'There you are, Massingberd,' said Conynghame. 'If you go and work for Peter on the new *Landed Gentry* you can put things straight.'

The plan was for me to work on the genealogical books for nine months until matriculating at Cambridge. As things turned out, I stayed on there and – like a frightened steeplechaser running out to the side of a fence on the second circuit of the course – shied away from Selwyn. My mother was mortified; my father could not conceal his relief. My friends and contemporaries were baffled. This was, after all, 1968 – the so-called Year of Protest – and I chose to immerse myself in compiling the pedigrees of *The Landed Gentry*.

Jonathan Pearce, who did proceed to Cambridge as planned, was particularly mystified by my apparent lack of qualifications for the occupation I was pursuing.

'I mean, Monty, here you are – the most antisocial person in the whole of London, proposing to spend your life working for the social arbiter of the season. How on earth will you fit into Townend's stable of debs' delights?'

'I won't, of course. I wouldn't go to a party for a thousand pounds. I hate all that nonsense. But you don't seem to realize, Pearce, that I am genuinely interested in family history—'

'Only your own. Like Sir Walter Elliot!'

'Just because you don't know anything about your own genealogy . . . You should study the subject one day.'

In some respects Pearce was right about the social side of the job not proving to my taste. Soon after I joined the firm I had a telephone call from a godmother of mine, not heard from in many years.

'Can you do me a great favour, dear Hughie, and get me "the list"?'

'I beg your pardon,' I said pompously. '*What* list?'

'You *know*, "the list". I'm sure darling Peter keeps it in the office. Why, you must be on it yourself, of course. I need it for my girls, you see.' She was alluding to the formidable brood of daughters, the youngest of whom eventually shared a flat with Lady Diana Spencer – a cohabitation that must have caused undreamed of pleasure in the maternal bosom.

'What Mr Townend does in his spare time,' I said with what I hoped was a sneer if not a snarl, 'is *nothing* to do with me. I am a serious student of genealogical scholarship busily engaged on the narrative pedigrees of *The Landed Gentry*. I don't know about any "list". I'm certainly *not* on it myself. I never go to parties . . . Er, um . . . Goodbye.'

The trouble was that Townend did not confine his social interests to his spare time. In addition to his duties at the genealogical publishers he had also taken on the social side of a glossy magazine, which had recently been revived by a shady Old Etonian ('a former guest of *Her Majesty's*', as Townend would gleefully shout down the telephone to all and sundry). On its reappearance on the news-stands a Sunday newspaper article attacked the glossy roundly for its mindless content and obsession with 'titled folk'. These richly justified insults were eagerly adopted as a mantra by Townend.

'Mindless! *Mindless!*' he would shriek with rapture as another fat parcel of photo-contact sheets arrived from the magazine requiring his expert identification for the

captions. The sheets would then be spread – to his school-
boyish enthusiasm and my priggish disdain – across the
table where I was endeavouring to collate the voluminous
questionnaires returned by what Rogers used to call 'the
sprigs of the family tree' for the *The Landed Gentry*.

'Look, look! *Titled Folk*! Here they are, loads of lovely
Titled Folk – why, there's *the Hon* Peter Phipps-Knightley
(*Fits-Tightly*, by the look of it). And, yes, *the Hon* Sir Clive
Bossom – neither one thing nor the other, eh?'

In my prim way, I knew that only postmen were
supposed to know about such courtesy titles as 'Hon', but
Townend always delighted in deriving the maximum
pleasure from pronouncing the 'H' as if it were a separate
syllable.

'Eh? *Eh?*' Townend, like the old trouper he was,
always expected a response to his jests, or 'jousts'.

'Quite so, Peter. I think it was Churchill who first
made that joke about Sir Clive's father, Sir Alfred, later a
life peer as Lord Bossom.'

'And, *aaaah*, look, *look!*' implored Townend as he
jabbed a bejewelled finger at the smiling image of a
behatted dowager. 'It's Lady Sugden. Isn't she charming,
charming? Isn't she – charming?'

'Oh yes, of course . . . Charming.'

These all too frequent, teeth-gritting ordeals apart, I
was left largely to my own devices in my cubbyhole in the
corner. The pleasantly untaxing work (mindless indeed)
of pasting up the pedigrees from the previous edition and
then annotating them with up-to-date details compiled
from the questionnaires was perfectly suited to
accompany elaborate fantasies about life as a landed
proprietor. I would alternate alter egos between a princely
duke in a Palladian palace and a modest literary squire
still seated on acres that had yielded my surname in the
Middle Ages.

Another fantasy, born out of my occasional visits on genealogical business to the College of Arms, was to be an exotically named herald or pursuivant – Rouge Croix or Bluemantle, perhaps – housed in comfortable bachelor chambers at the College, a handsome Queen Anne building below St Paul's, during the week and retreating to my country seat at Gunby for 'Fridays-to-Mondays'. I longed for the publishers to return to their rightful place under the wing of the College, where the series had begun in the nineteenth century and flourished up to the 1930s. Monsignor Gilbey, who presented me with a print of the College, encouraged me in my heraldic leanings. Indeed both he and my Catholic landlady, Mrs Lloyd – who had kindly invited me to stay at her house in Chelsea after a chance acquaintance made in the publishing office – arranged for me to meet the then Garter Principal King of Arms, Sir Anthony Wagner, over dinner.

At the Chelsea dinner, Mrs Lloyd, uncowed by the great scholar's chilly manner (born, I later discovered, of crippling shyness which was to be cured by his blindness in old age), courageously came out with: 'Well, Sir Anthony, are you going to give this clever young man a job?'

'Dear lady,' he replied. 'He would need to be clever enough to have a good university degree . . . And now, if you will forgive me, I must take my leave.' I noticed that this was announced on the stroke of 10.15 – evidently the earliest time permitted in court circles for the exit.

As well as the College of Arms, I especially enjoyed my escapes to the Gilbert & Sullivan world of the House of Lords, where I would venture on the flimsiest excuse for information about new peerage creations ('Ruddy *day boys*', as one official described the dreary flow of life peers.) Uncle Hugh's old Berlin friend Patrick Barrington, 'the Vanishing Viscount', would regularly entertain me in

the comforting club-like dining room. A splendidly Wodehousian figure, with wing-nut ears and no discernible
chin, the eleventh Viscount Barrington became my new
hero.

His Lordship, in stud-book terminology, spoke in a
clipped, throwaway tone pitched so softly that it was often
impossible to decipher. Gurgling laughter was never far
from the surface, particularly when he broke into
impromptu verse or song.

I had a duck-billed platypus when I was up at Trinity,
For whom I soon developed a remarkable affinity.
He used to live in lodgings with myself and Arthur Purvis.
And we all went up together for the Diplomatic Service . . .

Such 'Songs of a Sub-Man' would pass the afternoon
most agreeably in the red leather armchairs of the Lords.
The Vanishing Viscount's fellow peers, such as the
luxuriantly moustachioed old Earl of Albemarle (born
in 1882 and a son-in-law of the last Marquess of Lincolnshire, a title I rather fancied reviving for myself)
and the somewhat distracted Earl of Longford (a fellow
campaigner with Lord Barrington in the anti-abortion, or
'pro-life', movement), courteously made me feel very much
at home. I was given plenty of material for my pipe
dreams on the 6.15 back to Cookham, where I was still
mainly based.

Sometimes, when watching proceedings in the crimson Chamber of the Lords, I feared that Their Lordships
may have been laughing at rather than with my prized
eccentric peer, the Vanishing Viscount. During an abor-
tion debate, for instance, he announced, to a curious
House: 'Like most of Your Lordships, I was born.'

When Lord Soper, the Methodist soapbox orator,
declared: 'I am at this moment responsible for fourteen

pregnant girls,' Lord Barrington observed: 'Unlike the noble Lord, Lord Soper, I am *not* responsible for fifteen illegitimate girls—'

'I meant that I *visit* them,' interrupted Lord Soper. 'And there are fourteen, not fifteen.'

'I beg the noble Lord's pardon,' said Barrington.

On another occasion, when moving an amendment to the Nullity of Marriage Bill, Barrington absorbed the House by recalling how, in the 1930s, a male servant in the employ of his sister (who was, to drag in an aristocratic connection, the mother-in-law of my half-sister Juliet) announced that he was changing sex – again. He had already changed sex before, apparently.

'He left with the cook-housekeeper and they went as a married couple but as to *who* was *which* I cannot say,' Barrington told the by now thoroughly bemused House. 'I understand they were both interchangeable.'

Although dingy to a degree in contrast with the Puginesque plush of the Lords, the publishers' offices also housed a promising contender in the Eccentric Peers stakes in the unlikely environs of a gardening magazine down the corridor. 'You might have mistaken the mag's adman for the *bus stop*,' explained Townend of the tall man with a haunted expression, 'but he's really *the Hon* Brinsley Le Poer Trench, heir presumptive (*consumptive*, more likely) to the earldom of Clancarty. He has written books about flying saucers – that's all he ever talks about.'

'So he earns his renown by gazing at space and his living by selling it?'

'I'll do the jokes, if you don't mind.'

At the office Christmas party I heard myself asking, as if in a Bateman cartoon, whether Mr Le Poer Trench had ever actually seen a flying saucer? This was unwise.

'I installed a UFO detector in the bedroom wall of my flat in Drayton Gardens,' he told me, at considerable length. 'At first the results were disappointing. It did buzz one Saturday afternoon but when I rushed out I found that the sky was cloudy and completely overcast. Presumably it was above the cloud . . . At last, I did spot my first UFO . . . It was an eerie white light zigzagging over South Kensington. I had to climb into the kitchen sink to get a good look at it through the window.'

The future Lord Clancarty, who was to found a UFO Study Group at the House of Lords, went on – and on – to induct me in his theory that in 63,000 BC beings from other planets had landed on earth in spaceships. Other aliens had emerged through tunnels from a civilization which still existed beneath the earth's crust. 'I haven't been down there myself,' he said, 'but from what I gather they are very advanced.'

Then, with a tremendous flourish, he produced a satellite photograph from his person showing a large circular blob in the North Polar ice. 'That,' he said, pointing to the blob, 'is the entrance to one of the tunnels.'

'Are you sure er, um . . . that it isn't just *part of the camera?*'

The eccentric Earl-in-waiting never spoke to me again.

As at the club, I relished the somnolent gloom of the publishing offices in Waterloo. Aged twenty-two, I longed to be like the quiet, pessimistic, sympathetically melancholy middle-aged figure of Mr James, the sales director, who took a refreshingly cynical view of Townend and his absurd season, with its pushy, social-climbing mamas and gormless, grasping debs' delights. Mr James was nicknamed 'Lord James of Rush-Home' by Townend (an allusion to the educationalist Lord James of Rusholme) as the regular announcement that the sales director was leaving the office 'to make a few bookshop calls' on his way back to Croydon fooled no one – least of all the assorted jolly sales ladies, variously nicknamed 'the Old Scold', 'the Old Bawd' and 'the Young Slattern'.

'I tried to be a writer once,' Mr James would confide in me mournfully. 'But there was no money in it.'

Knowing his love of my cousin Ralph Vaughan Williams's music, I presumptuously arranged a lunch in the Festival Hall restaurant for Mr James to meet the composer's widow, Ursula, who was escorted by my uncle Peter. This could not be judged a success as neither Mr James nor myself uttered more than a sentence between us. I was disappointed that others could not share my delight in Mr James's Eeyorish wit.

'Your problem, Massingberd,' said one of the breathtakingly self-confident young Etonians who came to help out with editorial chores as the production schedule fell further and further behind, 'is that you are in love with failure.'

'It's not so simple as that,' I protested. 'I like the idea that the spark was there once. It may have been extinguished by disappointments, but it could yet flicker into light once more. Mr James saying "I tried to be a writer once" puts me in mind of poor old Newman Noggs telling Nicholas Nickleby that it would be in order for him to refer to "Mr Noggs" at one of his old haunts – "For I was a gentleman, then."'

Notwithstanding the melancholy charms of Mr James and the Dickensian set-up in Waterloo, it was a relief when I persuaded Townend that I could make better progress with the Sisyphean schedule by working at home for at least a couple of days a week. Much as I was enjoying my genealogical labours, the constant downpour of 'mindless' contact sheets and 'jousting' patter from the irrepressible Townend were beginning to prey on my nerves. I lacked the confidence to tell him outright, as Conynghame or the young Etonians would have done, to

put a sock in it and let me get on with my job. Instead, I
continued to smile weakly and murmur assentingly
'Charming'.

Working at home, back at Cookham and fortified by
Biddo's overflowing dog bowls, proved phenomenally pro-
ductive. I became so obsessed with arranging the piles of
'paste-ups' in apple-pie order, and in lovingly listing the
most excruciatingly tedious (or 'worthy', as I preferred)
biographical details in meticulously correct sequence, that
I slaved away around the clock. I was high on adrenaline
as I whipped myself up into close identification with the
head of the family – *of whom we treat*', as stud-book
terminology had it.

After the volume of *The Landed Gentry* – in which I
had the almost overwhelming thrill of seeing my name in
print for the first time – came a new edition of *The
Peerage, Baronetage & Knightage*, a vast undertaking
rendered even more formidable by a fiendishly punitive
production schedule. Honour, indeed the very future of
the *Peerage*, was at stake, or so the publishing firm's
manager warned me. Could I bring in the book on time to
save it from extinction? Young, keen and for the first
occasion in my life totally focused and committed, I dedicated myself to what my uncle Graham would have called
'a job of work'.

What I relished about compiling narrative pedigrees
was the satisfaction of tidying up history into neat little
parcels. For someone particularly interested in people and
their peculiarities (which could be evoked, historically at
least, by inserting pithy quotations and anecdotes amid
the straight curriculum vitae), yet who was pathologically
shy of meeting them in the flesh, this proved the ideal
exercise. It also served as the perfect platform from which
my daydreams – crystallized in the mugshots of my

heroes looking down from the walls of my Cookham cell on my ceaseless labours – could take wing.

On and on I toiled right through to the dreariest dregs of the *Knightage* (fortunately the *Companionage* was left to our rival publication) until the mammoth tome was completed, on schedule. I basked in my new official status as Assistant Editor proudly proclaimed in the 105th edition (the last, as it turned out, for nearly thirty years) and treated myself to a short holiday staying in the club, to which I had finally been elected.

A fully-fledged clubman at last, I wallowed in the leathery gloom of Sir Charles Barry's palazzo. Aged twenty-three going on seventy-three, I savoured the solitary fogeyish pleasures to the full; indeed for the ten days of my break I do not think I uttered a word to a soul. Not for nothing had Sir Arthur Conan Doyle based his description of the Diogenes, the misanthropic haunt of Mycroft Holmes where no one speaks to one another, on the club. After breakfasting in the coffee room (porridge, kippers, mixed grill), where the only excitement would be Monsignor Gilbey's arrival back from Mass at the Brompton Oratory (by 'omnibus'), I would proceed downstairs to the outer morning room to peruse the morning newspapers and attend to my desultory correspondence. Then upstairs to a chaise longue in the library overlooking Carlton House Gardens for a delicious Walter Mitty session; by this stage I had transported myself back to a Victorian/ Edwardian lifespan, ending with a dignified death on the *Titanic*. Lunch (kipper pâté, grouse-and-steak pie, rice pudding) would be followed by a visit to the cinema (a vintage Garbo season was in progress) or a matinee, or a descent into the cellar television room to watch the racing. In the evening came dinner (smoked salmon and lamb cutlets in what would subsequently become known as the Lord Lucan mode) and more daydreaming in the library. Altogether it was the best holiday I have ever had.

Yet it turned out to be the lull before the storm. Back at the publishing office, Townend's twitterings and tattlings were turning my nerves into a tightly compressed coil. Work on the latest volume of *The Landed Gentry* was piling up to impossible proportions. Even Mr James's pithy sarcasm, which so often punctured Townend's wilder fights of fancy, and the Etonians' self-confident attitude ('Don't let it get you down') were not easing the pressures I felt. My landlady, Mrs Lloyd, lent a kindly ear to my woes and tried to bring me out of myself by inviting a series of alarmingly 'proper' Catholic girls to supper at her little house in Chelsea. Following these rather sparse repasts (sausage rolls seemed to be the staple main course), I would be deputed to escort the young ladies back to Sloane Square Underground Station.

These perambulations provided the girls with a chance to relieve the frustrations of having spent such a tedious evening by being offensive to their unwilling companion. 'Are you an *Australian*?' enquired one.

'No. Why on earth would you think I was?'

'Well, for a start, you are wearing a funny green suit – and I once met some extremely boring creeps who turned out to be Australians, so I thought you might be from Down Under too . . .'

Another of the former convent girls (Mrs Lloyd was a pillar of the Sacred Heart) snarled as soon as we rounded the corner of the Royal Hospital: 'I am *quite* capable of finding my own way back to the Tube, thank you very much. So why doesn't Diddums toddle off back home to tuck up old Ma Lloyd into beddy-byes?'

This last crack was closer to the truth than the young

vixen realized. Mrs Lloyd, who must have been at least forty years my senior, had developed the disturbing habit of coming into my room while I was undressing and then sitting on the bed, with her back half turned away from me in a stagey gesture of modesty.

'No peeping, no peeping – I promise,' she would say in her most arch tones as she made a show of covering her face with her hands. The fingers would then spread unmistakably open. 'I'm not looking. Just carry on as if I weren't here, my dear. Now, *do* tell me all your worries. Do tell . . .'

My neurotic ramblings finally reached such a pitch that she summoned her doctor, a wiry old New Zealander who had specialized in venereal disease during the Second World War. (I thought of one of Townend's anecdotes about a respectable spinster, daughter of a naval commander, who had allegedly stormed his office with the complaint: 'I'm very upset that you omitted to mention that my father had the VD' – otherwise the Volunteer Decoration.) I could not really grasp what the medic was saying – he spoke very quietly, and the word 'debility' was unfamiliar – but it gradually dawned on me that I had been officially diagnosed as having suffered some sort of nervous breakdown. Feeling rather mystified, and heavily dosed on Valium (the better part of discretion), I retreated to the Wye Valley where my reveries were interrupted by news of the death of Uncle Hugh.

En route for the funeral, I stopped off at Roger's farm in Somerset for a night, only to be greeted by a telephone message that sent my newly settled mind into confusion. While idling by the Wye, I had formulated a plan for my future which seemed to hold out the hope of peace and serenity: to write novels in the mornings, and work as a waiter in a restaurant in Bath (where a cousin had

connections) at lunchtimes and in the evenings. What, as
the urbane Kenneth Clark used to say in his *Civilisation*
series on television, could be more agreeable?

Suddenly this scheme took on the shape of yet another
silly fantasy, an impractical daydream, in the light of
this stark message. Would I telephone Christine, from the
office, urgently on her home telephone number that evening? I had a strong premonition that if I did so the whole
path of my life would follow quite another direction to the
one I had sketched out at Symonds Yat. After much
dithering, curiosity overcame me.

'Er, is that Miss . . . um, I mean, Christine?'

'Ah, Hugh, at last! I thought you had disappeared off
the face of the earth and I would *never* track you down.
Look, can you come up to London tomorrow?'

'Er, no . . . I don't think so. I've rather finished with
London, really. Anyway, I've got to bury my uncle later in
the week.'

'I really do believe it would be well worth your while
to come up.'

Christine, whom I barely knew, sounded strangely
seductive and inviting. 'What do you mean?' I said in a
less snappy tone.

'Well, do you want to take over the genealogical series,
or don't you?'

'*Gosh.*' My head suddenly swam with visions of glory.
'But what's happened?'

'While you've been away the management have finally
decided that they want a complete change of direction.
The production schedules are up the spout. They want to
get rid of Townend and they've sounded me out as to who
should take his place. Knowing how much hard work
you've put in over the last three years and something of
your ideas for the expansion of the series, I naturally said
that Massingberd was their man.'

'It's very decent of you to think of me, but I don't know whether I'm up to it. I've got other plans now . . .'

'But wouldn't you regret it if they gave the job to one of the Etonians? I know Trelawney is sniffing round for it.'

This certainly cast a different complexion on the problem. While I did not wish to be party to stabbing Townend in the back, for, in spite of everything, I still entertained a nostalgic fondness for his idiosyncrasies, if he was really on the way out it might indeed be galling to see the Etonians scooping up the cream. After more humming and hawing, I agreed to meet Christine for lunch the next day opposite the Old Bailey (which played nicely on my perennial guilt complex) but was distracted from the business in hand by her feline eyes.

The only child of a French father, who became an American citizen, and an English mother, Christine had a cosmopolitan and commercial background which had evidently impressed Bill Cathles, the managing director of the publishing company. In effect, she had been installed as a sort of editorial troubleshooter by this beady old Fleet Street hand who liked to spend most of the day at his usual table in El Vino's. The job, Christine told me, was mine. All I had to do was drop in for a chat with 'Bill' on 'the Street' later that afternoon.

In the meantime, by arrangement, I met Mrs Lloyd in the windswept brutalist modernist environs of St Paul's Cathedral to review my position. My landlady confessed to having spied on my lunch companion.

'She's quite a pretty little thing, isn't she?' she said in unsympathetic tones. 'I'd be very careful of that mademoiselle if I were you.'

'I think you're being very unfair, Mrs Lloyd. Christine is clearly on my side, and without her I wouldn't be offered this great opportunity.'

'But can you really cope with such a responsible, wearisome post? Is it what you long to do? I thought you were going to be a *proper* writer, not just the compiler of pedigree books. Remember how ill it made you before. And ponder on what price you may be expected to pay with your new friend, the mademoiselle.'

Flushing crimson, I stammered out: 'I don't think I have anything further to say to you, Mrs Lloyd.' Then I turned melodramatically on my heel towards Fleet Street and a new future.

'Come in, old boy, take a pew.' Bill Cathles smiled. 'You've made a hit with our Chris, it seems. Bit of a corker, isn't she?'

Seeing that this brand of geniality was not breaking the ice as effectively as he had hoped, Cathles swiftly switched to management-speak. 'The brand needs a new, fresh image. You're young, er, dynamic' – hurriedly consults notes – 'full of bright ideas and with the right team – co-ordinated by Chris, no doubt – you can give the product a more meaningful market profile. What about it?'

'I'm rather concerned about Peter Townend.'

'Don't worry about him. He's history. We've had our sights trained on him for years. No, forget Mr Townend – we'll bung him some sort of "consultancy" to keep him quiet.'

Townend was duly given a retainer before being officially declared redundant, whereupon he sued the company for wrongful dismissal. The petition made some references to my 'nervous breakdown'. An old, loyal friend of his wrote me an angry letter complaining of my lack of chivalry ('Never betray your chief,' as Uncle Hugh had advised me before he lost his marbles), and the whole messy business troubles my conscience to this day. During our last uneasy encounter, Townend issued a curse that was to haunt me over the next thirty years: 'Just wait until some young *cat* [he always referred to Christine as 'that cat'] puts the skids under you . . .'

That heady afternoon in the summer of 1971, though, I was consumed by the unfeeling arrogance of youth. For the first time in my life one of my secret daydreams had, quite unexpectedly, come true. I was, in effect, now in charge of the genealogical series at the age of twenty-four. The insecure fourth child of a hearty family who had never achieved any sort of personal success in any field was suddenly somebody – or so I felt. Fantasy had collided with reality.

Drunk with power (as Mr James would have put it), I repaired to the library of the club and wrote out my editorial manifesto. With Cathles's corporate clichés still ringing in my ears, I priggishly declared that 'any suggestion of a "snob's bible" image must be firmly squashed and the series clearly established as the work of history and scholarship that it is . . . We must not be diverted from our course of publishing family histories into irrelevant byways of metetricious journalism, social frippery and the guidance of social climbers, snobbery and other mindless activities.'

Doubtless influenced by my unfortunate meeting with Mrs Lloyd earlier in the day, I went on to inveigh against the casual callers – 'mainly from the ranks of the unhinged brethren and sisterhood' – who, in the future, would 'never be accommodated'. Mrs Lloyd, a pathetically lonely and essentially kind person, had been just such a caller to the office in the first instance.

Next, I ranted on about the 'ludicrous' editorial policy that had so damaged the reputation of *The Landed Gentry*: 'The pushy, pseudo-smart social climbers on the one hand and the cranky, suburban genealogists (whose middle-class pedigrees are of interest to no one but

themselves) on the other have propelled themselves into
the pages of what should be the supreme authority on
the squirearchical county families . . .' And so, embarrass-
ingly, on.

Warming to the possibilities before me, I drew up
absurdly ambitious lists of spin-off books that would
popularize, and subsidize, the two main tomes, *The Peerage & Baronetage* and *The Landed Gentry*. These plans
included new studies of World Royalty and the Presidential Families of the USA; a multi-volume Guide to
Country Houses; collections of Irish, Scottish and Welsh
pedigrees; revised editions of the Extinct Peerages and
Baronetcies; and even a multi-media project on Oral
Social History covering living testimony on the British
Empire, Life on a Country Estate – and other topics too
humorous to mention.

At the time I confess to having taken all this very
seriously indeed. Somehow I managed to impress others
with the earnestness of my missionary zeal. Together
with Christine, to whom I soon became engaged, I assembled an efficient team of contributors. Even the Etonians
seemed to be caught up in this onrush of enthusiasm for
the brave new series – though the younger of them, Hugo
Vickers, noted in his diary that 'Massingberd was, as
usual, play-acting the part of "the Publisher" at his club,
while he copiously plied his contributors with claret.'
After one meeting of what I pompously called 'the Editorial Board' at Vickers's stockbroker father's house in
Knightsbridge, I murmured my approval of the opulent
interior to the elder of the Etonians.

'I wouldn't care to have a tap in *my* drawing room,' he
drawled, alluding to the bar-basin hidden behind one of
the bookcases.

Play-acting the part of publisher enabled me to fulfil
a fantasy which I had never anticipated – that of meeting

some of my favourite writers in the flesh. The ruse was to invite them to contribute an introductory essay to some genealogical volume or other. My first hero on the list was John Betjeman – whom I had glimpsed in the Hungry Horse restaurant on one of my visits to the College of Arms nearby – but he declined my request to celebrate the squirearchy. The right-wing journalist Anthony Lejeune ('At Oxford I knew him as Tony Thomson,' one of the heralds told me), revered for his role as deputy to the supreme satirist 'Peter Simple' (Michael Wharton) of the *Daily Telegraph*, proved more amenable. I thrilled to his acute and witty conversation ('civilized' seemed to be his favourite word) over lunch at Simpsons-in-the-Strand, though I made a fumbling hash over tipping the carver of our saddle-of-lamb and coins rolled around the floor. After the treacle roll, the sage pronounced, out of the blue: 'I think I'll change my mind and have a glass of port.'

As I had not actually offered him this courtesy, I was somewhat baffled by his 'change of mind', but managed to blurt out: 'Of course. I'm so sorry.' I was aware that I had committed some sort of clubland faux pas and only later did it dawn on me that he was, sensibly enough, merely trying to recoup something extra on top of the measly fee being proffered by his oleaginous table companion.

When the Lejeune essay for *The Landed Gentry* was duly delivered, it began with the arresting opening sentence: 'A male member of the landed gentry is a gentleman; which, in England, is an interesting thing to be . . .' Unfortunately I failed to spot the double entendre until it was in print and another contributor, Mark Bence-Jones, whose lavatorial humour is highly infectious, delighted in harping on about Lejeune's 'male member'. Mark, an old family friend from Ireland who had been taught briefly by Uncle Hugh as a boy at Ampleforth, became a stalwart supporter. I had relished his romantic, aristocratic novels as an adolescent and never tired of his fruity anecdotes about life in the Raj and Ascendancy Ireland, about which he is a great authority. A special joy of his company is that when he talks of, say, the '80s or the '90s you can be confident that he is referring to the 1880s and 1890s (the decade of his parents' birth), rather than the end of the twentieth century.

Although there are those who mock Mark for his antediluvian approach to the modern world (most of which, in the form of television and newspapers, he simply ignores), I have always found him full of fun and laughter. Once, on one of our research trips across the length and breadth of Ireland looking at family seats, Mark was at the wheel of a temperamental old Volkswagen Beetle which backfired every few yards. Every time it did so, Mark would be 'reminded' of yet another anecdote from his apparently limitless repertoire of farting stories.

Barp! *Barp*!

'That reminds me of the occasion when the Governor-General's lady forgot herself in Madras, and the ADC was obliged to . . .'

'Shouldn't we be turning right here, Mark?'

'Never believe an Irish signpost, my dear fellow – I just tend to follow the sun, anyway . . .'

Phlutt! *Phlutt*!

'A sound strangely reminiscent of the time when the Joint Mistress of the Galway Blazers – in more ways than one, you might say – was jumping a high stone wall . . .' And so on, all the way up to the north-west of the island.

Although we did not call upon Admiral of the Fleet Earl Mountbatten of Burma at his ill-fated holiday home in those parts, I had dropped in on him in London shortly before his murder by the IRA. For Lord Mountbatten, a passionate genealogist, was the biggest lion I lured into the fold. As my first new venture for the revamped series I devised a *Guide to the Royal Family* and asked Lord Mountbatten if he would write the Foreword. I was told to report to the Mountbatten bolthole in Belgravia at 1000 hours.

The tiny mews house seemed awash with young, muscular and suspiciously good-looking Naval ratings bustling about the place to no apparent purpose. I sat and awaited the arrival of the great man. Suddenly this whirlwind of erect bearing strutted into the small sitting room.

'Ah, good morning, Montgomery-Massingberd – presumably you're the General's grandson? Townend's been sacked, has he?'

My attempts at interjecting answers to those rapid-fire questions floundered hopelessly. He carried on as if I hadn't uttered, which I don't think I had.

'Yes, good riddance from what I heard about the feller. He wouldn't play ball with me over this *vital* question of the Royal Surname. Done your homework on that, have you? Well, don't worry, I'll put you in the picture. The thing is I *will* do your Foreword if you guarantee that you will give maximum positive exposure throughout the book to the House of Mountbatten and the correct Royal Surname of Mountbatten-Windsor. Got that: "*Mountbatten-Windsor*"! But, of course, no one is to know that I played any part in this and what I am telling you now is *strictly* off the record. As you must know, I loathe personal publicity. Deep background, non-attributable, as our friends in the press say.

'Well, here's the story. Princess Elizabeth married my nephew, Prince Philip, in 1947 and had two children, Prince Charles and Princess Anne. Then in 1952 Princess Elizabeth became Queen and so should have begun the reign of the House of Mountbatten on the throne. But that old drunk Churchill, backed up by that crooked swine Beaverbrook (who paid off all Churchill's debts), objected to this and forced the Queen to announce that the 'House of Windsor' would continue as before. My nephew was furious, as you can imagine. "It makes me into an amoeba," he said, "a bloody amoeba." Have you ever wondered why there is a ten-year gap between the births of Princess Anne (1950) and Prince Andrew (1960)?'

While Lord Mountbatten paused momentarily for dramatic effect, I struggled to collect my thoughts. Here I was, a greenhorn aged twenty-five having just walked in off the street, listening to a heroic national figure confiding in me the intimate secrets of the Sovereign and slagging off the most celebrated Prime Minister in history as an 'old drunk'. I had to pinch myself in order to assume a suitably man-of-the-world guise.

'The answer is that because it wasn't until 1960 we managed to persuade the Macmillan Government that the royal surname should properly be "Mountbatten-Windsor" not Windsor. But it has taken two bosh-shots to establish this, and even now there is, I understand, some constitutional confusion on the precise meaning of these declarations. But the experts maintain – and I agree with them – that while it is argued that Royal Highnesses have no need for surnames as such and that "Mountbatten-Windsor" will only come into play for their non-royal descendants there is actually one medium in which surnames *are* required – in documents of civil registration. That is why I am going to make damn sure that the name "Mountbatten-Windsor" appears on the marriage certificates of Prince Charles and Princess Anne.' Mountbatten's obsessive machinations were to bear fruit in the case of Princess Anne at Westminster Abbey, but he had been blown up two years before Prince Charles's wedding in 1981 so was unable to fix things behind the arras at St Paul's.

'It would be of great benefit to the cause if *The Peerage*, the nation's premier work of reference, were to push this point. I know that dear Lilibet – Her Majesty the Queen – would take notice of what you say and be very gratified.'

Duly flattered, I fawned in agreement. Mountbatten flashed a film-star smile and put his arm on my shoulder as I stood up to go. 'Now here's the debriefing, Massingberd: explain why the royal surname *has* to be Mountbatten-Windsor; give the House of Mountbatten a jolly good show; send the draft to me; and when I'm happy I'll do your Foreword. Understood?'

'Yes, Sir.'

Poor Dermot Morrah, the veteran Arundel Herald Extraordinary and an ornament of that bizarre breed known as 'constitutional experts', was given the unenviable task of grafting Mountbatten's thesis into his magisterial overview of the Queen's reign for the book. It took several attempts before this was achieved to Mountbatten's satisfaction. While discussing the minute detail in the club library with Dermot – this seemed safe enough as Dermot tended to speak in a hoarse whisper, only occasionally swooping up and down the vocal register, and I confine myself mainly to inaudible mumbling – we were suddenly set upon by Mr Buckingham, the Terror of the Club. 'SHUSH! SHUSH!' he hissed. 'This is a place of SILENCE! Moreover *this* is a *gentlemen's* club and you appear to be doing *business* in it. Out with the pair of you.'

We retreated shamefacedly across Pall Mall to the old United University Club. Dermot was in gentle protest mode: 'I don't *really* see why we have to keep dancing to Dickie Mountbatten's whim merely to compensate for all the insecurities he feels on account of his morganatic ancestry and the unfortunate sacking of his father as

First Sea Lord because he was a German prince, do you?'
Before I could murmur my sympathies with his frustra-
tions over this fraudulent Polonius of the Court, Mr
Buckingham was upon us again. 'SHUSH, SHUSH and
SHUSH *again*,' the ubiquitous clubman hissed, looking
for all the world like a bald eagle disturbed in his nest.
'This is *also* a gentlemen's club, to which I have the
honour to belong, and the same rules apply.'

Mr Buckingham continued to dog my footsteps in
clubland. When I was confirming the arrangements for
the launch party of the *Guide to the Royal Family* in the
club bar with Robin McDouall, the secretary, I failed to
grasp what Robin's agitated facial gestures and unexpected awkwardness signified.

'So it will be all right if there is a television crew in
attendance?'

'No, no, no. Let's forget all about that, shall we?'

'What – but surely, Robin, you said—'

Then, at last, I spotted the bald eagle glowering
behind McDouall's moon face. Steam appeared to be rising from Mr Buckingham's pate, and it was not difficult
to imagine the flapping of mighty wings.

'My dear,' simpered Robin in his more usual tones
once the eagle had flown off, 'I could have *throttled* you
for talking about parties and TV crews in front of that old
beast Buckingham. You know he hates any form of social
intercourse in the club.'

My true nature would have found me firmly on Mr
Buckingham's side in the best Diogenes tradition, but
the thrill of becoming a micro-celebrity (I had recently
made a small splash in newspapers and on the wireless
and television promoting *The Peerage's* 'new puppies', as
William Hardcastle rather breathlessly put it on *The
World At One*) was giving me a swollen head. On the
night of the launch party at the club I cavalierly failed

to greet the guest of honour, Lord Mountbatten, at the front door.

'My dear Hugh,' admonished Robin McDouall, who had to come to the rescue, 'don't you know *anything* about royal protocol?'

The truth was that I knew nothing about parties in general, having scrupulously avoided them all my life. Overcome with nerves, I had cut myself badly while shaving and blood was still oozing on to my blotchy chin as I essayed the role of host – preferable, I soon learned, to that of guest as you can remain constantly distracted on the verge of the action.

'I like the *red* motif, Hugh,' trilled David Williamson, the doyen of genealogists who is the spit of Ronnie Barker and sometimes almost as funny. 'Shirt, tie, carnation – they all go so nicely with the blood. "Blood Royal", you might say!'

The joy of the enterprise for a suburban fantasist who had dreamed of mixing with famous writers while reading library books on the Paddington train was the chance to encounter one's heroes in the flesh – even if sometimes they did not quite live up to expectations. For sheer force of personality none could match A. L. Rowse. 'I'm a very well *remunerated* author, my dear,' he miaowed as he insouciantly doubled the standard fee. Norman St John-Stevas, whose preening egotism, camp wit and striped shirtings I confess to having rather admired on television chat shows in the '60s, also tried it on.

'I couldn't *possibly* pen my words of wisdom on the Constitution for that *derisory* fee,' he sneered.

Later in our conversation while swanking about his intimacy with the Royal Family, he declared: 'Of course, I'd do absolutely *anything* for our dear, dear Queen.'

'Then perhaps you'd do the piece for the fee on offer, Mr St John-Stevas?'

'Oh, you *cheeky* boy!'

Perhaps, I reflected, it might help him buy another pair of Queen Victoria's knickers, which he was reputed to collect. To cover the 'Royal Image' I recruited Dr (as he then was) Roy Strong, formerly reputed to be a rather mousy researcher in the archives of the College of Arms but by now the flamboyant, self-publicizing director of the National Portrait Gallery. Over lunch at the Garrick (my own club was shut for the summer), where I failed to rustle up some Cumberland sauce to adorn the Doctor's cold ham, he laid into the Prince of Wales's dress sense. 'Just *look* at him! That *ghastly* short back and sides, those dreary "sports jackets". Why isn't he allowed to blossom as a *dandy* with flowing Cavalier locks. He should become a leader of *Fashion*! I was only saying to dear Xandra Rhodes the other evening . . .'

My mind wandered off to a more amusing club lunch, at the old 'Senior' (the United Service) when the cosy waitress was convinced that Hugo Vickers, then compiling the current royal biographies for the book, was in fact Prince Charles himself – complete with short back and sides and sports jacket which Dr Strong found so objectionable. Young Hugo, who had followed the Prince to Hill House school in Chelsea and formed a lifelong obsession with royalty which extended to dressing miniature models in mini-Garter robes, was beside himself with excitement at this misidentification and played up to the hilt.

On publication I asked Roy Strong if he would be prepared to plug the book on Radio 4's *Today* programme, which had expressed an interest. '*Today*,' he mused. 'Now is that good image or bad image, one wonders.'

Among the other eminent contributors to whom I paid assiduous court were Sir Charles Petrie, a pompous little man with an Imperial beard, and Sir Philip Magnus, who gave me fairly short shrift in the stately hall of Brooks's

Club. 'He obviously didn't fancy you, dear,' one experienced bookman told me later. 'You know Sir Philip is a terrible pouncer.' By far the sweetest and most straightforward authors I dealt with were dear old Roger Fulford, a friend of Uncle Hugh's up from Westmorland, with a scruffy sweater under his battered grey suit, and the refreshingly down-to-earth and practical Lady Longford.

My special hero and mentor in genealogy was 'the Ilk,' that gloriously life-enhancing figure Sir Iain Moncreiffe of that Ilk, Bt, Albany Herald of Arms and great genealogical scholar. As he never tired of pointing out to ignoramuses who use the phrase 'that Ilk' to mean of that sort or kidney, it actually signifies a place of the same name. The Ilk, who had contributed rollicking narrative accounts of such families as his own, the Stuarts and the O'Neills (complete with a Gaelic chieftain known as 'the Lazy-Arsed Youth') which enlivened the *Peerage* no end, was an inspiration in my campaign to make genealogy amusing and diverting. Family history, too often the preserve of the batty, the boastful and the bore, was sheer fun to the Ilk. He urged me to transform the series into 'a treasure-house of family tales', to put some flesh and blood into the traditionally skeletal stud books. 'Above all,' he would say, 'remove all the eyewash and the whitewash.'

The difficulty was getting the Ilk to put some of his encyclopedic knowledge on to paper. Once an essay I had commissioned from him on 'The High Kings of Ireland' for our *Irish Family Records* was so late that I sent an emissary up to Easter Moncreiffe to chivvy him along. Knowing his love of blondes in horror films – particularly Ingrid Pitt in the role of his ancestress Elisabeth Bathory, 'the Blood Countess' who tops, as the Ilk delighted in reminding one, the list under 'Murderer' in the *Guinness Book of Records* – I chose my luscious fair-haired assistant, Susanna Osman Jones. Susanna reported that when, on arrival, she headed for the lavatory, she spotted the Ilk's beady eye pressed to the keyhole. 'I can't hear anything yet,' he said. Susanna, a nicely brought-up girl from Surrey, stuffed the keyhole full of paper and turned the taps full on before resuming her place on the throne.

For my part, after peeing beside him in the 'stand-ups' of the Turf Club, where he had invited me to lunch, I shocked my host by my suburban gentility in crossing the floor to wash my hands afterwards.

'Why on earth are you doing that, my dear fellow? It suggests that you have been handling something unclean. As the world's Master Snob, take a tip from me: very non-U, I'm afraid.'

It was typical of the Ilk to face the charge of snobbery head-on instead of the usual wriggling about 'social history', though nobody knew better than he that genealogical scholarship is actually the antithesis of snobbery. 'No family,' he would say, 'is older than any other family, though some lines can be traced back further than others.'

On our 'club crawls', as he called them (others might have categorized them as 'benders'), the Ilk also taught me such niceties as how to eat gulls' eggs and regaled me with snippets of his colourful life.

'As a boy in Kenya I had two pythons and a boa constrictor put round my neck to teach me not to be alarmed by snakes ... In my Game Book during the war I entered under "Bag", at Monte Camino, "15th Panzer Grenadiers: 1?" But I had no time to pick him up if he was bagged. I probably missed him as I am a rotten pistol shot ... At my marriage to Puffin [the Countess of Erroll in her own right] I wanted a live falcon, the Erroll crest, at the ceremony but my bride's Sackville relations were too English to permit anything so Celtic and bizarre.'

Frequently I would try to lure the Ilk back to the office for a spot of work but somehow he would always contrive to stop the taxi outside White's en route. 'Here's ten bob, my good man,' he would say to the cabbie. 'Just wait for us here while we have the one.' Then, in an aside to me, he would say: 'Now if he's the right sort he'll stay. If he's a shit he'll bugger off.'

Hours later when we emerged from this holy of holies in clubland to find no trace of our taxi, the Ilk would exclaim: 'I knew he was a shit.' The intervening period was spent uproariously in the bar, that haven of happenings where Wheeler, the veteran barman, was once asked by a new member if it was open. 'Bless my soul, sir,' this stalwart replied, 'it has been open for 200 years.'

Among the regulars propping up the bar was Lord Boothby – doubtless between his various encounters with the Krays – who would unfailingly enquire in his growling tones what relation I might be to the Field Marshal. During these club crawls I felt rather like P. G. Wodehouse's character Pongo Twistleton nervously escorting the Ilk's irrepressible Earl of Ickenham around the fleshpots. Like the immortal 'Uncle Fred', the Ilk certainly spread 'sweetness and light' – and he would have been the first to point out the genealogical connection between Wodehouse and Matthew Arnold, the originator of that happy phrase.

The secret of the Ilk's charm is that he never grew up. 'Goodness,' he would say, 'I feel sorry for grown-ups: chairmen of companies, social democrats, civil servants ("No longer servants and no longer civil", in Churchill's phrase), retired majors, etc. Hold on, I am a retired Major of the Perthshire Home Guard myself.'

Sadly when he died in 1985 so much wonderfully recondite knowledge and scholarship died with him. Some of his best writing appeared in the form of rambling book reviews for the eclectic *Books and Bookmen* magazine, edited by the eccentric Philip Dossé, who eventually killed himself. The Ilk's 'review' of the *Guide to the Royal Family*, for example, ran to some 20,000 words of anecdotal reminiscence. After his death I cobbled together some of these pieces in a miscellany to his memory.

Another genealogical mentor of mine, Patrick Montague-Smith, editor of a rival genealogical book of reference, died in the same year and, like the Ilk, well before his time. Although not as colourful a personality as the Ilk, Patrick was no less a genealogical scholar and a brilliant sleuth. He was also the kindest, gentlest and most modest man I ever met. In appearance, he somehow resembled a friendly, furry and irresistibly endearing little animal of the forest with his bright, dark eyes, bushy eyebrows and busy movements. When Sir Anthony Wagner, the pre-eminent herald, invited us to lunch with him during his mastership of the Vintners' livery company in the City, he made an elaborate play of introducing us as 'The Rivals' in a manner worthy of Patrick's kinsman, Richard Brinsley Sheridan. Sir Anthony was rather put out when we revealed that we already knew each other, lived on either side of Richmond Park and met regularly.

By that time I was married to Christine and living in an unappealing modern 'town house' next to Kew Gardens, where we would perambulate our baby daughter. Patrick and his wife Annabelle were installed in a substantial semi-detached villa in Kingston that rejoiced in the name of the great Cheshire dynasty of Brereton of Brereton and formed a family shrine to the celebration of Patrick's myriad ancestors and cousins. Overflowing with books, pedigrees, coats of arms, portraits, prints, view of seats and assorted memorabilia, Brereton was an antiquarian's paradise, a treasure trove of the past, an exchange of anecdotal family history.

We used to lunch halfway at Valchera's, a delightful old-fashioned Austro-Swiss restaurant in Richmond with stout, elderly waiters in ill-fitting penguin suits, and chat away about our shared love of Lincolnshire (Patrick's maternal family came from a village down the road from Gunby), Ireland, country houses and the idiosyncratic nature of genealogy.

'As a boy I would bicycle around the country gathering information from distant cousins,' he recalled. 'On one occasion, I had to beard a crusty colonel in his Turkish bath.'

Bubbling with infectious enthusiasm, he would pore over family trees between courses at Valchera's. 'There, now you see how this lot ties up with that lot and – I *say*, do look at this – from that link you can see how your lot and my lot tie up.'

Patrick's unworldliness was memorably illustrated when he appeared on the television magazine programme *Nationwide* to discuss forms of address. The production team had hit on the wheeze of lining up a collection of suitably robed and ermined 'extras' for Patrick and the presenter to hail. Unfortunately, just as the two of them approached a heavily bewigged lady judge, this worthy began to sway alarmingly and then fell down in a faint at Patrick's feet. The learned genealogist blinked and glanced at the presenter, who anxiously motioned him forward. Without a word, Patrick and the presenter then proceeded to step gingerly over the prostrate female form before continuing their discourse on the finer points of etiquette.

On one of our excursions to country houses we set off to find a seat tucked away in the unlikely depths of urban Middlesex. Patrick's map-reading went hopelessly awry and we somehow found ourselves proceeding along what

looked suspiciously like a runway within the perimeters
of Heathrow Airport. 'Perhaps it is along here, somewhere?' said the ever-hopeful master genealogist.

It was always our wish that the rival genealogical
publishing firms should be combined: the only sensible
solution when such works of reference were becoming so
expensive to produce. This was one of the dream schemes
I outlined to the new management when Bill Cathles's
company decided to offload 'the genealogical brand'.

Under the new regime we were happily installed in
some huddled rooms above a wine shop in Chelsea.
Indeed the atmosphere was the most relaxed and harmonious I have ever experienced in a workplace. Thanks to
the imperishable esprit de corps of all who worked there,
fun and laughter kept us afloat. And, despite the financial
restraints, we did manage to produce at least some of the
'dream list' including the *Irish Family Records*, a *Family
Index* (to mark the series' eagerly celebrated 150th anniversary in 1976), the *Royal Families of the World* and the
start of the *Country Houses* series.

Unfortunately, the *Presidential Families of the USA*
did not prove the runaway hit that the new management
had hoped – though it won a prize from the *Library
Journal* as 'Reference Book of the Year'. The upshot was
that they decided to put *The Peerage* (which was eventually sold off) and *The Landed Gentry* indefinitely 'on
ice' and dabble in picture-book packaging. The editorial
team was declared redundant and I resigned in dismay to
go freelance. The publishing dream had turned into a
nightmare.

Troubles came not in single spies but in battalions . . .
My marriage to Christine had already come under strain
when she nearly died of peritonitis while six months
pregnant with our daughter in 1974. It was not helped by
my staying up in the London office half the week before

returning home to Wiltshire, where we had impulsively moved in order to be close to the publishers' designers and printers. The arrival of our son in 1977 seemed to augur better times ahead, but increasingly worried by work and money troubles I retreated more and more into a fantasy world. The proximity of Wincanton Racecourse was all too tempting. The garden was left undug, the leaking roof ignored. I turned a deaf ear to Christine's complaints and imagined myself to be the Knight of Glin in my Gothick castle (where, to my intoxicating delight, I had now stayed).

As a freelance, I continued to edit the now limited list of genealogical publications, including Mark Bence-Jones's compilation of Irish houses for the *Guide to Country Houses*. Mark came to stay with Christine and myself in Wiltshire to collaborate on the 2,500 picture captions. Under pressure from the management we had unwisely agreed to knock these out in a few days (and nights). In the watches of our second night without sleep I noticed Mark writing something strange on the back of one of the pictures.

'What's that, Mark? It's supposed to say "west front", isn't it? Who's this *"Dear Cousin . . ."*?'

'What an extraordinary thing,' said Mark, as if in a deep sleep. 'I was writing a letter to a cousin who died in the '40s.'

'Would that be the *Eighteen*-forties, Mr van Winkle?'

Having enjoyed our collaboration, we then pooled resources for a bash at a general ('proper') book about the British aristocracy. At the end of the summer of 1978 I set off for Ireland to work with Mark on the manuscript without any undue fears as to the future, even though the publishing fiasco had hit hard and my freelance prospects seemed precarious to the more practically minded Christine. At the local station I scribbled my telephone numbers in Ireland on the blank side of a page from my diary which listed my New Year resolutions, among them 'Cease daydreaming and live in the real world.'

I ended my Irish tour at Blessingbourne, where Uncle Peter's health had collapsed. My father had come over to give support. The night before heading back to England I telephoned Christine to tell her which train I would be catching down to Wiltshire the next day. I was told not to bother coming home. She had filed for divorce, citing 'unreasonable behaviour'.

As I shook with shock at the terrible prospect of losing my adored children, and my father plied me with brandy, I mused that living in the real world – as publisher and husband – had not worked out too well. It was back to daydreaming with a vengeance.

EIGHT

Saint Jim

Bᴀᴄᴋ ᴀᴛ ᴛʜᴇ club, my marital misadventure elicited scant sympathy. 'Well, my dear,' simpered Derek 'Dazzle' Jennings, a flamboyant figure who worked for the Historic Buildings Council, 'if you *must* get married . . .'

Prone to hysterical outbursts, Dazzle had been in the forefront of the campaigns to prevent a bar being installed in the inner hall and to block increased access for lady guests – or, as he put it, 'to save the club from becoming a speakeasy pulullating with women'. At one tempestuous meeting Dazzle constantly heckled the chairman, a retired diplomatist accustomed to a smooth ride on such occasions. An angry altercation ensued with another member, Colonel Hale, already a sworn enemy of Dazzle's and notorious for his complaints about the club being 'full of giggling Catholic queers'. On this point, I mused, the Colonel would have seen eye to eye with my erstwhile father-in-law, who had heard it on good authority from some business acquaintance that the club was a hotbed of homosexuality. I had visions of rustling up a phalanx of heterosexual fellow members – Alec Home, Anthony Powell, Kingsley Amis, Colonel Hale, indeed – to serve as character witnesses if needed in court.

After Dazzle had worked himself up into a veritable frenzy of rage (I had seen him, by chance, in similar form at a stormy 'ecumenical seminar' at York Minster addressed by a liberal Ampleforth monk), a note of asperity crept into the chairman's silky blandishments. 'Mr

Jennings,' he said, 'I am endeavouring to run this *gentlemen's* club to the best of my ability for the benefit of its members . . .'

'Well, sir, run it properly!' shrieked Dazzle. 'RUN IT PROPERLY!'

He then exited at a brisk pace. The doors of the smoking room swung on their hinges in the embarrassed silence. Dazzle, not encountered again, became a priest and cropped up in Sir Alec (otherwise 'Dame Alice') Guinness's memoirs and journals as the actor's father confessor before going to an early grave.

The doyen of the club Catholics, Monsignor Gilbey lent a more kindly ear to my woes. 'I am concerned about you, Hugh,' he said. 'You have a strangely haunted look. What is the matter, my dear?'

Regarding the Monsignor as a link with my much-missed Uncle Hugh, I felt that I could confide in him. 'The truth is, Alfred,' I blurted out, 'that I am terrified of going to prison if I can't keep up with the maintenance demands made by my wife's lawyers.' Hearing myself articulate these hidden demons I realized that I was hardly in a position to label Dazzle an hysteric. The Monsignor looked bemused.

None the less, with great generosity Alfred Gilbey entertained me to numerous lunches (oops, 'luncheons') and dinners at the club which helped to keep me afloat. Yet, much as I admired his Edwardian elan and enjoyed his company, I never felt entirely at ease with the Monsignor. Try as I did, I could not quite manage the role-playing required to perfect the part of the elegant, erudite, buttoned-up bachelor which I believed was what he sought as an ideal companion. Having not been one of his flock at Cambridge, I did not fit in and was plagued by feelings of inadequacy. While approving of Alfred's

archaic pedantry in principle – or, at least, pretending to
do so – I was constantly tripping over it in practice.

'When you say "mutual friend", dear boy, you mean,
of course, "friend-in-common"?'

'Of course, Alfred. A slip of the tongue.'

Once when I returned from collecting a volume of *The
Landed Gentry* on the other side of the outer morning
room for the Monsignor's perusal (he was celebrated in
the club for padding down in the late evening in his bare
feet and a virtually see-through old silk nightshirt in
order to consult such works of reference), I found him in
high dudgeon. 'In all the years I have known and admired
you, my dear,' he said in a reproving tone, 'you have never
shocked me by uncouth conduct. That is, until a moment
ago.'

'Why, Alfred, what have I done which is so shocking?'

'When you picked up that esteemed publication in
your hand just now, and opened it in what I regret to say
was a *brutal* manner, you virtually broke its back, my
dear.'

Having learned one or two technical terms during my
stint in publishing, I countered: 'You mean I may have
strained its spine?'

'A gentleman,' intoned the Monsgnor, ignoring my
impertinence, 'treats a bound volume with respect.'

Heraldry, supposedly the subject which was our
strongest bond, proved full of pitfalls. 'You are familiar,
no doubt, with the canting coat of the FitzUrses?'

'Eh? Oh, er, quite . . . a nice touch of armorial wit.'

'By "nice", naturally, you mean "deft"?'

'Naturally, Alfred.'

The ultimate cul-de-sac in our friendship, though, was
religion. Alfred made much play of his lack of prejudice
towards non-Catholics – 'Some of my closest friends in

the beagling field have been Black Protestants from
Ulster, like yourself, dear Hugh' – but my failure to
advance towards Rome tended to put a dampener on
proceedings. Every now and then he would slip into a
curious trance when, with eyes closed, he would mumble
a rapid-fire homily on the philosophy and inestimable
advantages of the Old Faith. At least, that is what I
imagined he was burbling about because I could not
actually hear, let alone comprehend, his message of belief.
As far as Alfred was concerned, I was a lost lamb.

Like Uncle Hugh, Alfred Gilbey took a dim view of my
ingrained tendency to hero-worship, and especially dep-
recated any suggestion that I might transfer my idolatry
in his direction. While remaining on the best of terms, we
somehow drifted apart and by the time of his sad (and
unnecessary) departure from the club to a nursing home,
where he soon died, aged ninety-six, we were no more
than nodding old acquaintances.

Another long-standing hero figure from clubland
whose supreme powers of sympathy and friendship came
to my rescue at the time of my divorce was James Lees-
Milne. 'Quite frankly, Hugh, I was rather surprised when
you married,' he told me over lunch at Brooks's. 'I didn't
think you were really of the marrying kind.'

This was said with such simplicity and concern, and
without any suggestion of sexual undertones, that, in my
naivety and innocence, it never occurred to me even to
think of some coarse reply like 'Look who's talking,
matey?' or 'D'you mean I'm a poofter like my Uncle Peter?'
Not, of course, that I would ever in a million years have
uttered such crudities to Jim (as I had eventually learned
to call him, after initially addressing him as 'sir' when we
first met through *The Landed Gentry* in the late 1960s).
Even to the end of his life, in 1997, we were always far
too shy of each other to engage in heart-to-heart con-

fessions – though occasional startling confidences would suddenly erupt, as in his remark about the 'marrying kind'.

Typically, I failed to respond. Instead of politely explaining that though, in fact, I was *not* a homosexual (despite the more or less obligatory adolescent bout or two at Harrow), that I had probably been far too immature for marriage but that it was now the loss of my children which was destroying me, I stammered some inanity and changed the subject. Rather than deal in reality with Jim, I wanted to submerge myself in thrall to this great Hero of the Heritage, the single-handed saviour of country houses for the National Trust and a revered gentleman of letters.

Indeed his enchanting, hilarious memoir *Another Self*, published soon after I first met him, had become one of my favourite books and featured prominently in my thoughts. It struck a special chord with me not only on account of its romantic depiction of an 'outsider' struggling to survive the embarrassments of an eccentric, hearty background and the rigours of private school, Eton, Oxford and a hostile adult world, but because it contained tenuous links to my own family.

My father, for instance, had taken over from Jim in the 1930s as private secretary to the empire-builder and sometime Colonial Secretary Lord Lloyd, the brother-in-law of my landlady in Chelsea. Jim was intrigued to hear my scabrous tales of her invading my bedroom while I was undressing for bed. As I prattled merrily away about Mrs Lloyd's erratic behaviour I was blissfully unaware that Jim kept a detailed diary. And when the particular volume setting out my indiscretions about my landlady were duly published many years later, in the 1990s, Jim himself was unaware that poor Mrs Lloyd (with whom I corresponded occasionally) remained very much still with us. 'Oh dear, oh dear,' worried Jim at one of our regular lunches. 'What *shall* we do?'

'"*We*", Jim?' I was becoming bolder in middle age. 'It was *you* who published it, without checking with me first!'

'But naturally I assumed the old girl had died ages ago. After all, my and your father's old boss, George Lloyd, must have been born in the 1870s.'

My uncle Peter, who together with Jim had been one of Harold Nicolson's coterie of young men in the 1930s, also complained of Lees-Milne's frequently cavalier way with the cold facts. He was not best pleased by Jim's description in *Another Self* of how the pair of them had been bombed out of the Piccadilly Hotel, where they were sharing a room, during the worst blitz of the Second World War in April 1941 (the notorious night pinned in my mind as the time when Lady Molly Jeavons, her niece Priscilla Lovell and her estranged husband 'Chips' were all killed in *A Dance to the Music of Time*).

'The mention of the sleeping arrangements – not that we got any sleep that night – is hardly calculated to improve my standing on the Bench in Northern Ireland,' muttered Uncle Peter, for ever troubled by his double life.

'Don't you *sit* rather than stand on the Bench, Uncle Peter?'

'Tee-hee . . . But the trouble with Jim is that he makes everything up. All this stuff about how I was fussing around because my tie was out of place as the bombs fell, or there was some dust on my overcoat. I mean, really! And as for all this boloney about his mama disappearing skywards in a balloon and Jim dancing, in drag, with one of his beaks from Eton at a roadhouse in Bray – well, it's sheer fantasy.'

To a daydream believer like myself, though, it was a fantasy which seemed infinitely appealing. From my earliest days on *The Landed Gentry* Jim Lees-Milne lit up my life with his powerfully romantic vision of the squire-archy – 'the best form of government ever invented', as he put it to me over our first lunch at Brooks's. Mr Lees-Milne, as I still thought of him, had written an inspiring paean to the landed gentry by way of an introductory essay to the new edition and I was only too glad of the opportunity of meeting my great hero. How I thrilled to his articulating all the unspoken feelings I had nurtured since boyhood about 'the rare and indefinably proud distinction in holding no constitutional title and yet enjoying the prescriptive right to call yourself, for example, the Knight of Glin, the Hereditary Captain of Dunstaffnage, or the twenty-third Dymoke of Scrivelsby, Queen's Hereditary Champion and Standard Bearer of England'. Here, too, was a fellow fantasist who could swoon to the romance of territorial surnames when their holders are still associated with the places from which they derive – like Craufurd of Craufurdland, Craster of Craster, Cruwys of Cruwys, Enys of Enys, Fulford of Fulford, Langton of Langton, Plowden of Plowden. Beachcomber's *List of Huntingdonshire Cabmen* had nothing on the roll-call exchanged between Lees-Milne and myself over the years of lunches alternating between our respective clubs.

Jim confided in me that, as a boy, he had longed to be Rouge Dragon Pursuivant at the College of Heralds (a vision I have long dabbled with myself) and had written passionate poems about the extinction of long-established Catholic gentry families. 'Did you ever publish any of your poems, Jim?' I asked.

'Oh no. I fear they were frightfully bad. Though I did once show some sonnets of mine to Vita Sackville-West. She told me they reminded her of Tennyson's younger brother.'

'But I remember some literary lady in Lincolnshire claiming that he was actually rather good.'

'Ah, Lincolnshire,' said Jim, adroitly steering the conversation away from his verse. 'How is dear Gunby? I can see it now, beckoning me like some friendly Star to the East. I long to go back.'

In his essay for *The Landed Gentry* James Lees-Milne had earned my undying devotion by placing 'the Massingberds of Gunby' at the front of a list of families ('like . . . the Lucys of Charlecote and the Throckmortons of Coughton') who had come to terms with the National Trust during his own years as the first secretary of the Trust's pioneering Country House Scheme. Although in my private dream world such an unfortunate eventuality had never been necessary, I was happy to forgive Jim his entirely sympathetic role in the transfer to the Trust by my great-uncle and great-aunt – 'the dear old Field Marshal and Lady M.-M.,' as Jim referred to them. His devotion to Gunby, with 'its air of feudal well-being and content', and to 'the sweet old couple' ('true county squirearchy whom I would have gone to the ends of the earth to help', as he put it to me) was an unbreakable bond between us.

Yet I could only grind my teeth when he related how the elderly Field Marshal had been almost over-keen to divest himself of every conceivable object at Gunby. 'The old boy would even look rather hurt,' Jim recalled, 'when we showed a disinclination to accept some watercolours of the "honeysuckle-over-the-cottage-porch" kind.'

Meeting James Lees-Milne in my early twenties was as much a turning point in my life as the drunken Maurice Hastings peppering the private parts of the statues in the great garden of Rousham had been in his. As an Oxford undergraduate Jim had been the impotent, mute witness of a philistine assault on the work of William Kent (himself originally a protégé of the Massingberds, as Jim told me) which, as he described in

Another Self, 'brought home to me how passionately I cared for architecture and the continuity of history, of which it is the mouthpiece'. After watching this gross exhibition of vandalism, Jim had vowed to devote his energies and abilities, 'such as they were', to preserving the country houses of England.

My own vow followed a chance observation Jim made at one of our early club lunches. In his mild way he was grumbling (John Betjeman nicknamed him 'the Worcestershire Grumbler') that *Country Life* seemed to have lost interest in the smaller seats of the squirearchy. 'It's an awful bore, as I'm really only interested in writing about very *dim* houses lived in by long lines of landed gents. They may not always be architectural gems but their loss is much more significant than the so-called experts appreciate.'

This was my vision on the road to Damascus. I determined to devote myself to cataloguing lesser-known country houses and the families who created them. Jim generously agreed to act as a sort of 'honorary godfather' to my *Guide to Country Houses*, when we finally managed to get the ambitious project off the ground, and he allowed me to consult his own country-house albums which he had installed in William Beckford's old marbleized library in Lansdown Terrace, Bath. Jim used to commute here to write from his small late seventeenth-century house near the gates of the Duke of Beaufort's seat at Badminton. 'A curious arrangement at my time of life,' he said.

On one of my visits to Bath I met Alvilde, Jim's legendarily formidable wife who had been an intimate friend of Vita Sackville-West. Mrs Lees-Milne struck me as brusque and direct in an old-fashioned, military way; indeed her father had been a general. With her slightly squat figure and helmet of blue-rinsed hair, she made a curious contrast with Jim's willowy, wispy, whippet-like

presence – he was prone to shudder as if in sympathy
with their pets of that breed. Yet much to my, and to
Jim's, surprise, I seemed to hit it off with Alvilde. We
chatted away very affably. Crippled by shyness, I sometimes seem to have been capable of coming out of my shell
when faced with blunt, potentially awkward customers. 'I
say,' Jim told me when we next met in London, 'you've
made a hit with Alvilde. There have been times when she
has banned my friends from the premises but she said of
you that you had the "manners of another age".'

'That will be a surprise to my family – and everyone
else who knows me.'

On a later visit to their house at Badminton Alvilde
took me to one side and asked if there was anything I
could do to obtain an honour for Jim. 'Of course the old
boy pretends he doesn't care a hoot for such baubles and
gongs. But, deep down, I think he's rather miffed about
it. Dammit, his chum Robin Fedden at the National Trust
got a CBE and Jim – who really started the whole
Country House Scheme going years before – has never
even got so much as a measly MBE. It's *extraordinary*;
quite scandalous, really. Can you think of any reason *why*
he hasn't received some official recognition?'

'No, Alvilde. It seems absolutely outrageous that Jim,
who saved much of what everyone now takes for granted
as the so-called National Heritage—'

'What has the bloody *nation* ever had to do with it, I
would like to know,' interjected Alvilde.

'Quite. Exactly. But perhaps some bureaucrat Jim
upset in one of his conservationist campaigns may have
put the black spot against his name . . .' (I thought that
this might be a safer speculation than hinting at some
homosexual activity which could possibly have upset the
authorities – though this had not finally prevented his old
flame John Gielgud's knighthood.) 'After all, Jim doesn't

mince his words when roused. Some Stalinist in the Civil Service might not have forgiven him for writing that the sound of "Churchill on the radio magnifying the virtues of our new ally Soviet Russia marks without question the nadir of my whole life".'

'Or his regret that he did not go to Spain to fight for Franco?'

'Yes, well . . . I'll see what I can do, Alvilde.'

With laughable self-importance, I duly lobbied the then Arts Minister, whose name now eludes me (it wasn't my old friend Norman St John-Stevas), and over the years wrote various articles banging on about a gong for the great man. Nothing happened, and I subsequently wondered whether Jim, the most modest and unassuming of men, might actually have turned down an honour years before, never to be offered another.

'Perhaps if Jim is not to receive any temporal honour ("Lord Jim"?),' I said to Alvilde over a kitchen lunch at Badminton, 'we can console ourselves that Lady Colefax was right to conclude that he must be a saint. "Saint Jim" has a certain ring to it, don't you think?'

Turning to Jim, Alvilde said: 'You're always saying how beastly journalists are about you, how horrid the reviews of your books always are, but at least you can't complain of the charming articles Hugh has written about you.'

Although my sucking-up to Alvilde had her purring with pleasure, Jim's claws were now out.

'Oh, do *shut up*, the pair of you! I hate all this vulgar talk of honours. I couldn't give a fig. And I loathe this harping-on about hero worship and heritage (*how* I hate that word). As for your articles, Hugh, with their sugary praise and deferential politeness, I am afraid they make me feel extremely uneasy. Quite frankly, they make me *squirm*. Yes. SQUIRM!'

'Oh dear,' I murmured sotto voce. 'The Worcestershire Grumbler strikes again.'

'What utter poppycock, Jim,' barked Alvilde. 'You really must stop moaning all the time.'

Such was Jim's place of imperishable honour that well-deserved rockets from the pedestal had no effect whatsoever on my admiration for him. I received another blast when I became entangled in a plot to dramatize his *Diaries* for a touring National Trust show. The scenario was for an actor – I suggested one of my gentleman-actor heroes, Jonathan Cecil – to portray Jim as a youngish man against a backdrop of the library at Brooks's while he wrote up his account of the day's travels in his temperamental old banger to decaying family seats. The actor, in character as Jim, would then break off his scribbling to enact the eccentricities he had encountered. I envisaged a national tour culminating in a lengthy West End run at, say, the Criterion – like Roy Dotrice's *Brief Lives*.

Unfortunately Jim was having none of it. When someone at the National Trust in Queen Anne's Gate let the cat out of the bag one morning, chance had it that Jim was going on to lunch with me at the club. I received the full force after he had walked across St James's Park. 'I absolutely forbid you to have anything further to do with this hare-brained scheme. I *forbid* you, do you understand?'

'Yes, Jim, I'm so sorry . . .'

'How could you possibly have imagined that I would ever consent to such a ghastly charade? To see myself protrayed by an actor on stage would make me *writhe* with embarrassment and shame. *Writhe . . .*'

'Even Jonathan Cecil?' (This was an unwise interjection, as I suspected that the physical charms of Cecil, famed for playing silly asses, hardly measured up to Jim's idea of himself as a young Adonis.)

'*Especially* Jonathan Cecil!'

A more promising idea for a collaboration between Jim and myself was an elegiac study of the squirearchy to be called *The Last of the Squires* – the title taken from a memorial tablet erected in the 1970s by a son to his father in a church in Gloucestershire, which Jim had pointed out to me on one of our country-house jaunts. He sent me off, solo, to discuss the project with his then publisher, Norah Smallwood of Chatto & Windus. Ushered into a dusty eyrie behind the Strand, I found myself confronted by a gimlet-eyed dragon who made Alvilde seem like a pussycat.

'Well, who are you and what do you want?' she snarled.

'Erm, Massingberd's the name . . . and, er . . . I was hoping to collaborate with Jim Lees-Milne on a book about, um, the sort of old squires, you know . . .'

'Indeed. Mr *James* Lees-Milne happens to be *my* author, and he does *not* need a *collaborator* on this or any other book, for that matter. Good afternoon.'

Not for the first time with Jim, I had the feeling that I had been set up. On one of our jaunts we called at a country house in the Forest of Dean where the owner, a ponderous retired businessman, manoeuvred me into forking out some vast sum for an immensely dreary tome he had produced on the exhaustive history of the old Abbey going back to its Cistercian foundation in the twelfth century. 'You fell right into the old crasher's trap, didn't you?' chortled the impish Jim as I beggared myself.

The highlight of the visit for Jim, though, was the châtelaine's bizarre obsession with his old sparring partner Oliver Messel, the designer. Having fallen in love with Messel's theatrical flair on a trip to the West End, she had become convinced that this exotic bird of plumage was just the man to transform the Abbey – already

Georgianized by Anthony Keck – into the fairy-tale home of her dreams. Messel, captivated by the Abbey's capabilities and its châtelaine's devotion, had obligingly camped the place up and had been about to take up her generous offer of permanent accommodation for his retirement, in the best bedroom, when he died. 'Poor Oliver,' mused Jim as he struggled to suppress his *fou rire* at this extraordinary saga. It was fascinating on such visits to see at first-hand how Jim, the beady-eyed country-house chronicler who never missed a trick and whose curiosity about the vagaries of human nature was inexhaustible, gathered his material. Ostensibly a model of good manners and sympathetic concern, he would swoop imperceptibly on the inherent absurdity and unconscious hilarity of his guides.

At one house in the Midlands, though, I savoured the satisfaction of seeing the tables turned. The bachelor owner, jumping to quite the wrong conclusion about the proclivities of Jim's companion (myself), led us to a garden building adorned with a graphically explicit fresco in the muscular modern neo-classical manner. 'What d'you think of that meaty young piece, eh, Jim?' nudged the pederastic squire.

'I find it all faintly embarrassing, if you must know.' Jim shuddered, by now blushing on my behalf. We managed to avoid eye contact before edging towards the exit.

Jim's most engaging and instructive quality away from the country-house trail was his humble simplicity. When I foolishly attempted to impress him with lavish five-course lunches and magnums of vintage wines, he would quietly shame me by asking for some grilled fish and a glass of cider. He spoke with disarming candour about his shyness and loneliness when young; of how he had felt rather frightened of his family; and of how happy he was to escape into the servants' hall as a small boy. 'I can still hear their screams of laughter,' he said.

His devotion to an old retainer, portrayed as Goddard, the golden-hearted parlourmaid in his novel *The Fool of Love* (the publisher of which made him strike out the true account of dachshunds being stoned in the village street during the Great War), found an echo in my own adoration of my beloved Biddo. Sometimes, in the most abstract way possible, we would talk of love and the dangers of searching for affection. 'Love is a terrible affliction, a deadly disease,' he would muse. 'When you are in the grip of it you are virtually insane.' Some of the views he expressed to me on love found their way into his novels – such as how 'the object of affection always recoils from the lavisher thereof' and 'So long as one is madly in love, one is living in a fool's paradise.'

For the most part, though, we skirted around real emotions. After I had taken him to see the film of *The Remains of the Day* (we had both admired Ishiguro's novel, but Jim's identification of all the houses used in the interior shots rather distracted our fellow cinema-goers in the Curzon Mayfair), he used a discussion of the poor butler's frozen impotence to urge me out of my shell. 'When will you ever reveal your true self, I wonder, dear Hugh? Some of us both long, and dread, for you to do so.'

The truth was that I much preferred to coax Jim into telling funny stories about the famous people he had known than to become embroiled in any deep discussions about the meaning of life or love. I particularly enjoyed his account of dining with his fellow Worcestershire Grumbler, Sir Edward Elgar, Bt, at Brooks's. 'The old boy looked like a Poona colonel, which I think he would really rather have been than a musician. Before we went into dinner, he warned me that he was expecting an urgent telephone call. Then the hall porter emerged from his booth.

'"They are on the line now, Sir Edward."

'"Thank you . . . Hullo, hullo . . ."

'Down the line,' continued Jim, 'I could overhear strange noises. *Woof! Woof! Woof! Woof!* – barks and snuffles. Sir Edward admonished: "Now, be good dogs and *don't* bite the cushions. Good night, good night."

Woof! Woof!'

Another favourite story featured G. M. Trevelyan, the historian, whom Jim escorted to various National Trust functions. On one occasion, as the local mayor and reception committee waited patiently by the motor car, Trevelyan remained contentedly in the front passenger seat polishing his false teeth on his lap. Trevelyan had written the introduction to Jim's first book, on the work of the National Trust, and, at Jim's urging, stressed that the Trust was opposed to 'museumization' but wished to preserve the face of England as it was under private ownership. Jim himself always emphasized that his loyalties were to 'the houses, the families and the National Trust (which I regard as the instrument of the others' preservation) in that order'.

It was fitting, then, that my happiest memories of my hero worship for Jim revolved around his return to Gunby while I was fortunate enough to be 'house-sitting' there for Jack and Betty Wrisdale, who had by now long since taken over the National Trust tenancy of the house from my father. On the first night of his stay, I came across Jim, now into his eighties, ascending the staircase to the north wing, instead of the central one leading to his bedroom, 'the squire's room'.

'You're going the wrong way, Jim.'

'How extraordinary. What an old fool I am. Most

houses one revisits in old age seem to have shrunk but for some reason Gunby seems bigger than I remember. I must say it is all looking absolutely splendid, and so well cared for.'

'That's thanks to you, Jim.'

'No, all the credit should go to the Wrisdales. It really does appear to be the happiest of all collaborations.'

For a jaunt across the vast, remote and still undiscovered county, I unwisely recruited another hero of mine, the great local antiquarian the Reverend Henry Thorold, to join us. As I realized far too late, it is always a mistake to cast two stars, let alone hero-figures, in such close proximity. While in theory Jim shared my admiration for Henry (whom he memorably described as having 'a profile like George III's and a stomach like George IV's'), in practice a little of Henry and his set-piece anecdotes went a long way. As I ferried these two eminent Old Etonians around the unknown sights of Lincolnshire I detected a certain tension in the air. All too audibly, at various stops, Jim persisted in referring to Henry as 'the dear old boy', even though Henry was actually thirteen years Jim's junior. It was evident that Henry's stories – which usually combined an antiquarian point with a sense of reverence for long-established families and a dash of the macabre in the M. R. James manner – were beginning to try Jim's nerves. 'The poor old boy's *not* really that much of a *scholar* is he?' hissed Jim at one stage.

Matters came to a head when Henry employed one too many of his extraordinarily elongated pauses while relating the saga of Harlaxton. 'To save from demolition,' Henry intoned from memory the advertisement in *The Times*, 'a purchaser required for Harlaxton Manor near Grantham [pronounced, in true Thorold style with a hard 't'] . . .'

The seemingly interminable pause was impatiently

interrupted by Jim. 'Ah, yes, Harlaxton. I bicycled up the
drive there in the 1940s but Mrs van der Elst, the dotty
owner who spent all her fortune on psychical research
and campaigning against the death penalty, wouldn't let
me in, and sent me packing.'

'Mrs van der Elst? *Dotty?* She bought it. She saved it.
She should be *canonized*!' thundered Henry in the orator-
ical tones of the pulpit. 'But, as I was praying – er, *saying*,
or rather quoting from *The Times*: "The labour of an age
in piled stones . . ."' Another very long pause. '"Definitely
it ranks as one of the stately homes of England—"'

'I say, Henry,' interrupted Jim. 'Isn't that Belvoir over
there?'

'It is. But that is in Leicestershire. We are in *Lincolnshire* and if I could be allowed to continue . . .'

By the end of the day the hostility between my two
heroes was virtually out in the open when Jim suggested
that Lincolnshire must be the coldest county in England.
'Nonsense!' responded Henry.

Some years later, when Jim's description of staying
with Henry was published in his *Diaries*, I found myself
reading the passage aloud to Henry. The sentence 'Is
rather greedy and hogs his food', which I found endearing,
did not go down terribly well with Henry.

At Jim's memorial service at the Grosvenor Chapel in
Mayfair in 1998 I experienced a frisson of pride and
affection when Martin Drury, the director-general of the
National Trust, announced that in Jim's memory, and
with the proceeds of his own book collection (sold by John
Saumarez Smith of the booksellers Heywood Hill), the
library was to be restored in a 'beautiful little-known
house in a remote corner of England, of which he had
such fond memories'. This was Gunby.

As I write these words, on another house-sitting visit
to the place we both loved, I can look up and see his alert,

beady yet gentle eyes in the photograph that commemor-
ates his generosity which restored the library (dismantled
by my great-aunt in the 1920s) where I am currently
installed.

In his will, Jim also generously bequeathed me a
Worcester porcelain tea service hand-painted with
country-house scenes. His hope was that one day this
would go with me to Gunby. Not long after I had collected
this treasure from his executor, though, I was sitting
upstairs in my Bayswater cell when I heard two strange
sounds. The first was the warbling of a sentimental number from the musical *Blood Brothers* by our temporary
cleaning lady from Liverpool – *'Living on the Never-Never /
Constant as the stormy weather'* – followed immediately by
the tinkling, surprisingly musical but long drawn-out and
shattering sound of porcelain under demolition. I squirmed
and I writhed. Yet, as I thought of dear Jim, I somehow
found myself smiling ruefully as I reassured the Scouser
that these things happen in the best of places.

NINE

Sage of the Chantry

M Y GREATEST THRILL during my association with the
genealogical series was coming into contact with
Anthony Powell, my chief literary hero since schooldays.
When I first came across his books in the early 1960s I
was in the thrall of Evelyn Waugh's novels and somehow
imagined that he could be bracketed in the same category.
It took me some years to grasp that whereas Waugh dealt
in fantasy, Powell was essentially a realist.

Initially, Powell's books proved an acquired taste. I
made a false start with *The Acceptance World*, the third
volume in his panoramic sequence of novels *A Dance to
the Music of Time*, which seemed to be written in a sort of
secret code that I was incapable of deciphering. Yet when
staying at Blessingbourne with Uncle Peter I noticed the
first volume of *Dance, A Question of Upbringing*, on the
bedside table.

'Have you read that?' asked my uncle. 'It's set at Eton
– though it never actually says so, only "School" – and
there's this brilliantly sophisticated dialogue between
the boys. Pole has a deliciously dry wit – I think you'd
like it.'

'*Pole?* I thought his name was Po-well.'

'Ah, yes, but it's pronounced *Pole*. And by the way I
heard you refer to *Ralph* Vaughan Williams yesterday –
our cousin only answered to *Rafe*.'

I blushed at my suburban solecism. Although I had
my doubts as to whether Uncle Peter had actually read *A*

Question of Upbringing himself – he was prone to parrot
the opinions of smart friends in his Arts Council circles –
his outline of Etonian elegance was irresistible. Within a
few hours I was immersed in *Dance*, deep in the early
twentieth-century universe Powell had created and
savouring its own special inner mythology, jokes, network
of ramifications and recurring characters. In my dreams I
was swallowed up into this parallel Powellian world. The
Eton schoolboys – Nicholas Jenkins, the elliptical narrator, the charming Charles Stringham, the brash Peter
Templer, the extraordinary Widmerpool, notorious for
having worn 'the wrong kind of overcoat' – became more
familiar to me than my own acquaintances in real life. So
powerful was the pull of Powell's fiction that the diverse
gallery of characters encountered – and frequently, not
to say fortuitously, re-encountered – by Nick Jenkins
populated my own imagination to the extent that I felt I
knew them all. I found myself constantly choreographing
everyone in my daydreams from the Marxist critic J. G.
Quiggin and the manipulative don Sillery to the prank-
ster gentleman-rider Dicky Umfraville (just the sort of
amateur jockey I most admired) and the frigid femme
fatale Pamela Flitton; from the quixotic Lord Erridge
to the effeminate nightclub entertainer Max Pilgrim; from
the Fitzrovian novelist X. Trapnel to the enchantingly
witty composer Hugh Moreland. All these personalities
lived and breathed for me. I was utterly hooked.

I could not walk through, say, Bayswater without
expecting to bump into Jenkins's awkward Uncle Giles
(self-styled 'a bit of a radical') sloping out of the Ufford
Hotel; or through Shepherd Market, where Uncle Giles
might well be spotted slipping out of some less respectable
establishment; or Hyde Park without hearing Sillery's
shrill cry in the protest march of 'Abolish the Means Test!'
Or indeed Pimlico (where I sometimes lodged with Pearce)

without thinking of poor Maclintick, the embittered music critic and the wretched failure with whom I was to find it so easy to identify, gassing himself.

By the mid-1960s a printed photograph of Anthony Powell's distinguished features, captured in stylish repose, had been cut out from the *Listener* (which my father used to bring home from the BBC) and pasted up among my gallery of heroes on the wall of my cabin at Cookham. Any spare time at school (not, of course, Eton, alas) and subsequently as a commuter on the 8.12 up to Paddington was spent reading and rereading the Powellian corpus. As well as keeping up to the mark on *Dance*, I eagerly tracked down his early pre-war novels. In the first, *Afternoon Men*, which seemed to be a sort of Bohemian forerunner to *Dance*, I was struck by the author's description of an unprepossessing painter whose false nose at a party lends his face 'an unaccustomed dignity'. And I had never read anything funnier than the scene in *From a View to a Death* in which the moustachioed Major Fosdick (who found it 'restful' to repair to his dressing room in the afternoon in order to read *Through the Western Highlands with Rod and Gun* attired in a large picture hat and a black sequinned evening dress) absent-mindedly opens his front door to the local squire while still in drag, and then proceeds to conduct a conversation about the shooting rights to a nearby copse.

Such delectable gems ensured that Anthony Powell superseded Evelyn Waugh in pride of place among my heroes. Having read that they both lived in Somerset, I spent my train journeys to and from stays with Uncle Joe and Aunt Daisy in that county eagerly combing the compartments for possible sightings. I became hot and flustered over what seemed to be a Powellian prospect – a tall eminence in a tweed suit – but his face looked a little too weatherbeaten for a suave literary gent and fortunately

I lacked the nerve to buttonhole him with a copy of one of his own paperbacks. My efforts at hero-spotting on trains were redoubled after my parents reported that they had sat at an adjoining table to Evelyn Waugh at the Great Western Hotel by Paddington Station.

'He was extremely red in the face,' said my mother. (Perhaps writers were flushed around the gills, after all?) 'And he was behaving very badly towards the waiters.'

When Waugh died on Easter Sunday 1966 I experienced a shock equivalent to a death in the family. After all, for some years I had imagined that I actually *was* Evelyn Waugh, living (rather implausibly) on Barbados attired in linen suitings and striped red shirtings. I was staying with my old Port Regis friend and sometime cricket-album collaborator Robert Stokes in Surrey when the news came through. We had been playing about with his tape recorder laying down a spoof cricket commentary by E. W. Swanton, who had forgotten the identity of the box's scorer – 'What's his *bloody* name? Oh dear, I really must apologize, ladies and gentlemen . . .'

Suddenly the adolescent giggles stopped as a genuine radio announcement was broadcast. Waugh's death was a cold blast of reality cutting through my secret fantasies.

'What's the matter, Monty? You look as if you've seen a ghost. Why are you so upset – I mean you didn't *know* Mr Waugh, did you?'

'Er, well . . . not exactly. But my uncle Hugh was a sort of friend of his – through Ronnie Knox, actually, who was the subject of a biography by Waugh.'

'Who?'

'Oh, forget it . . . Let's have E. W. sucking up to Johnners because he went to Eton. "Now, Brian, you will recall those beautiful wickets at Agar's Plough—"'

'Don't you mean Upper Club, Swanny? Remember I was never in the XI.'

'Aaah, indeed. Upper Club, just near the Wat'ry Glade . . .'

Brooding later on what Stokes had said about my not knowing Evelyn Waugh, I conceded that my chances of ever meeting him had always been extremely remote. Yet now he was dead, at an age (sixty-three) that even I as a nineteen-year-old thought to be on the young side, it was sobering to reflect that they were now absolutely non-existent. Though perhaps it was all for the best that my daydreams on the 8.12 would never collide with real life. If I ever had met Mr Waugh, or in the equally unlikely event of being in the company of Anthony Powell, what could I have possibly had to say to such a revered figure?

As it turned out, one of my first tasks when I joined the genealogical publishers less than a couple of years later was to approach Anthony Powell in order to ask him to revise his introductory essay for *The Landed Gentry*, which he had generously summed up as 'an enormous and unique repository of individual families – something unlike anything else to be found in Europe, or possibly in the world'. I pored over the sage's reflections on the pedigrees which bore out the idea of the extreme social fluidity of landed families in Britain. 'Have we,' asked Powell in his piece, 'a deeply rooted, even ineradicable, taste for drawing social distinctions for their own sake and then disregarding them?' Powell's learned philosophizing made me feel as if I had accidentally landed in a serious, grown-up job, though my boss, Peter Townend, soon brought me back to earth.

'I say, you'd better do your prep before tackling Old Powell – sounds like *Old King Coel*, doesn't it? Actually I think he descends from him. Anyway, his own pedigree in the *LG* – *Powell of the Chantry* – is stuffed with Welsh kings, princes, bards, knights of the Arthurian Legend, and what-not.'

'Yes, Peter. I see he traces his descent from the Lord Rhys, who held the first recorded Eisteddfod at Cardigan in 1176 . . .'

'That reminds me of Frankie Howerd – "Welcome, my brethren, to the Eisteddfod . . ."'

I mused inwardly that no one could personify Anthony Powell's maxim that 'melancholy should be taken for granted in anyone with a true gift for comedy' better than Frankie Howerd. Out loud, I said: 'Is Mr Powell very keen on genealogy?'

'Keen? He's absolutely loopy about *G*! Obsessed. Takes it frightfully seriously. He's very thick with Garter, you know.'

'I suppose that he must have been at Eton and Balliol with Sir Anthony Wagner, though he would be a few years senior.'

'No doubt that explains why he was allowed to display the unadorned silver eagle of Llywelyn Crugeryr – sorry to spit – as his coat of arms.'

In my letter to the Sage of the Chantry (I was tempted to use this form of address on the envelope), not shown to Townend, I managed to insert a grovelling reference to what a tremendous fan I was of all his writings. His response stuck firmly to matters genealogical, but mentioned that we had 'an infinitely remote connection' through his maternal family, the Dymokes of Scrivelsby in Lincolnshire (the dynasty celebrated as hereditary Champions and Standard-Bearers of England). I learned, with a bursting sense of pride, that Anthony Powell's maternal great-grandmother, Ann Dymoke Welles (née Waterhouse), had been the sister of my ancestral aunt Elizabeth Hawksmore Massingberd. Dash it, we were related! There must, I felt, be something to be said for this genealogy business.

The letter from the Chantry, addressed to me and

containing this exciting item of intelligence, meant more
than Holy Writ. I lingered longingly over its typescript,
but eventually had no compunction in cutting off the
ballpoint signature 'Anthony Powell' and sticking it
underneath his photograph on my bedroom wall. I would
gaze adoringly at this shrine to the Sage before transporting myself to, say, Stourwater Castle, the seat of the
industrialist Sir Magnus Donners in *Dance*, adorned with
tapestries of the Seven Deadly Sins, one of which featured
'a goat of unreliable aspect'.

In subsequent correspondence with the Sage, he told
me that he had inherited a couple of letters written by
Byron to a 'Mrs Massingberd' of 16 Piccadilly, where the
poet unwisely took lodgings. Unwisely, as Anthony Powell
explained, because this Mrs Massingberd ('who obviously
brought confusion to all monetary dealings') acted in an
ill-advised manner in making it possible for Byron to
negotiate loans through moneylenders, when he was
under age. It had always been assumed by Anthony
Powell's family that these letters were sent to our ancestral aunt-in-common, Elizabeth Hawksmore Massingberd, but recent scholarship had now led him to believe
that actually they were addressed to her mother-in-law,
Elizabeth Massingberd, widow of Thomas Massingberd of
Gunby – my own direct ancestor. As Powell put it, 'the
blame has been shifted'.

My attempts to steer the Sage towards discussion of
his fiction continued to be played straight back down the
wicket. Believing his second novel, *Venusberg*, to have
been based in Finland where his father, Colonel Phillip
Powell had been a member of the Military Mission in the
1920s, I sought to waylay him with the discovery of some
beagle-breeding Massingberd kinsmen in Helsinki (where
their line had retreated after an ancestor had been out-
lawed in Russia). Besides earning me a compliment on

my genealogical enterprise and an admission that he had indeed visited Finland, my ploy to unravel the origins of the surreal cocktail conversation of *Venusberg* did not succeed. By way of a return, 'A. D. Powell' (as he signed his genealogical articles in the learned journal of the *Transactions of the Radnorshire Society*) sent me the result of his assiduous researches concerning a Midwestern branch of the Powells seated at White Eyes Creek in Ohio – 'and other even less smart states'.

Our relationship as strictly genealogical pen pals would doubtless have ticked over steadily for decades in this manner had it not been for the intervention of Monsignor Gilbey at the club. When lunching there with Alfred and another of his acolytes, one day soon after I had been elected in 1970, I expressed my passionate admiration for Anthony Powell's novels.

'I do *so* agree,' said the acolyte. 'His perceptive observation and understanding of society between the wars is quite unrivalled.'

'Now that poor Evelyn has been gathered,' mused the Monsignor, 'I suppose Tony Powell could be regarded as the Greatest Living Novelist?'

I sat awestruck. This was the first time I had heard the Sage called 'Tony'.

'Certainly, Alfred,' said this acolyte. 'I think we can safely omit the Communist Mr Greene from consideration – though he may still claim to be a member of Holy Mother Church.'

'*Especially* so, my dear, among co-religionists such as ourselves – oh, forgive me, Hugh, I always think of you as one of my own flock.'

'But,' I piped up, at last, 'Anthony Powell isn't a Roman Catholic, is he?'

'One might have thought so, as he is Frank Longford's brother-in-law,' said the Monsignor. 'But then Frank is a convert, of course.' As if to himself, the Monsignor murmured: 'Actually I suspect Tony may be a non-believer, something of a pagan, perhaps.'

More audibly, he continued: 'I have met him in the company of Ronnie Knox – who used to be a neighbour of his in Somerset, at Mells – and also of Alick Dru, Evelyn Waugh's brother-in-law who served with Tony in the Intelligence Corps during the war. Naturally, you both know Tony, don't you?'

'No,' chorused the acolytes.

'But he has been a member of this very club for forty years,' said the Monsignor. 'I must bring you together.'

The ever-generous and hospitable Alfred duly arranged for us all to meet for dinner. As I sat nervously in the smoking room waiting for this epic evening to begin, I envisaged the heroic figure my idol would cut. Our Greatest Living Writer and most eminent literary critic, whose witty novels had entranced me with their fastidious style, paradox, irony, worldly wisdom and throwaway dialogue. Surely he would be tall, grand and aloof, a formidable presence of chilling authority? I felt awestruck, certain I would be unable to articulate anything intelligible.

Instead, there bustled through the swing doors a rather bent, bespectacled sexagenarian of average height showing plenty of teeth and exuding a powerful sense of energy, friendliness and laughter. 'Sorry I'm late,' he said in a mellow, sibilant and singularly charming drawl redolent of the '20s. 'Came on from a very jolly party of Bob Conquest's – d'you know him? He's a member here – in Battersea. Extraordinary how everyone always seems to have a stint living on Prince of Wales Drive.'

As he renewed old acquaintance with Alfred, I caught the eye of my fellow acolyte, whose expectations of a smooth, languid man of letters had been equally confounded. He mouthed something along the lines of 'Life imitates Art' (or was it 'Art imitates Life'?) which I failed to comprehend. By this time, the great novelist was presenting a 'missal' to the Monsignor: 'I came across this and thought you might like it, Alfred.'

During the temporary absence of 'Tony' (as I still did not dare to think of him) in the Gents before we went upstairs to dinner, there was a distinct chill in the air. 'Fancy calling this work a "missal",' said the Monsignor sorrowfully. 'To show such ignorance of the greatest civilizing influence of the Western world he really must be a pagan.'

The acolyte tut-tutted in sympathy. For my (silent) part, I considered that Alfred was being strangely ungracious about a present so thoughtfully given. If battle lines were being drawn, I wanted to declare myself on Tony's side in the lists – and I began to regret that I was meeting my hero in such buttoned-up company.

Despite this sticky beginning, however, the evening passed genially enough on the basis that we were all members among members. Tony recalled the time he had served on one of the club committees concerned with the discipline of various peccadilloes committed by members. 'The usual things,' said Tony. 'Unsavoury divorces, bankruptcies, soliciting guardsmen in the park and so forth.'

'What about the transvestite activities of the Major Fosdicks?' I blurted out in the hope of impressing the Master with my knowledge of his novels. As soon as the words were out of my mouth I realized that I had made a fool of myself.

'My dear boy . . .' Tony winced in embarrassment at my crassness.

Alfred adroitly steered the conversation round to Evelyn Waugh. 'When Evelyn wrote a short story, "Basil Seal Rides Again", for the first issue of the *Sunday Telegraph*

in the early 1960s,' said Tony, 'it made a most frightful
stink at the club.'

'Was Seal a member of the club?' I volunteered with a
view to retrieving my position.

'Apparently so,' said Tony. 'As his wife tells him to
stop looking like a stuck pig and to go and sit there "with
all the other queers".' (Muted laughter from the Monsignor and acolyte, raucous guffaws from myself.) 'Well,
as you can imagine, that didn't play very well with the
committee. I was deputed to persuade Evelyn not to
publish the story in book form without altering the name
of the club to some fictional establishment. He took some
persuading. "Everyone *knows* the club is full of queers,"
he protested. "I'm not for a start," I replied (the same
answer I give when critics compare me with Proust,
incidentally). But he stuck to his guns; it took ages for
him to consent, very grudgingly, to think of an invented
substitute. Some time later, long after we had abandoned
the subject, I happened to mention that I had bumped
into his neighbour, George Wyndham, in the club the
other day.

'"George Wyndham, the Squire of Orchard Wyndham?"

'"Yes."

'"Didn't know *he* was a queer."

'That was typical of Evelyn: once he had a particular
tease in his head he would never let it go.'

Stupidly sticking to my carefully rehearsed script, I
thought I saw my cue. 'Would it be true to say that Alick
Dru, Waugh's brother-in-law and your mutual friend with
Alfred here—'

'Friend-in-common, *please*,' interjected the Monsignor.

'That,' I continued doggedly, 'Major Dru was the model
for your character David Pennistone in *Dance* – the one
who annotates the bureaucratic Blackhead's three-and-a-

half page memo on soap issues for the Polish Womens' Corps with the words – "*Please amplify*"?'

Tony raised his eyebrows impatiently. But failing to spot the warning signs, I blundered on: 'Perhaps you ought to include Alfred in the last few volumes?'

With perfect politeness, Tony replied evenly: 'Novels are simply not written in that way. You don't merely transplant real-life characters into fiction; some might work, most wouldn't. I'm always being asked whether such-and-such a character was based on so-and-so. People won't believe that you are capable of *inventing* characters. All right, a couple of real people *might* occur to you but to make it work you have to invent a third person to pull it all together.'

Unknowingly I had trampled over Tony Powell's most sensitive territory. For years I had been toying with a trainspotter's guide to *Who's* Really *Who* in fiction. Egged on by Conynghame, I compiled lists of characters in Waugh and Powell with their possible real-life models. Yet, as Tony Powell gently taught me over the lunches at the club that followed our dinner with Alfred, such a literal-minded approach had betrayed a disgraceful ignorance of the creative processes of fiction.

It was finally dinned into my dense skull that *Dance* was *not* a roman-à-clef. Naturally, the seventy years of experience crammed into the twelve-volume sequence, from the first decade of the twentieth century onwards, by the novel's narrator, Nick Jenkins, ran parallel with those of Tony Powell in some obvious respects – Eton, Oxford, publishing, scriptwriting, artistic and aristocratic life (Jenkins married Lady Isobel Tolland, Powell married Lady Violet Pakenham), the Army in the Second World War, literary magazines (Powell was literary editor of *Punch* in the Muggeridge era), home in the West Country.

But, as I learned first-hand and from his four volumes of memoirs, *Dance* was by no means straight autobiography.

Like someone scratching a sore, though, I could never resist returning to my favourite topic with Tony, who would occasionally let slip a few clues if not tackled head-on. After all, even he had to concede that Hugh Moreland in *Dance* was largely based on his great friend Constant Lambert. As for Widmerpool, Tony had to suffer the claims of his brother-in-law Frank Longford, who eventually decided that he must have been the original himself – though Erridge struck me as much more likely to have been inspired by the eccentric Earl.

'Originally,' Tony told me during one of our chats on the perennial question, 'Frank, who has a one-track mind on such subjects, put it about that Widmerpool was based on Reginald Manningham-Buller, whom actually I hardly knew at school – though we were once in the same French division. The beak called him "Bullyingham-Manner" – thus anticipating that little ass Levin by about forty years. It is true that Buller always sculled single-handedly on the river, rather in the manner of Widmerpool's solo runs, and indeed through sheer dint of effort and willpower, managed to gain a place in the Upper Boat, or 2nd VIII, which was a remarkable achievement by someone in a dry-bob house. And Buller did indeed get someone sacked – a beak, though, not a boy, as in *Dance*, who promptly got another job at Charterhouse – for making a pass at a boy. But the idea – as some people have claimed – that *Buller* was the object of the pass is fantastically wide of the mark. As a boy he looked just the same as he did when he sat on the Woolsack as Lord Chancellor Dilhorne. I sat next to him at Pratt's once.'

'Did you touch on the subject of Widmerpool?'

'No.'

'I've played cricket with his son. He had a strong look of "Bullying-Manner".'

'Yes. He looks just like his father in his younger days. I lunched once at a bank with him and his wife, but there was no danger of Widmerpool being brought up as the Dilhornes looked as if they had not only never read a book but as if they did not know what a book looked like.'

Not that Tony had much time for most professional book readers, the critics. 'One complained recently that Widmerpool's ending up in a hippie commune was quite unbelievable. But, in fact, in real life, the boy at the deb dance who – like Widmerpool in the novel – had sugar poured over him was a very conventional young man, and *he* ended up in some peculiar religious order wearing a special uniform.'

When Desmond Seward put up the name of Denis Capel-Dunn (known as 'the Papal Bun') as a likely candidate in the Widmerpool Stakes at Brooks's Club the rumour soon found its way into Kenneth Rose's 'Albany' column in the *Sunday Telegraph*. Tony cryptically conceded to me that Seward was 'a clever fellow and might be on to something'. He and Capel-Dunn had briefly served together at the Cabinet Office during the war.

'I only knew the Papal Bun for nine weeks,' he said. 'But he certainly made an impression. I've never met anyone so materialistic in outlook. But then, of course, he wasn't at school with me so he was only *partly* the inspiration for Widmerpool. Fiction, as I keep reminding you, isn't as straightforward as that.'

Tony's slighting reference to 'that little ass Levin' during his Widmerpoolian reflections about 'Bullying-Manner' had been provoked by a piece Bernard Levin had written in *The Times* ticking off the Sage of the Chantry for being so touchy as to fall out with his old friend Muggeridge over a review of *The Valley of Bones*, the first

of the war trilogy in *Dance*. 'Levin obviously hadn't read
Malcolm's article before attacking me,' Tony told me. 'If
he *had* read it, he would have seen what purported to be
a review was an all-out onslaught – nothing to do with
the novel. I knew Malcolm like the back of my hand. He
had clearly decided to break off relations. But, pace Levin,
Malcolm and I still corresponded during the period he
claimed that we were incommunicado. I was very fond of
Malcolm, but really he was the most awful humbug, the
humbug of all time – like something out of *Pilgrim's
Progress*, Mr Humbug. All those girlfriends of his!'

'Did you remonstrate with Levin?' I asked.

'I wrote to *The Times* pointing out that Levin, then in
his early sixties, still had some lessons to learn later in
life. But they pompously wouldn't let me pull his leg –
though he had pulled mine.'

The characteristically shrewd final word was delivered by Lady Violet Powell, when I took the Powells out
to lunch in Somerset to mark the seventieth anniversary
of the founding of the Eton Society of Arts. 'What enraged
a failed novelist like Malcolm,' said Violet, 'was the
thought of Tony going on with more novels in the series.'

The Society, of which Harold Acton and Tony were the
last survivors, produced a remarkably precocious magazine called the *Eton Candle* to which Tony contributed, as
he put it, 'a not very interesting drawing (influences of
Beardsley and Lovat Fraser unconcealed)'. The drawing
was captioned by Brian Howard (part-model for Evelyn
Waugh's characters Anthony Blanche and Ambrose Silk)
'Colonel Caesar Cannonbrains of the Black Hussars'.
Tony had a highly developed visual sense, as was strik-
ingly evident when I made my first visit to the Chantry
in the early 1970s. I was startled to find that the gentlemen's lavatory downstairs had been completely covered –
cistern, pipes and all – by Tony with an elaborate collage

of faces from glossy magazines. I was even more startled when Tony, standing beside me, suddenly announced: 'I am going to do some peeing.'

Affecting a naturalness I did not feel, I waited until he had finished and then – without pulling the chain, which I feared would look prissy – followed suit. The best I could do to ease my tension was to mention Sir Iain Moncreiffe of that Ilk's strictures over washing my hands after urinating.

'Does Moncreiffe really know his stuff, do you think?' asked Tony.

'What – about peeing?'

'No. Genealogical investigation, properly conducted.'

'Oh yes. He knows too much, probably. Can't get it down on paper.'

'The only time I ran into him he was pretty tight.'

Our shared interest in genealogy was a great bond between us. Tony knew only too well that anyone keen on the subject risks being branded a snob, a crashing bore – and probably 'off his rocker', as Peter Templer in *Dance* would have put it.

'My own father was not merely bored by genealogy,' he said. 'He was affronted. He possessed little or no sense of the past; still less curiosity about the circumstances of other people, alive or dead.'

Tony was quite the reverse. 'Genealogy teaches much about the vicissitudes of life,' he used to say, 'the vast extent of human oddness.' As for the lazy label of 'snob', he pointed out the paradox that 'the chief lesson of genealogy is how extraordinarily close the classes are – and have always been – together'. As his salty *Journals* confirm, he was equally interested in the giggling girls who delivered the Sunday papers to the Chantry as in the local duke, who burped his way through the National Anthem.

Tony's inexhaustible curiosity about other people –
and not only people but animals, particularly his beloved
cats, Trelawney and Snook – was the mainspring of his
genius as a novelist. Indeed he regarded an interest in
other people as the sine qua non of novel-writing – an
attribute lacking in not a few novelists whose interest in
people extends only to themselves.

It was typical of Tony, for instance, to cross-examine
a photographer who came to the Chantry in order to
illustrate some journalistic piece I was writing. 'He was
called Tim Richmond,' reported Tony afterwards. 'I
noticed that he had painter's hands – and, sure enough,
he turned out to be descended from that dynasty of
Richmond artists – you know, George and that lot. One of
them was Yeoman of the Stables. Came from Bawtry,
near Doncaster.'

'Just near the seat of our kinsmen, the Waterhouses,
eh, Tony?'

'Exactly.'

Nicholas Shakespeare, on the other hand, did not
satisfy the Sage's rigorous genealogical viva voce on the
exact nature of his kinship to the Bard and relations
between the *Telegraph*'s chief reviewer and its literary
editor were consequently never quite what they might
have been. Tony concluded that young Shakespeare did
not have 'much idea as to how to run a books page'. After
Shakespeare had mischievously commissioned Auberon
Waugh to review a collection of Tony's *Telegraph* notices
– which resulted in an extraordinarily vitriolic attack –
Tony severed his long links with the paper, or at least the
books page. He continued to chip in pithy appreciations of
old friends for the obituaries page, which I was then
editing and, by way of a peace offering, the *Telegraph*
acquired a bust of his head by William Pye. I told Tony

that it was exhibited in the so-called writing room, a retreat in Docklands for hacks in search of silence.

'You mean where people go to sleep it off after lunch?' said Tony with his customary acuity.

Pursuing one of my pet theories – about novelists tending to be only children – I once put it to Tony that his solitary childhood might be the key to his imagination. 'In my experience,' he replied, 'it is the children of *large* families who tend to exhibit the traditional foibles of the only child.' Among the multitudinous family he had married into, he noted 'the Pakenham habit of contradicting anything anyone else says'.

Yet anyone as privileged as I was to overhear some of the hilarious and harmonious conversation between Tony and Violet, which had begun in September 1934 when they first met in County Westmeath and happily carried on until his death in the spring of 2000, will know how much Tony and his work owed to Violet's encyclopedic knowledge, insight into human nature and zestful love of life. On my first visit to the Chantry, my wife Christine and I were a jittery bag of nerves – a young suburban couple completely out of our social and intellectual depth. But the Powells put us at our ease with the promise in their kindly manner – unfailingly fulfilled – of constant amusement, stimulation, subtle, original and often oblique observation. Every minute in their company bucked you up.

To break the ice, Tony asked us to sign our names in his treasured copy of *Lt-Col Secombe's Army & Navy Birthday Book for Children*. 'I bought it when I was eight in the Gloucester Road,' he recalled, 'and promptly signed under "21 December", the winter solstice.' I appended my own signature under 30 December, beneath L. P. Hartley. 'Another Harrovian,' noted Tony. 'And as one of his

increasingly erratic servants – Leslie seemed to take
pleasure in employing alarming domestics – put it in her
parting shot, with her small daughter beside her: "Take a
good look at him, Emily, an Oxford man, and a cad."'

Meanwhile, Violet was perusing the *Guide to the
Royal Family*, which I had brought down as a present. 'I
see several of these Normans were killed out hunting in
the New Forest,' she observed. 'You would have thought
after the first few deaths in the field they might have
chosen a different country.' And in the biographical entry
for Princess Alice, Countess of Athlone, she noticed that
HRH was patron of the Society of Gold and Silver Wyre
Drawers. 'Rather uncomfortable, I would have thought,'
mused Lady Violet.

Over lunch we talked of the amazingly debauched
Evelyn Waugh *Diaries* currently causing a sensation in
the *Observer*.

'Presumably you can identify quite a few of the un-
named characters, Tony?' I cheekily suggested. (Later he
showed me the original of a Mark Boxer pocket cartoon
he had been given with the caption: 'He knows who all
the asterisks are in the Waugh *Diaries*.')

'I could hazard a few guesses,' Tony said. 'Though I
am *not* the unidentified "Tony" described as taking part
in an Oxford orgy.'

'Isn't it rather worrying, though, to think of what
might be published next week, or the week after?'

'I don't care in the slightest what Evelyn may or may
not have jotted down in a drunken moment about me,'
said Tony. 'I can take it. But what one really dreads is
being quoted by him making some disobliging remark
about a third party who might be very much still with us.'

'I suppose that without such scurrilous gossip,' I said,
'history, and genealogy for that matter, would be pretty
dull. As you said in your biography of John Aubrey, so

much of the picturesque detail of the seventeenth century was plundered from his *Brief Lives*, that extraordinary jumble of biography.'

'Yes,' said Tony. 'With all due modesty, I never felt I got enough credit for rediscovering Aubrey. That one-man show "devised" by Patrick Garland, for instance, does not even acknowledge my books on the subject.'

'Do you remember the moment when Roy Dotrice, who played Aubrey, picked up a work of reference, read out an ineffably dull biographical entry about a barrister – Recorder of this, Bencher of that, and so on – and then snapped it shut with a *Tchah* or was it a *Pshaw*? – and the comment: "He got more by his *prick* than his practice"? That was the blinding light in my quest to make reference books more lively.'

'But the point is that Aubrey was a *gent*,' said Tony. 'He was not portrayed on stage as one.'

Like Aubrey, Tony had a relish for quirky anecdotes. A particular favourite of mine was the one he had heard from his old friend Wyndham Ketton-Cremer, the Squire of Felbrigg, about a Norfolk parson who was officiating at a funeral in a church not his own. He arrived early to have a look round. Above one tomb he spotted a medieval iron helmet and, as there was time to kill (as it were), tried it on. Assuming this headdress was easy enough; removing it proved impossible. And so when the mourners and the coffin arrived at the church they were (as Tony, with typical understatement, put it) 'surprised to be received by a cleric wearing a knight's bascinet'. Thus accoutred, the priest duly pronounced the burial service – but Tony was characteristically exercised by the question of whether or not the helmeted parson had 'contrived to lift the vizor' in order to conduct the ceremony.

A regular feature of visits to the Chantry was a walk with Tony down to the lake and overgrown grottoes which

had a strong flavour of the ancient world that so
bewitched his imagination. As indicated in *Dance*, he took
an interest in the local folklore and delighted in the fact
that his property was bordered by Dead Woman's Bottom.
This historic name proved too fruity for the bureaucratic
Blackheads of the modern world ('the plansters', as John
Betjeman called them) who announced that it would be
changed to the ever so dainty 'Chantry Vale'. Tony countered by saying that he would have his letterhead
changed so as to incorporate Dead Woman's Bottom as
part of the address.

He never stood for any nonsense of that sort. It was a
tonic to hear Tony's bracing views on the absurdity of
power, politics and public affairs – so witheringly
potrayed in *Dance* through the ambitions of Widmerpool,
who yet always managed to back the wrong horse,
whether it be Mrs Simpson, National Socialism, Stalinism
or '60s student revolution. I found much solace over the
years in his strictures on the idiocy and incompetence of
subeditors, publishers and journalists. 'One notes again
and again,' he used to say, 'what amounts to censorship
of any original idea in a piece.'

For public consumption, at any rate, Tony tended to
eschew making literary judgements about his contemporaries, though he made an exception in attempting to
promote the poetry of the novelist Kingsley Amis and the
novels of the poet Roy Fuller. 'Needless to say,' he would
complain, 'not a single interviewer ever picks up this
point.' On our walks, however, Tony would occasionally
let slip some trenchant remarks about other writers
in the tetchy tones that were to startle readers of his
Journals in the 1990s. The targets included Graham
Greene ('absurdly overrated'), Virginia Woolf ('what a
dreadful woman she was'), Laurie Lee ('utterly unread-

able'), Gabriel Garcia Márquez ('essence of pretentious middlebrow verbiage of the worst kind'), Salman Rushdie ('characteristic of a particular sort of successful bad writing'), Dorothy Hodgkin ('left-wing old hag') and, of course, the ghastly Auden Gang ('woolly minded in what might be called a public-school manner, without the supposed public-school virtues').

To hear such literary home truths from the horse's mouth, as it were (Philip Larkin, summed up by Tony as 'not really a very nice chap', notoriously nicknamed the Sage of the Chantry 'Horse-faced Dwarf' for Kingsley Amis's benefit) gave me a tremendous buzz. Here indubitably was a hero well worth worshipping, a wise mentor. Above all, Tony took a robust approach to the Arts. Real aestheticism called for toughness, discipline. An essentially practical man, Tony was prepared to get his hands dirty – whether hacking away at the undergrowth around the grottoes, preparing one of his 'farmhouse curries' (ideally lamb, with no shortage of garlic), bottling *'vin très ordinaire'* from imported hogsheads or handling dusty genealogical documents on one of his scholarly quests.

True to his military background, the former Major was intolerant of sloppiness and had no time for sentimentality. 'Self-pity,' he used to say, 'is the unfailing ingredient of every best-seller.'

I always enjoyed hearing how he dealt with importunate fans. As one myself, I was glad of tips on conduct unbecoming. One especially dotty fan took to telephoning at strange hours. 'I suggested that he should consult a psychiatrist,' said Tony. 'He said he had. Told him to do so again.'

Yet only the humourless could fail to detect a Bowraesque element of leg-pulling and self-parody in such astringency – and indeed in his celebrated last paragraph wiggings in his reviews for the *Telegraph*. A typical one, correcting some howlers in the edition of *The Letters of Evelyn Waugh*, read:

> The note on p.90 should read Lady Diana
> Bridgeman, not Bradford; the Princess de Caraman-
> Chimay on p.430, the same as she on p.559, was
> née Hennessy, not Hamilton; the dog that acted in
> *La Dolce Vita* belonged to Iris Tree, not Mrs Taffy
> Rodd.

But my own favourite was a magisterial dressing-down of Geoffrey Grigson (described by Tony as possessing 'an uncontrollable vanity, combined with lack of humour'):

> Look here, Grigson, this is the umpteenth time
> you've been up before the beak for Insulting
> Behaviour. A clergyman's son ought to know better,
> but you're not so young as you were, and in your
> day you have produced some good anthologies and
> collections of pictures, so this time you'll just be
> Bound Over in your own recognisances to keep the
> Peace. Next case.

On the whole, I merely acted as a prompt in any literary conversation with Tony by chipping in cues for his pronouncements – almost all of which chimed with my own infinitely less formed views, or prejudices. But occasionally, fuelled by the club claret, I would be bold enough to disagree.

'Kingsley says he can't take Martin's novels, a judgement I heartily endorse,' he said once over lunch. 'Though he's a goodish critic.'

'I can understand why you dislike them so much,' I

ventured. 'But have you tried *Money*? It really is rather a tour de force on the way we live now.'

Next time I bumped into Tony in the club he button-holed me, and I feared the worst. 'I bought a paperback of *Money* on your recommendation. I felt that you would be reliable on that question—'

'Oh dear, Tony, I'm so sorry, I shouldn't have chanced my arm—'

'No, no, my dear boy. You were right. It's not at all bad in its genre – admittedly not my favourite one. I've sent Martin a fan postcard – of a naked lady playing with herself, in keeping with *Money*'s subject matter.'

When Tony won the T. S. Eliot Prize for Creative Literature, the citation for which from the Ingersoll Foundation curiously mentioned his contribution 'to upholding Judaeo-Christian standards and the Ten Commandments', I plucked up the courage to ask about his religious views. He smiled rather wearily: 'Basically *non-croyant*, you could say.' Otherwise I tended to steer well clear of metaphysical matters with Tony whose mild fascination with spiritualism, psychical research, the occult, astrology, tarot cards and so forth I did not share. In fact, these topics gave me the creeps and their airing in *Dance* remains the one element of my annual fix (to this day I reread Tony's masterpiece every year) that I find unsympathetic.

While I was still, just, married to Christine and living near Shaftesbury, the Powells came to tea at our cottage on their way back from lunching with Lord David Cecil, Tony's former fagmaster at Eton ('he hasn't changed a bit', Tony reported). Unfortunately the visit, over-eagerly anticipated by me, could not be said to have been a roaring success. I heard myself blurting out that I had spotted one or two solecisms in *Dance*. As Tony looked on

resignedly, I stammered: 'Yes, I'm afraid so. Dicky Umfraville refers to "the *Saint* Leger" when he would have
merely said "the Leger"—'

'Only if he had been in Turf circles,' interjected Violet.

'And,' I idiotically continued, 'Quiggin says "lavatory
paper" instead of "toilet paper".' Both these points had
actually been drawn to my attention by Mark Bence-
Jones, whose lavatorial humour embraced a particular
interest in the various euphemisms employed. Happily,
before the omniscient Violet could gently put me straight
on this prickly question, my four-year-old daughter Harriet made her entrance down the stairs in her party frock.

'Why, she's the spitting image of you, Hugh, isn't she,
Violet?' said Tony.

I beamed with paternal pride, and felt an inner glow
that Harriet might possibly remember having met the
greatest novelist of the twentieth century. Christine, on
the other hand, bridled alarmingly. 'Oh, do you *think* so?'
she said in a chilling tone. The tension was palpable.

After the ensuing divorce, the Powells, by now firm
family friends, rallied round supportively. John Powell,
Tony and Violet's younger son, generously gave me shel-
ter in the basement of his house in Kennington. John,
who had been working on the City pages of the *Daily
Telegraph*, was a fellow member of the club, but our
association went back to boyhood. In one of those characteristically Powellian coincidences that trouble plodding
critics but actually form the pattern of real life ('so much
so,' as Tony used to say, 'that they have to be toned down
for fiction'), we discovered that we had played on opposing
sides in the needle cricket match between Port Regis and
Sandroyd in the summer of 1957. 'I was run out for a
duck,' ruefully recalled John. 'I don't think I've ever got
over it.' Somewhere deep in my subconscious is the nag-
ging fear that I may not only have been responsible for

this traumatic dismissal, but that I achieved it through unsporting means.

The proximity of the Oval to my new chambers in John's basement was a life-saving advantage. My depression over the divorce, and a subsequent disastrous infatuation, was kept at bay by afternoons spent day-dreaming under the gasometers of the friendly 'People's Ground'. In the close season I would hibernate in my burrow weaving fantasies about my wholly illusory success as a reclusive best-selling author. At least I had no shortage of the magic ingredient for the formula identified by Tony – self-pity.

The Chantry remained my ultimate Shangri-La. After one of my visits down there, I was amused to read years later in the published *Journals*, Tony noted: 'Both V & I noticed that living in this proximity [in Kennington] had caused both Hugh & John to develop a certain similarity of manner, hard to say who influenced whom.' It was reassuring to read also that 'Hugh seemed in excellent form'. The truth was that Tony and Violet were so extraordinarily funny and so sympathetic ('The only sort of writing worth reading,' he would say, 'is *sympathetic* writing') that I always felt in excellent form when at the Chantry.

Perhaps in a subconscious attempt to provide Tony with amusing copy, I played up my gluttony into a running joke – though the reality was that my gross 'comfort-eating' had spiralled out of control. Of one visit, Tony recorded: 'Hugh had Creole soup, beef and mushroom pie, gooseberry crumble, so with a couple of slices of plum cake at tea one hopes he kept from fainting before reaching the restaurant car on the way back.'

When I landed a job on the *Field*, then still a weekly, Tony sportingly entered into the spirit of the magazine during an interview he gave me for his eightieth birthday.

'I suspect,' he said, 'that the *Field* could have featured
among Major Fosdick's reading matter on those afternoons he found it "restful" to repair to his dressing room
in drag. And, come to think of it, Dicky Umfraville might
have claimed to have once written for the *Field* on some
recondite subject.'

On my pilgrimages to Powell a perennial topic was
the progress – or, more usually, lack of it – of various
schemes to adapt *Dance* for television. At one stage Dennis Potter (soon to be briskly alluded to by the Sage as
plain 'Potter') was involved; then Ken Taylor of *The Jewel
in the Crown* fame and Jonathan Powell of the BBC. 'No
relation,' reported Tony. 'He pronounces his surname
Pow-ell.' (Enunciated with theatrical distaste.) As one
projected adaptation after another bit the dust, Tony
traced a saga of 'lettings-down'. Yet he remained keen on
the prospect of a television airing for *Dance* on account of
its effect on ordinary book sales. After all, he had begun
life as a publisher – 'in the sense,' he would deprecatingly
point out, 'that I used to empty the inkpots, interview
wrapper-design artists, deal with lunatics, that sort of
thing'.

Even when Channel 4 finally went into production
for an eight-hour screenplay by Hugh Whitemore in 1996,
I found Tony, by then in his nineties and confined to a
wheelchair, half relishing, in Eeyorish gloom, the improb-
ability of the television version ever coming to pass. 'I feel
like a woman who has been seduced so many times that
she'll never marry,' he said chortling. 'It will be a race to
the tomb.'

Out of sheer presumption – not to mention my own
dreamy demands – I took it upon myself to act as a sort
of authorial spy on the production, in the guise of a
reporter hanging round the set. I furnished Tony with the
intelligence that James Purefoy, who played Nick Jenkins

as a young man, was a scion of the Squires of Shalstone in Buckinghamshire. Tony's genealogical antennae were still as acute as ever. 'That name, Purefoy, always seemed next to Powell in lists of documents when I was researching my disreputable ancestry.'

John Standing (otherwise Sir John Leon, Bt), who played the older Jenkins, told me that his grandfather, Sir Guy Standing, had failed to convince in *Lives of the Bengal Lancers* when he announced in his best 'old actor-laddie' tones that he had been 'in the Blues'. I duly passed this snippet back to the Powells, old Hollywood hands, but Violet was unimpressed. 'I think you'll find that it was actually Franchot Tone who spoke that line.'

Violet also had to put Hugh Whitemore straight over the singing of 'Happy Birthday to You' at the party for Mr Deacon, the pederastic painter and dealer in curios. As she pointed out, this American ditty did not reach these shores until some years after Mr Deacon's jollifications (at which he took a fatal tumble downstairs). Why not substitute 'For He's a Jolly Good Fellow'? On such punctilio does the *Dance* subtly turn: every name, every title, every nuance is unerringly spot on, in a deftly choreographed chronicle at once comic and profound.

Struck by the sympathy and intelligence of Simon Russell Beale, who gave a definitive performance as Widmerpool, I passed on a charming vignette squirrelled away by the actor. 'I noticed a passage in Anthony Powell's *Journals*,' he told me, 'in which a Widmerpoolian doctor bids goodbye to the author in hospital by shaking Powell's feet ("an authentically Widmerpoolian gesture", as he describes it). I managed to slip in an echo of this as a bit of business in one scene. It's my little tribute to Anthony Powell.'

I also picked up the titbit on set that Miranda Richardson was said to have prepared for her part as the terrifying Pamela Flitton by studying the career of the late Barbara Skelton, sometime wife of Cyril Connolly and George Weidenfeld. 'Not too wide of the mark there,' commented Tony when I relayed this on my next Chantry visit.

'I may say,' Violet added, 'that Barbara Skelton was the most sinister person ever to have stayed under this roof – and that's saying something.'

Although some of the critics claimed to be confused by Hugh Whitemore's ingenious and skilful compression of the twelve-volume sequence into four two-hour films – for my part, I would have welcomed at least four hours per novel – all that really mattered was that Anthony Powell himself had the satisfaction of seeing it on screen before his death. And he undoubtedly enjoyed the experience.

'It's really not too bad, is it?' he said when I telephoned with gossip about the screening at Channel 4. 'What did you think?'

I burbled and bumbled incoherently about my enthusiasm. 'Oh, I think – well, er . . . it's absolutely the best thing – um, the best thing – the *best thing I've ever seen*, Tony!'

'Eh? *What?*' And then, without covering the mouthpiece, he shouted across to Violet: 'It's Hugh – his stammer is *worse* than ever!'

'Hugh *who?*' I overheard Violet's voice echoing in the background. 'Lloyd-Jones? Trevor-Roper?'

'No,' said Tony *fortissimo*. 'Merely Massingberd.'

My feeling of well-deserved deflation was gloriously dispelled when Tony did me the honour of dedicating the last volume of his *Journals 'For Hugh Massingberd'*. This gave me a thrill beyond my wildest dreams. I was on such a cloud of happiness about it that I managed to rise above the regrettable impression given in one of the entries

('enjoyable, but extremely exhausting day') that I had
been party to the notion that Max Hastings had ruined
the *Telegraph* by dragging it downmarket. On encountering Max at a special *Evening Standard* preview of the
Dance film, when he grunted of his dismay, I could only
apologize feebly – and reflect ruefully on Tony's comment
a quarter of a century before about the worry of being
misrepresented in Evelyn Waugh's *Diaries*.

When I went to congratulate Hugh Whitemore on his
excellent work, he told me that the compliment he cherished most came from the Sage of the Chantry himself
after the novelist had seen some rushes. 'Did you write
that joke,' asked Tony, 'or was it one of mine?'

I asked Hugh Whitemore for his favourite line in
Dance and he quoted the macabre reaction of the catering
officer in the war film to news of Captain Biggs hanging
himself. 'In the cricket pav, of all places,' said Captain
Soper. 'And him so fond of the game.'

Back at the Chantry I passed this on to Tony, who
could not resist a guffaw. My abiding last image of the
Sage was of him sitting in front of his television set and,
at last, being given the richly earned honour of laughing
at his own jokes.

Living up to his family motto, *True to the End* ('I
always think it's rather a feeble sentiment,' Tony used to
say), Tony bore his long years of immobility with great
fortitude and never lost his sense of humour. 'At least,' he
would console himself, 'it's better than being back with
my old Regiment.' Neither did he lose his curiosity about
people ('I don't think we've ever met,' he said to my second
wife when she came with me to the Chantry not long
before his death), nor his courteous hospitality. 'Help
yourself to a drink' were his penultimate words, according
to his elder son, Tristram. And his genealogical instincts

survived to the end. On his final appearance in the library
of the Chantry, he noticed Violet seemingly reaching for
The Landed Gentry. He said: 'What are you looking up?'

On the day of Tony's funeral, 4 April 2000, spring in
Somerset suddenly turned to winter. Thick snow ('doubtless laid on by A. P. himself', as his biographer Hilary
Spurling put it to me) delayed the arrival of mourners
from London, including my wife and myself. As Tony's
ashes were scattered from a boat into the Chantry lake,
it was, by all accounts, like a vision of the ancient world.
Tristram read the dirge from *Cymbeline*: 'Fear no more
the heat o' the sun . . .' John half expected a mailed arm
to rise up from the water. And everyone thought of the
closing passage of *A Dance to the Music of Time*: 'Even
the formal measure of the seasons seemed suspended in
the wintry silence.'

This was read at Tony's memorial service the next
month, at the Grosvenor Chapel, by Simon Russell Beale.
Harold Pinter, Tony's nephew by marriage, read – after
some difficulty in gaining entry into the seemingly impen-
etrable pulpit – the sonorous passage from Ezekiel about
'the Valley of Bones'. Emma Fielding, who played the
young Lady Isobel in the *Dance* film, read an appropriately agnostic extract from 'The Garden of Proserpine' by
Swinburne (another Eton and Balliol man). Jonathan
Cecil, son of Tony's old fagmaster, read from *Measure for
Measure* and reminded the congregation that Tony constantly reread the works of William Shakespeare in the
last part of his life. And Karl Daymond sang 'If You Were
the Only Girl in the World' from the Great War musical
The Bing Boys Are Here, which Tony had seen as a
schoolboy and was judged by Ted Jeavons in *Dance* to be
a 'top-hole show'.

My main concern in my own heartfelt eulogy to Tony
on this occasion was to pay tribute to the devoted care

given to him in his last years by Violet and the family, especially John, whose selfless commitment and dedication were nothing short of heroic. As Tony had written in the last entry of his *Journals*: 'I realise more than ever how much I depend on V., and the rest of my immediate family.'

In conclusion I could only echo the feelings of Nick Jenkins in *Dance* when he sees his boon companion and great friend Hugh Moreland for the last time. 'It was also the last time I had, with anyone, the sort of talk we used to have together.'

It was then my intention to retire in good order (to employ a favourite phrase of Tony's) from the pulpit, but whereas Harold Pinter had found access difficult, egress proved to be my undoing. In the manner of a low comedian of the music hall, I tripped down the spiral staircase and for a moment thought that I might share the fate of Mr Deacon at his birthday party. On landing awkwardly, my next worry was that I might let out an involuntary curse reminiscent of Sir Maurice Bowra's epithet, which had rent the Mediterranean air during a cultural cruise when he and the Powells realized that they had missed the last lift down to sea level. As I limped away, I murmured to myself: 'Funnier than *anything* I managed up in the pulpit.'

Shortly afterwards, when up at Gunby for another house-sitting stint during the absence of the Wrisdales, I received a letter from Violet saying that she and the family had decided that I should have Tony's two letters from Byron to Mrs Massingberd. I felt quite overwhelmed by the generosity of this gesture. My own correspondence with Tony going back more than thirty years had come full circle. My plan is for the letters to be added to Gunby's literary treasures preserved for posterity in the James Lees-Milne Memorial Library, alongside Boswell's autographed *Life of Johnson*, the manuscript of Tennyson's lines celebrating the 'haunt of ancient peace', Kipling memorabilia and the rest. Yet, with all due respect to the poet described by Tony as 'your fellow Harrovian cricketer', the proudest literary association of all is with my hero, Anthony Powell.

A year later, the newly formed Anthony Powell Society held its first conference at Eton. Assorted fans, including myself, revelled in the opportunity of retracing the steps of Jenkins, Stringham, Templer and Widmerpool around 'the Wat'ry Glade'. In the last session, I was to deliver a paper on A. D. Powell's preoccupation with genealogy, but an unexpected announcement from the platform virtually deprived me of the power of speech. It seemed that I had been appointed president of the Anthony Powell Society.

TEN

Highly Satirical

'AT LAST,' WROTE my form master at Harrow in 1963 at the top of my general essay, 'you seem to have found a subject that *really* interests you.' That subject was 'Satire', then – thanks to the Profumo Scandal which was spluttering along like a bowl of porridge on the boil – at the height of its boom. After a brisk canter through mugged-up literary history – Juvenal, Dryden, Pope, Swift, Byron and so forth – I had dragged in my favourite novelists Waugh and Powell and then luxuriated in the thrill of describing the satire industry that had sprung up in the slipstream of *Beyond the Fringe*.

I had first heard of this ground-breaking satirical revue a couple of years earlier when staying with my old prep-school friend Robert Stokes in Surrey. As usual, we were fooling around with spoof cricket commentaries – much as we were doing, *mutatis mutandis*, five years later, when Evelyn Waugh's death was announced – and Mr Stokes, Robert's father, a droll, shrewd man, observed: 'I'd say, Hugh, that you have rather a "Beyond the Fringe" attitude to life, wouldn't you?'

In my customary manner when addressed by grown-ups, I blushed uncomprehendingly and mumbled unintelligibly. Was he making some sarcastic allusion to my curly hair, which was incapable of being brushed forward into a fringe? Noticing my discomfiture, the kindly Mrs Stokes came to the rescue. 'I don't think you know what the old man is on about, do you?'

'Er, not really,' I murmured.

'Well,' said Mrs Stokes. 'The other night we went to this extraordinary little show in a tiny theatre in London – it was called *Beyond the Fringe*. "The Fringe" is the offbeat part of the Edinburgh Festival apparently, where these four young men – just undergraduates, really, made a hit last year. They were *so* funny. It was all wonderfully fresh and irreverent. They send things up – rather like you and Robert with your imitations of E. W. Swanton. That's what you meant, isn't it, dear?'

'Yes, of course. The star of the show is a brilliant young chap called Peter Cook – and I'm proud to say, Robert, that he is an Old Radleian.' Robert, some eighteen months my junior (an age gap that had so exercised our headmaster that he felt compelled to humiliate me in front of the whole school), was due to follow his father to Radley the next term.

'D'you know,' continued the affable Mr Stokes, 'he imitates the Prime Minister?'

'What! Mr Macmillan?'

'That's the fellah.'

'Gosh!' These were sensational tidings.

'Yes. He shuffles on and reads out a letter from a Scottish old-age pensioner, which he then proceeds to tear up.'

'And,' chipped in Mrs Stokes, 'there's even a sketch about the war.'

'Some of that was in rather poor taste, I thought, Elizabeth. I don't think that bespectacled bloke should really have taken off Douglas Bader's walk—'

'I heard some people hissing at that. But wasn't he a *scream* as the clergyman giving the school sermon? "But my brother Esau is an hairy man."'

'That was spot on. And I enjoyed the cod Shakespeare skit – "Oh saucy Worcester, dost thou lie so still?"'

Spoofs of school sermons and Shakespeare? Suddenly I felt new horizons opening up. I took the Stokes' programme of the revue off to bed and pored longingly over its contents. The *'Fringe* boys' were to be my new idols. Whereas Jonathan Miller, Dudley Moore and Alan Bennett all looked amusing in a 'funny-face' sort of way, Peter Cook exuded style and glamour, even danger. Mr Stokes had been right: the Old Radleian was the star. He rose even higher in my estimation when I worked out that he must have overlapped at the school ('College' it liked to call itself) with my cricketing hero, the dashing 'Lord Ted' Dexter. And the programme note intimated that Cook had been a wizard soccer player. I tabulated all this information away for future daydreaming sessions, with myself assuming the role of master satirist.

By the time Robert Stokes and I managed to see *Beyond the Fringe* on the stage, the cast had changed – Cookie & Co. had gone to New York – and the revue failed to live up to my fantasies. I had seen snatches of the original stars on television; their replacements would not find their way into my gallery of heroes. I consoled myself by memorizing large chunks of the script, which I bought. Unfortunately much of it passed well over my ignorant teenaged head, though I did my best to pretend that this was not the case. At least I could be grateful to Michael Frayn's introduction to the script for the explanation as to the proclivities of the 'aesthetic young men' in the sketch about 'Bollard: a man's cigarette'. Apparently the original stage direction had read 'Enter two outrageous old queens' but was altered at the command of the Lord Chamberlain, who was to remain in control of theatre censorship until *Hair* in 1968, seen by Stokes and myself, wearing City suits, to mark his coming of age.

Back at Harrow, I enthusiastically spread the word about satire, but my hearty contemporaries were not to be distracted from their concentrated absorption on the playing fields. 'You say this chap Cook was at Radley with Dexter, Monty. Big deal! I'd rather just watch Lord Ted batting, wouldn't you?'

A solitary exception was an amiable apple-cheeked boy from Lancashire who had a keen eye for the way the wind was blowing. Later, it was he who first alerted me – from local intelligence gleaned in Liverpool – about the Mersey 'beat' groups making a name for themselves at the Cavern – though typically I backed the wrong horse by preferring The Searchers to the other combo with that embarrassing name, The Beatles. 'If you like satire,' said Apple Cheeks, 'you'd probably enjoy this. I picked it up in London.'

He handed me a rough-looking agglomeration of apparently roneoed sheets of paper crudely stapled together. It bore the legend *Private Eye* and was adorned with a silhouette of the Albert Memorial beside the banner headline: 'Britain's First Man into Space'. In the bottom right-hand corner was a caricature of Queen Victoria with a bubble coming out of her mouth saying 'Ho Ho Very Satirical'.

This and subsequent issues of what became 'the Fortnightly Lampoon' were scrutinized, as the *Beyond the Fringe* programme and script had been, in the manner of sacred texts. If the *Fringe* script had passed over my head, the *Eye* appeared to be written in an undecipherable code – 'pseuds', 'pooves', and so forth. And who were these people being satirized? C. P. Snurd, Smarty-Boots Eccles, Perishing Worthless, Baillie Vass, Eric Buttock? At least I could enjoy the cartoons, seemingly drawn by someone called William Rushton. I stuck doggedly to my task: after all, this was satire and I knew that I should be laughing. I noticed, in my methodical way, that the magazine was printed at Wembley, just down the hill. Perhaps if I loitered outside some of this satirical magic might rub off on me and I would be able to get the jokes.

My fascination with the *Eye* took on a new dimension when my half-sister Juliet told me that its editor, Christopher Booker, was the brother of a great friend of hers. The Booker parents had run the preparatory school where Juliet had boarded in Dorset, Knighton House, not far from my own prep school, Port Regis. Christopher, Juliet explained, had been at Shrewsbury with 'a very clever and funny group of boys who all worked on the school mag, the *Salopian*'. They included Richard Ingrams, Willie Rushton and Paul Foot.

'You mean, you *know* some of the people on the *Eye*?'

'Of course – I've known Christopher since I was so high. In fact, I think you must have met him when you were a baby – *Lovey-Boy*.'

'That's enough of that. Tell me more about *Private Eye*.'

'Well, these Salopians met up with some other clever and funny chaps at Oxford – though actually Christopher had gone to Cambridge, like Peter Cook – and then, when they all found themselves in London, they thought they would carry on with the same sort of undergraduate japes. I remember picking up an early copy of *Private Eye* in a bistro when I was nursing at St Mary's. I couldn't understand a word. It's all rather left wing, isn't it? Christopher used to be in the Young Liberals.'

'Is it? I thought it was just satirical – and funny.'

It never occurred to me to ask Juliet for a fresh introduction to Booker. I would have been far too shy and nervous of being in the presence of such a brilliant figure. In fact, I have never met him face to face to this day – though he once telephoned me nearly thirty years later when I was working on the obituaries desk of the *Daily Telegraph* in order to tick me off for publishing an uncharitable obit of a clergyman of his acquaintance.

My obsession with *Private Eye*, and frequent recourse to its secret lingo, had made me increasingly unpopular at Harrow – or at any rate in the narrow confines of my own hearty house. To the school at large, naturally, I remained an utterly anonymous figure. 'My God, there goes a *grey man*,' I overheard one swaggering 'blood' observe to another as I negotiated my way as imperceptibly as possible past them in the school tuck-shop. Too ostentatiously for my own good, I would take my treasured copies of *Eye* into 'Reader', the house library. 'What's that bolshie comic you're reading, Monty? Why don't you bugger off to Soho, where you arty-farty types belong?'

One evening when I retired to my own study at the top of the rickety structure that could only have been designed for institutional use, I found a crude caricature of myself – curly hair, bulbous nose, cheeks in full crimson blush, poppy, madly staring eyes, that sort of thing – complete with the caption 'HIGHLY SATIRICAL'. Instead of interpreting this as a warning to pipe down and resume my customary low profile, I took it as a compliment. My hero worship for the bright new satirists of the *Fringe* and the *Eye* was one daydream that I felt proud to share with the world.

Undaunted in my enthusiasm, I suggested to the amiable Apple Cheeks that we should introduce some satirical touches to the end-of-term *House Revue*, traditionally a dire entertainment characterized by rugger players pretending to be a line of chorus girls. I set to work on a searing series of sketches about the hearty hypocrisies of our housemaster and other crucial topics, but then received a formal visitation from the producers.

'We hear, with no small measure of surprise,

Monty—' began the most senior, a portly figure who was later to become a judge.

'Bloody *amazement*, more likely,' interjected his chirpier sidekick.

'That,' continued the producer, his jowls wobbling magisterially, 'you have the presumption to think that you can, in common parlance, muscle in on *our* revue . . .'

'"Muscle" is hardly the mot juste, old cock,' said the assistant producer. 'Have you seen his arms? They're like ruddy matchsticks – Belsen Billy had bigger biceps.'

'My understanding,' carried on the producer, regardless of these interruptions, 'is that you propose not only to write disobliging material about our esteemed housemaster but also to presume to perform it.'

'Pull the other bollock,' said the other half of the double act. '*Monty* – on stage, in front of an audience?! He's so spastic – he couldn't even look at himself in the mirror.'

How wrong you are, I mused to myself. As part of my escapist routines, I would regularly act out imaginary scenes in front of what I had learned from study of Nancy Mitford was supposed (unconvincingly) to be called 'the looking-glass'. During this reverie my persecutors looked at me strangely. I realized that it was about time I struggled to say something. 'Um, er . . . well, I thought perhaps I could have a go. Just a little bit of satire, perhaps? It's all the rage now.'

'No, Monty,' pronounced the future judge. 'I once speculated, when I heard that you had opened a book on the Grand National, that you might – contrary to all appearances – possibly possess hidden depths but I soon learned that I was mistaken.' He moved towards me, with offensive intimacy, and tried to look into my averted eyes. 'There are *no* hidden depths there.'

Seemingly disconcerted by his self-important friend's

courtroom charade, the breezy understrapper reverted to the locker room for his parting shot: 'Yeah, just bugger off with your stupid "satire" – and leave us to do the revue how we like.'

As things turned out, it was just as well that I had no association with the excruciating entertainment that followed. In one sketch, as I recall, a parody was essayed of *Juke Box Jury* – retitled 'Joke Box Jewry'. The oleaginous host, 'Jewboy Jacobs', was portrayed by another budding lawyer wearing a rugger cap back to front, so as to resemble a skullcap, and speaking in a heavily Faginesque accent.

A nasty whiff of anti-Semitism also hovered over the live television incident that electrified me late one Saturday night during the holidays when I was staying with Uncle Joe and Aunt Daisy in Somerset. This was the first time I had been allowed to watch *That Was The Week That Was*, television's first satirical revue. It would never have been permitted at home by my father, who strongly disapproved of Hugh Carleton Greene's eagerness to recapture the *Kabaret*-style diversions of his younger days in the Weimar Republic.

Bernard Levin, perched on a stool, was about to begin a discussion with a group of pacifists in the studio – an environment shown for the first time on the box in all its naked glory, complete with overhanging lights, cameras, equipment – when a tall, menacing figure loomed over him from the left of the screen. 'Mr Levin? Will you stand up, please?'

Levin duly did so. 'Good God!' exclaimed my cousin Julian, who had been up at Cambridge with *TW3*'s compère David Frost ('a bloody hard worker, I must say'). 'I don't think *this* is in the script ...' The tension was palpable.

'You reviewed a production, Mr Levin,' proceeded the

mysterious stranger in ominously measured tones, 'in which my wife appeared—'

'I don't think this is the time or place to discuss that,' interjected Levin.

'It was the most *vicious* . . .' Then, suddenly, the large man's buttoned-up rage overflowed. As the camera kept rolling, we saw a flail of fists as poor Levin was knocked flying. In an instant, his attacker was apprehended by a scrum of men wearing headphones and dragged away. Levin, resuming his perch and adjusting his glasses, smiled with heroic sangfroid and said: 'After that warlike interruption, we shall now resume our discussion on unwarlike subjects . . .'

At the end of the item, Frostie disclosed to the viewers, none more agog than myself, that Levin's attacker was associated with a concept calling itself *Musique Concrète* – and that 'we must all hope he soon finds himself in something else concrete'. I soon learned that he was called Desmond Leslie, and was a son of the novelist Sir Shane Leslie of Glaslough, a neighbour of Uncle Peter's in Ireland – one of the characters I had cried off from meeting as a boy through shyness (or 'carsickness'). In a later incarnation I visited Glaslough, where Desmond Leslie virtually incarcerated me in a room where I was compelled to endure some of his *Musique Concrète* and to express admiration of photographs of a subsequent wife. 'Look at those magnificent *globes!*' he roared in my ear, already damaged by the reverberating *Musique Concrète*.

'I fear that I really must be on my way now, Mr Leslie,' I spluttered.

He gave me a hard look eerily reminiscent of the basilisk glare he had bestowed on Bernard Levin before lashing out at him. Eventually he said in tones of melancholy menace: 'I had expected you to stay well into the night . . .'

The Leslie-Levin punch-up passed into my fantasy folklore. Back at school, I managed to persuade a boy called Tudor – a surgeon's son from Wales with a passion for rhythm and blues – to stage frequent re-enactments of the unforgettable scene. 'Mr Levin. Will you stand up, please?' As Tudor wore glasses and had dark hair with an unruly quiff, he was usually cast as Levin, though as my own curls proved equally unamenable to flattening (resulting in what became known as a 'Bernie') I did my share of stool-perching. By way of a trade-off, I would dutifully sit through Tudor's dreary records of Leadbelly, Howling Wolf and Muddy Waters, but I could not emulate his soulful finger-clicking and sympathetic moaning. As he kept his eyes reverentially closed during these ghastly emissions, I did not see the necessity of doing so. Eventually I would lure Tudor back to the Levin stool. 'Let's improvise some of the insults Leslie might have been spouting at Levin once Frostie got his mitts over his mouth . . .'

By this time, satire had finally permeated Harrow. In one school revue, Michael d'Abo – already a hero on account of his fronting a raffish pop group which performed before film shows in 'Speecher', or the speech room, as I priggishly insisted on calling it – put on a dog collar and did a very passable imitation of Alan Bennett's sermon sketch from *Beyond the Fringe*. His rendition of how he had been accosted on his way out of the station – '"Hey, mate," he shouted. '"Where do you think you are going?" That at any rate was the gist of what he said . . .' – and of how his friend, at the top of the mountain they had climbed together, 'very suddenly and violently vomited' struck me as the funniest thing I had ever heard.

However, my minor efforts to introduce satire into the Cadet Corps were not a success. The idea that our famously keen house should deliberately sabotage its own unrivalled record in the annual Drill Competition by putting on a farcically shambolic display in front of the inspecting officers from the Brigade of Guards was dismissed out of hand by the future judge and his pals. 'Why should we let the side down like that? It would be a disgrace.'

As part of the officer-training procedure we were obliged to give 'lecturettes' on subjects of our choice. Naturally, I opted for 'Satire'. Yet even while I was still waffling my way through the Juvenal period, the talk soon floundered into a fiasco. 'Even if we could understand a *word* Monty was saying,' complained one squaddie, 'we wouldn't be able to hear it, anyway.' I was marked down as *'Not* officer material' – and doubtless 'LMF' (Low Moral Fibre) too.

With nothing to lose, and releasing years of pent-up frustration, I unexpectedly found my voice on the parade ground. I heard myself giving tongue to some ferocious drill commands. 'Good heavens! I never knew Monty had it in him,' observed one bustling beak. 'Perhaps he could live up to his name after all.' For a moment, visions of Sandhurst – the Sword of Honour, the white horse ascending the steps – floated before me. All those uniforms would look rather jolly in my daydreams. Yet my heart remained in Soho, the Mecca of Satire.

There I would go to worship. I loitered around outside the offices of *Private Eye* and Peter Cook's Establishment Club in the hope of spotting some of my heroes making their entrances and exits. I would gaze up longingly to the upper windows above the plaque announcing 'Pressdram', the *Eye*'s publisher, with a view to catching a glimpse of Booker, Ingrams or Rushton at work. Then (unlike later, during my stint as an articled clerk, a career path the great Rushton himself had briefly pursued) I would turn a deaf ear to such Soho street cries as 'Looking for business, dearie?' and 'Live show. Twelve lovely girls. They're naked *and* they dance. Come along in, boys. Live show . . .'

In my innocence, much of the smuttier material on *TW3* passed me by. By now I had managed to wheedle my way into procuring parental permission to watch the show in Biddo's room, where the television set was kept, on Saturday nights. During one of the many sketches about the Ban the Bomb marches, a shifty-looking jailbird played by Roy Kinnear was asked if he had been arrested in Parliament Square or Trafalgar Square. 'Neither,' replied Kinnear with a knowing leer. 'Leicester Square.'

Or at least it was unknown to me. 'A good example of a pointless joke, that,' I piped up.

'Not *quite*, I think, Hughie,' said my mother cryptically.

Kinnear and Rushton, both built on the generous side, were my two special favourites. I particularly relished the former's turn as 'Cuddles' Kinnear, an old-style music-hall comic desperately trying to keep up with the new satirical fashion. ''Ere – a prison warder said to Earl Russell: "What do you do, then, mate?" And His Lordship replied: "*I think*." So the warder came back, quick as a flash, with "Well, d'you think you can clean out those toilets?"'

Then, retiring in good order with a song, Cuddles warbled a ditty in the dotty old philosopher-earl's honour:

> *He behaved just like a toff*
> *As the coppers led him off.*
> *For the future of the masses*
> *We sat upon our – backsides*
> *And for Bertie Russell –*
> *Yes, Bertie Russell, ladies and gentlemen*
> *He's a Grand – Old – Man!*

I would lovingly memorize all this material in my own cell at Cookham. How exciting to daydream that I was masterminding the Satire Boom that embraced the *Eye* (several of whose stalwarts were involved in *That Was The Week*), the Establishment and all the rest of it. Yet the alter ego I imagined for myself was certainly not the egregious Frostie – seemingly an ambitious creep on the make – but rather the dashing, glamorous Cookie, then still in America and fearing that the sceptred realm was about to submerge giggling into the azure main.

One of the perks of my father's job with the BBC was that he could wangle free tickets to the recordings of some of the television shows. Two of Biddo's favourites were *The Billy Cotton Band Show* and *The Dick Emery Show*. I enjoyed escorting Biddo to these; it was a particular pleasure to watch the bottle-nosed bandleader relying on idiot cards for his supposedly impromptu patter, whereas the sight of Emery in drag was to give me an uncanny foretaste of one of my future mothers-in-law.

The golden day came one Saturday afternoon when my father took us on a tour of the spanking new Television Centre. Through one door we unexpectedly found ourselves in a viewing gallery overlooking a hangar-like but strangely familiar studio. I recognized it as the set of *That Was The Week That Was* (soon to be taken off the air because of its controversial content).

'I don't think we should be here,' said my father. 'They seem to be rehearsing something or other.'

'Oh, please, Dadda,' I pleaded. 'Can't we just stay for a few minutes?'

Down below I had spotted Rushton and Kinnear being put through their paces by the producer Ned Sherrin for a soft-shoe-shuffle number called 'Fat Men Are Coming Back'. Kinnear, an experienced old trouper, was proving surprisingly light on his feet, but Rushton looked uncomfortable with the routine. 'It's no earthly good, Neddy,' he was bleating in his tweedy, reedy voice. 'These pedal extremities weren't designed for tripping the light fantastic.'

I watched, rapt, as the rehearsal continued. It was exhilarating for a besotted fan. Indeed, those few minutes in the viewing gallery were virtually the highlight of my youth.

As the years passed, and *TW3* was replaced on the box by *Not So Much a Programme, More a Way of Life*, and that in turn by *The Late Show* (in which Barry Humphries and John Wells, a former Eton beak, immediately joined my galaxy of satirical heroes), my passion for satire rather dwindled. The *Eye* did indeed lurch to the left – much as Juliet had feared – and my hormone-driven trips to Soho during my time as an articled clerk were more concerned with answering the familiar street cries than with stalking satirists.

Yet I continued to cherish my special idols, such as Peter Cook in his television show *Not Only . . . But Also* (I always found Dudley Moore too obviously winsome) and Alan Bennett in the exceptionally literate, witty and much underrated series *On the Margin*. One of Cook's typically cruel sketches cheered me through many a depressing hour in the office. An arrogant, brutal boss (Cook) takes a grovelling supplicant (Moore) out to lunch and then proceeds to spill wine over him, throw spaghetti over his head and so humiliatingly on, while the pathetic toady apologizes profusely for his clumsiness. In my daydreams, I was the Cook character; in reality, I was Moore.

Bennett moved onwards and upwards from satire to write one of the funniest and most elegiac plays in the English language, *Forty Years On*, though some critics damned it with faint praise as a series of sketches. For me, seeing it with the original cast in 1968 – starring Sir

John Gielgud as the headmaster and Bennett himself as
the junior master ('I wish I could put my hands on the
choir's parts') – was the finest night I have ever had in
the theatre. I spent my savings in making a block booking
for family and friends. My half-brother Antony, lured by
the prospect of hearing the Harrow School Song, arrived
late and missed its rousing chorus *'Follow up!'* The assembled party apparently did not share my taste for Bennett's
old jokes, literary spoofs and bittersweet nostalgia, but I
was well away into a daydream of my own.

I committed the entire script to memory and to this
day have to restrain myself from quoting it in extenso. I
cannot, for instance, pass Claridge's without thinking of
Hugh, Moggie and Nursie sheltering in its basement
during the Blitz; or Park Lane without seeing the Grenfell
motor en route to hear the nightingales sing at Kimber;
or go up the staircase at the London Library without
expecting to bump into Mrs Woolf 'outside the changing
rooms . . . all flushed and hot after a hard day's reading'.
And in White's I look out for a member of the Breed
'dining alone': 'Once met you will always know them, for
their hand is firm and their eye is clear and on those rare
occasions when they speak it is well to listen for they
choose their words dangerously well.'

Rushton, to my delight, cropped up as the squire in
the Mermaid Theatre's musical version of *Gulliver's Travels* in 1969, starring my old schoolboy crush, Michael
d'Abo, then the lead singer with Manfred Mann. D'Abo –
now democratically styling himself 'Mike' – was the only
one of my Harrovian contemporaries to have made it big
in the world of showbiz, around which my fantasies
increasingly revolved. His friend and fellow revue performer Andrew Barrow had repeatedly died the death as
a stand-up comedian in the Northern clubs and Simon
Williams was yet to make his mark as James Bellamy in

Upstairs, Downstairs. In the audience at the Mermaid, together with my sister Mary, I basked in d'Abo's starry aura. It would never have occurred to me to go round afterwards.

My passion for *Private Eye* was rekindled the following year, 1970, when my great journalistic icon Auberon Waugh joined the magazine, having been sacked from the *Spectator* for altering George Gale's name in the table of contents to 'Lunchtime O'Gale'. I had enjoyed Waugh Junior's novels as a schoolboy well enough, but his supremely funny and robust journalism struck an immediate chord as soon as I read his blistering attack in the *Spectator* on the trendy frauds who had sneered at his father on Evelyn Waugh's death in 1966. In his 'Diary' for the *Eye* – originally intended as a spoof of a Sunday paper offering by Alan Brien, a bearded old Leftie who had claimed that anyone reading Evelyn Waugh in the future would require footnotes – Auberon Waugh found an inspired comic voice that went beyond satire into the world of surreal fantasy. As a more than half-crazed daydreamer myself, I felt the jokes were being freshly minted for my own benefit.

As Patrick Marnham put it in his history of *Private Eye*, Waugh 'is one of the few journalists in the country who knows what to do when offered freedom of expression. He sets out what he thinks in a terrible stream of consciousness which thousands of readers recognise as their unexpressed, indeed carefully repressed, instinctive reactions.'

When Clive James made his celebrated crack about the *Eye* sending people's children crying from school, it was Waugh who had the best answer in his 'Diary':

It is probably time we had a law forbidding publication of any news or comment which might

embarrass the young children of those concerned. I
remember how a callous remark I once made at
school about Attila the Hun caused Sir Iain
Moncreiffe of that Ilk (a direct descendant of
Attila's) to burst into uncontrollable sobs . . .

Auberon Waugh duly joined my bedroom's pictorial
pantheon beside 'the Ilk' – who had, in fact, been at school
at Stowe with yet another of my heroes, 'Perishing Worthless' (Peregrine Worsthorne) and, incidentally, always
argued that Attila was actually *left* wing, not, as popu-
larly supposed, a man of the right.

It was Auberon Waugh's taste for genealogy – one of
the *Eye* diarist's absurder conceits was to colour in the
coat of arms in the *Peerage* of every peer he had met –
that ultimately led me in from the streets of Soho
through the portals of *Private Eye*. In 1976 Waugh wrote
an extraordinarily flattering column in the *Spectator*
(where he had resumed his prolific output) about my new
edition of *Irish Family Records* under the headline 'To
Kill a Massingberd'. Hardly able to believe my eyes, I
dropped the magazine from my lap in the outer morning
room of the club and turned a shade of puce. Once I had
recovered my senses – and reread the piece a thousand
times – it finally dawned on me that it must all have
been in jest. After all, the headline was a pun on
'mockingbird'.

Waugh seemed especially delighted in the book's revelation that his brother-in-law, Giles FitzHerbert – once
the Liberal candidate in Fermanagh and South Tyrone
supported by Uncle Peter at Blessingbourne – was a
Ruxton in the male line. 'Aha, Ruxton, I know your
secret!' he chirruped, in echo of the disclosure in *The Code
of the Woosters* that the fortune of the Fascist leader Sir
Roderick Spode, notorious for swanking about in footer

bags, derived from a lingerie emporium known as 'Eulalie'.

Too overjoyed to care about making a fool of myself, I wrote a letter of gratitude to Waugh at Combe Florey (hallowed precincts for an old Wavian fan like me), suggesting, in Wodehousian vein, that he might care for a spot of lunch at my club. He replied: 'In homage' (this had to be a wind-up, surely?) that he made it a rule never to accept hospitality from 'publishers' (not something I had ever thought of myself as, other than in my daydreams), but why didn't we meet on neutral ground at a *Private Eye* lunch?

I had heard about such gatherings, where hardened hacks from the Street of Shame unburdened themselves of stories too juicy for their own papers to handle. I would indubitably be way out of my depth. Was this all an ingenious set-up to make me into a figure of fun? My instincts, always very faint, were whispering that I would be wise to walk away.

None the less, on the appointed day and well before the appointed hour I finally managed to pluck up enough courage to overcome my growing feelings of guilt and fear and push through the swing doors into the appointed place, a Soho pub called the Coach and Horses – soon to be immortalized by Jeffrey Bernard, whose battered cherubic features were no doubt those glaring at me as I blinked nervously about me. Two of the faces I focused on seemed familiar. Why, they belonged to two of my most favourite gentlemen-reprobate actors, good old James Villiers and Ronald Fraser. Were they part of the *Eye*'s network of informers too? I looked forward to reading some of the inside scandals of 'the Avenue'.

My theatrical reverie was, to say the least, rudely interrupted by the landlord from behind the bar. 'You look like a fucking dying duck in a thunderstorm,' he snarled. 'What the fuck are you doing in here, you fucking stupid cunt?'

I was about to confide in this charming character, who bore a strong resemblance to Walter Matthau, that I was 'here for the *Private Eye* lunch' when it occurred to me that it would be more prudent to keep mum. The gathering was probably a secret. 'Could I have a tomato juice, please?'

'Fucking hell!' exclaimed the landlord, rolling his eyes in a manner that Matthau would not have disowned.

'Last of the big spenders, eh, Norman?' chipped in a wag from across the bar.

'Fuck off, you cunt,' said Norman. 'Leave the gentleman alone to enjoy his fruit juice.'

I endeavoured to disappear into the gloom as I waited for some secret sign. Eventually, after what seemed like an eternity, I spotted the craggy features of Richard Ingrams, the *Eye*'s editor (recognized from television) advancing towards the bar. With barely a nod to Norman, he lifted up the hatch and disappeared out the back. It was now or never. 'Erm . . . er, I think I'm supposed to . . .'

'WHAT!' yelled Norman. 'Are you going to the *Eye* lunch? Well, for fuck's sake, why didn't you bleedin' well say so, you fucking stupid cunt!'

Safely upstairs, I introduced myself to Ingrams, a genial schoolmasterly type with a ravishing smile and a corduroy jacket. 'Ah yes, Massivesnob. You're Bron's new hero.'

'He's certainly mine.' This seemed to be an effective conversation-stopper. Panicking, I blurted out: 'Yes, er . . . I rather go in for hero worship, I'm afraid.' I heard myself cackling like a hyena. 'There's Anthony Powell—'

'Don't mention that to Bron,' Ingrams said, laughing. 'He can't stand him. Thinks *Po-ell* frightfully precious.'

'But surely he and Evelyn Waugh were old friends . . .'

'Bron doesn't tend to like his father's chums very much.' This was disconcerting. How on earth could I reconcile my daydreams if two of my principal heroes couldn't stand the sight of each other?

I thought it best to change tack. 'Well, James Lees-Milne is another of my special heroes. Have you read *Another Self* – it's wonderfully funny . . .'

'Lees-Milne?' bumbled a pleasantly Pickwickian figure. It was Auberon Waugh, who had now joined us. 'Is he a homosexualist?'

Rather taken aback to hear the ever-fastidious Jim described in such uncompromisingly stark terms, I stammered incoherently: 'Er . . . he's *married*, you know, to Alvilde, a friend of Vita Sackville-West's, actually – whereas Jim, of course, was a friend of Harold Nicolson's. So, erm . . .'

'Stand easy,' said Waugh in his gentle, mild, yet precise voice. 'I think we get the picture.'

'Can you explain why *Waugh of Combe Florey* did not feature in the last, peculiarly unsatisfactory, edition of *The Landed Gentry*?' Fortunately, before I could proffer any sort of explanation as to this most regrettable oversight, the Squire of Combe Florey proceeded to give me the benefit of his own conclusions. 'Is it, as I suspect, due to the unhealthy influence of the fashionable North Somerset novelist and knitting specialist, Major 'Toni' *Po-ell*, who was, I understand, some kind of editorial adviser?'

Although feeling outraged by these gratuitous insults to the Sage of the Chantry, I tried to attune my answer to the Squire of Combe Florey's lightly bantering tone. 'No, no, absolutely not at all, I assure you. Major – I mean *Mister* – Anthony – Tony – Po-ell – no, Powell, no, sorry, POLE – was not an editorial consultant.'

'But he wrote one of the introductory essays. "Reflections on the Landed Gentry", I believe he called it? And then he filled page after page after page with his unspeakably dull Welsh ancestry – which left no room at all for the wretched Waughs.'

Remembering what Tony Powell himself had said about the Wavian habit of never letting a hobby horse go, I sought to laugh politely without implying any form of agreement with Waugh's nonsensical thesis. Happily, another thorny question was exercising the *Eye* diarist's imagination. 'Can you throw any light, in your capacity as a genealogical authority, on the vital matter of whether my Lady Forkbender's two children are permitted to use the courtesy title of "Honourable"?'

'I didn't know that Lady Falkender had any children.'

'Oh, yes. When Marcia Williams was secretary to Mr Wislon she had two children by Walter Terry, then political editor of the *Daily Mail*.'

'Illegitimate children – "natural", as we say in the *Peerage*?'

'Precisely. I have been badgering the College of Arms, even Garter himself, for a ruling on whether these children are entitled to the honorific. In fact, I was awaiting an answer on this crucial point from the previous Earl Marshal, the great Duke of Norfolk (Bernard, of course) when the shattering news of his death overtook me.'

'If she were to marry Mr Terry, then the children would be legitimated and thus would almost certainly be granted the style of "Honourable" out of courtesy, or indeed chivalry.'

'And if Mr Terry, say, were to be made a peer himself, having already married my Lady Forkbender, the children might be "Hons" twice over. Is that right?'

Not for the first time in my new friendship with my hero 'Bron' (as I wondered if I would ever dare to address him), I asked myself if my leg was being pulled. In his diary entry for the day, he wrote: 'A GOLDEN DAY, one that I am unlikely to forget for as long as I live. Today, at lunch, I met Mr Hugh Montgomery-Massingberd . . . one of the few men able to talk with authority and wit about the great issues of the day.' He went on to describe my solution to the Falkender issue as 'miraculous'.

The allusion to my ability 'to talk with authority and wit' must, I realized with shame, have been meant satirically as I hardly uttered during the lunch. Fortunately, everyone else round the table was heavily preoccupied with the 'Goldenballs' affair – hardly surprisingly, as the megalomaniac grocer Sir James Goldsmith was threatening to have Ingrams and Patrick Marnham (who had written the original offending article 'All's Well That Ends Elwes', about an alleged conspiracy among the friends of the vanished Earl of Lucan) imprisoned for libel.

Feeling that I had failed miserably to sing for my supper, and by now rather tipsy, I finally gave tongue. Primed by Jonathan Pearce with two tiny titbits of gossip about the Goldsmith-Lucan axis, I blurted them out. Silence. A stony glare from Sir John Junor, then still editor of the *Sunday Express*. 'Both these stories have already appeared in the *Eye*,' murmured Ingrams. 'Collapse of Massivesnob.'

As I stumbled to the door, Patrick Marnham put out a friendly hand. I gathered my wits enough to say that his cousin Nicky had been a childhood friend in the Thames Valley. 'What's he up to now?' asked Marnham, his eyes attractively alight.

'I believe he is working for the United Nations.' It had been Nicky who had deputed some other student to show my suited self round the University of East Anglia – and had addressed me as 'sir'.

'What a thoroughly bad idea,' said Marnham, laughing. His warm smile saved me from complete despair after my first, and surely my last, *Eye* lunch.

Fortunately, though, my poor showing was soon swallowed up in the march of time and, while never becoming a regular, I was asked again. After one lunch, Bron Waugh took me on to the Colony Room, the Soho drinking club, where I had the opportunity of studying the barman Ian Board's magnificent nose (shaped and nourished by his breakfasting on brandy and knocking off a bottle of crème de menthe at a sitting). I also bumped into a bogus Irish baron posing as a film producer who asked me on to dinner with Peter Ustinov. Like several hero-figures I had always longed to meet, though, this celebrated monologuist turned out to be something of a disappointment in the flesh.

As the years went by, I somehow seemed to have become accepted as having joined the *Eye*'s circle of supporters. 'Massivesnob' and its variants (from 'Massivefees' to the equally untrue 'Massivepecker') became a fairly frequent spoof byline in the news parodies, often attached to absurd 'How They Are Related' charts. Each 'mench' afforded me far more pleasure than seeing my real name in print above the hackwork I was having to churn out in order to keep afloat as a freelance after the genealogical publishing debacle.

I shared to the hilt the *Eye*'s contempt for power and for the self-important, even more psychologically flawed people than myself who sought it so ruthlessly. I thrilled to the unmasking of such villains as the corrupt architect John Poulson, the Gannex manufacturer Joe Kagan and the monstrous 'Cap'n Bob' Maxwell. I cheered the constant sniping at such figures of fun as Frostie, Quintin Hogg and 'Desi' Wilcox. Yet I could not help noticing that journalists who affect to despise the world of power and politics often derive a power complex of their own from being privy to so many sensational secrets.

In due course the Jeremy Thorpe case replaced the

Goldenballs Affair as the *Eye*'s principal preoccupation.
The publisher Anthony Blond, a vibrant hobgoblin of a
man, regaled everyone round the table with the yarn of
how Thorpe had extracted himself from National Service.
'Instead of admitting his homosexual tendencies,' said
Blond, 'which would have got him out straight away, he
decided to *pee* his way out of the Army. He would drink
gallons of water before retiring and then wet his bed on a
monumental scale.'

It was fun to watch the *Eye*'s collaborative process at
close quarters as instantly the editorial team's antennae
for a story twitched into action. 'Now look here, Thorpe,'
Marnham said, improvising a conventional officer's
accent. 'You're letting the side down. Damn it, you were
at Eton, weren't you?'

'Yes, sir.'

'Radley, m'self.'

As more revelations were exchanged about politicians
dodging National Service it dawned on me that the *Eye*
stalwarts' own experiences in the military were a vital
component of their humour. In my eyes they represented
ideal elder brothers who somehow stood apart as real
men whereas I felt more like Peter Pan, a callow, immature youth who could never grow up.

Although Bron Waugh had been an officer in the Blues
– and nearly died in Cyprus after jiggling with an only
temporarily out-of-order machine-gun at point-blank
range – significantly, Ingrams and Rushton were 'other
ranks'. When I had the great thrill of meeting Willie
Rushton – he did a caricature of me to accompany a well-
merited hatchet job on a picture book I had cobbled
together about the squirearchy – the decisive influence of
soldiering on a comic view of life was amply confirmed.
'The Army is, God bless it,' wheezed Rushton, 'one of the
funniest institutions on earth and also a sort of microcosm

of the world. It's split almost perfectly into our class system. Through serving in the ranks I discovered the basic native wit of my fellow men – whom, basically, to tell the truth, I'd never met before.'

I wondered what Rushton made of Marnham's assessment that he was a man heavily disguised by his bluff exterior, who had an interest in serious ideas but a dread of pretentiousness: 'This prevents him from ever discussing anything in other than humorous terms.' Rushton conceded that: 'In the main, my basic defence is Blitz humour.'

When I suggested to Rushton that – notwithstanding his celebrated parliamentary candidature against 'Baillie Vass' (Sir Alec Douglas-Home) in the Kinross by-election of 1963 – he was not really a political animal, he replied in a voice markedly different from his usual fruity, mock-bufferish tones: 'I do my bit for the Labour Party every now and then but I'm not very good with organizations.' He sounded mild, even apologetic.

Carried away by impertinence, I asked him why he had appeared on all those ludicrous quiz shows on television in the 1970s. 'I know they were appalling,' he said with his trademark reedy chuckle, 'but funnily enough I met everybody doing them.' His best showbiz friend and cabaret partner, the comedian Barry Cryer, told my favourite Rushton story of the time he was due to give a talk at a dinner. The chairman was talking loudly into Willie's left ear as he ate, with Willie murmuring 'Good Lord!' and 'I can imagine' at suitable intervals. Finally the man said, in front of the whole table: 'You'd better be funny tonight, Mr Rushton, we're paying you *a lot of money.*'

'Well,' responded Willie, 'most of it's for sitting with you.'

How I wish I had the nerve to say that when I was

experiencing similar humiliations as an occasional
speaker on the 'ladies' luncheon lecture circuit'.

Naturally I could not resist boring Rushton with my
memories of watching him strut his stuff for *That Was
The Week That Was* back in the '60s. 'My body has done a
reverse,' he explained. 'I had middle-age spread when
young and now I have the figure of a seventeen-year-old –
thanks to diabetes.' He complained that everyone always
asked him about the '60s: 'It's as if I died of drink in
1966.'

Talented though he was as a performer – right from
his days at Shrewsbury playing Lord Loam in *The Admirable Crichton* – Willie Rushton's genius as an artist
tended to be underrated. 'I love drawing,' he told me. 'It's
the only job I do without looking at my watch.' I had
admired the bold confident line of his cartoons since
boyhood and when Richard Ingrams asked me to supply
the words for a 'Focus on Fact' strip in the *Eye* (previously
undertaken by my old school chum, Andrew Barrow) on
'Britain's Least-Known Peers' I was hoping that Rushton
might have drawn the pictures.

In the event, Barty Glenn, like most cartoonists an
engagingly offbeat character, was assigned the task and
we hit it off very well. The idea had been inspired by a
remark made by the *Eye*'s patron saint, Sir John Betjeman, who had started the magazine's hard-hitting column
on the ghastliness of most modern architecture, 'Nooks
and Corners of the New Barbarism'. Recalling the career
of Lord Trimlestown, who had served before the mast in
his youth, 'Betj' had chortled: 'He was Britain's least-
known peer!'

All I had to do was to set out in deadpan style brief
details of some of the bizarre or, more usually, very
ordinary characters who happened to have inherited
hereditary peerages. Thus we had bingo-calling peers,

policemen peers, dentist peers, bus-driver peers, night-porter peers, pigeon-kicking peers, brothel-keeping peers, bagpipe-playing peers – and, of course, my old chum the flying-saucer peer, Lord Clancarty – complete with often painfully inappropriate family mottoes ('Death Before Dishonour') and all the usual journalistic clichés about the peerage turned on their head. Glenn would come up with suitably absurd drawings. For example, to illustrate the fact that two peers both had elder (illegitimate) brothers living, he drew a Lucanish figure shaking someone in peer's robes and saying '*What* did you call me?' And underneath the intelligence that the bongo-playing Lord Moynihan 'describes his recreation as dog-breeding' were two burly hounds copulating.

Altogether the *Eye* proved an ideal employer – prompt with payment and generous to a remarkable degree. Free-lance contributors even received occasional bonuses. This reflected much credit on the 'hands-off' proprietor, Lord Gnome, otherwise the great Peter Cook himself. I finally met my satirical hero in the 1990s thanks to my dear friend Craig Brown, who had by then taken over the spoof diary column in the magazine.

Craig and I had both been in love with the beautiful, bewitching American writer Lesley Cunliffe (later to live with the cartoonist Michael Heath), but if anything this only increased the strength of our friendship. We also shared a passion for prep-school humour. 'Prep-schools,' as Craig once said to me, 'are the undervalued key to so much English humour. At my prep school, Farleigh House, the headmaster used to wear the same uniform as the boys – Aertex shirt, sandals and shorts – and the music master used to attach his wife's wheelchair, with her in it, to his car . . .'

With typical kindness, Craig arranged for me to join him and his wife Frances (daughter of Colin Welch, the founder of the revered 'Peter Simple' column in the *Daily Telegraph*, surely the forerunner of the Satire movement), and Willie Donaldson (otherwise 'Henry Root' of spoof-letter fame) for lunch with Peter Cook and his Chinese wife Lin at Cook's local Italian trattoria in Hampstead. Of all my heroes whom I have managed to meet, none was more friendly and relaxed, or put me so much at my ease, as Peter Cook. And unlike many of those previously worshipped from afar, he effortlessly exceeded all possible expectations with his complete lack of self-importance and his generous desire to amuse – and readiness to be amused.

Far from the raddled old drunk I had dreaded to see, there bounded in a still dashing figure in a T-shirt, tracksuit bottoms and trainers clutching a pile of newspapers. 'It's terrible – I look the spitting image of Des Wilson,' a sometime Liberal politican from New Zealand, he said at one stage during the long, leisurely lunch. But to my eyes he still had the cheerful, unaffected and enchanting manner of an undergraduate. I was so enraptured by his casually mesmerizing presence that I failed to remember almost anything that he said – apart from his expressing regret that he had never been asked to record a message for a fan in a coma. I only recall being deliriously happy in his presence, and laughing uproariously.

Initially, I made my usual mistake of trying to impress a hero with my trainspotterish knowledge of his curriculum vitae. Summoning up my swotting of the programme notes for *Beyond the Fringe* of thirty years before, I alluded to his Radleian soccer tour of France. He denied all knowledge of this. So much for my tabulating. Attempts to draw him out about the original production of the revue (by Donaldson) were also airily dismissed as of no conceivable interest to anybody.

Cook preferred to weave surreal fantasies about stories he had spotted in the papers, and we were treated to a brilliant impromptu one-man show. To my joy, he expressed himself a fan of the *Telegraph* obituaries page (which I was then editing) and improvised several hilariously funny spoofs of some of the dotty dowagers and bristling brigadiers who were the staple of the operation.

It was also clear from his conversation that he spent an inordinate amount of time watching trashy television. I could fully identify with this particular addiction. The ridiculous trivia of daytime viewing proved an instant bond. Would that I could replay the banter in the now oddly defunct tape recorder in my head; I was convinced that I would remember every syllable he said to my dying day. The trouble was that we were all simply having far too good a time to bother with memory.

When the party finally broke up and we reluctantly made towards our separate ways, Peter Cook turned to me and said: 'Want to come back and watch the golf on the box?' Suddenly my new-found courage and confidence failed me. I hesitated. Overcome with shyness, I stammered my refusal. The force of my regret at such stupidity multiplied manifold when I learned of my idol's death a few years later.

Not long afterwards Willie Rushton also died far too young, and then John Wells, another *Eye* hero. I had also met Wells thanks to Craig's introduction and – though he was already stricken with cancer – we had some delightful times together working on his last book, about the House of Lords. When I confided in him that several peers had made my life impossible by censoring my scurrilous accounts of their family histories for my picture books about their palatial seats, Wells immediately launched into an improvised sketch. 'Now, Mr Montmorency-Mockingbird,' he quavered, 'when you say here that the first

Marquess was described as "a squint-eyed, shifty, unprin-
cipled villain of the darkest hue", I wonder – ahem – I
wonder whether you would be so kind as *just* to make a
minor alteration so that it reads "was generally regarded
by his contemporaries as the soundest of fellows, a model
landlord and a pillar of the community". We don't want to
upset anyone, do we?'

At John Wells's memorial service at St Paul's, Covent
Garden ('the Actors' Church'), Richard Ingrams in a moving address said that he was beginning 'to feel rather
lonely'. At the last *Private Eye* lunch I attended there was
a distinct feeling of 'empty chairs and empty tables' (to
quote one of Herbert Kretzmer's fine lyrics for *Les Misérables*). Ingrams beckoned me to join him and Paul Foot
(whom I failed to interest in a rambling account of my
brush with Mohammed Fayed over my aborted text for a
book on the history of the Paris Ritz) at one end of the
upper room in the Coach and Horses. 'Come on, Massivesnob,' he said, 'you belong with the Old Bores.' I mused to
myself that I had fulfilled my dream by advancing from
adolescence to senility, bypassing maturity.

ELEVEN

Gentleman Hack

T O HAVE ENDED up among the Old Bores at the
Private Eye lunch table was, on reflection, fairly pre-
dictable. The absurdity of the name I had eagerly foisted
on myself as a young fogey was bound to project a crusty
image. 'I am plagued,' John Gross – then, in the late
1970s, editor of the *TLS* – complained to Lesley Cunliffe,
the Irish journalist Mary Killen and Craig Brown, 'by a
snobbish old bore from the depths of the West Country
called Montgomery-Massingberd, who keeps badgering
me to review books about the nobs.'

'Oh, no, J.G.,' chorused Lesley, Mary and Craig (or so
they assured me), 'he's really *not a bit* like that! He might
have been a silly snob once, but now he's quite a reformed
character. Do give him a break . . .'

I had indeed been badgering editors for freelance work
after the collapse of the genealogical series, and not
making much progress. Inspired by the liberatingly unfet-
tered reviewing styles of Sir Iain Moncreiffe of that Ilk
and Auberon Waugh for the idiosyncratic monthly *Books
and Bookmen*, I tackled its eccentric publisher Philip
Dossé, who generously allowed me to ramble on in print
in a manner that was merely a pale reflection of his two
star contributors. Dossé appeared to take the admirable
attitude of letting his mixed band of reviewers (from Tariq
Ali to Diana Mosley) say anything they wanted at whatever length they fancied. Such a laissez-faire approach
naturally proved too good to last and eventually poor

Dossé committed suicide at the gloomy Victorian mansion block where the magazine was so haphazardly produced – round the corner from Jonathan Pearce's old flat, where I had lodged in the 1960s, and also, of course, in my daydream world, the Widmerpool residence.

The *Field*, then still a weekly and hardly unchanged from the reassuringly rural paper I had fantasized over in the deep armchairs of my prep-school headmaster's study in the '50s, also proved amenable to my blandishments. Its devotion to country sports, though, cost me another column I had picked up while lecturing on the *QE2*. A fellow lecturer, Cleveland 'Clip' Amory, an endearingly curmudgeonly Bostonian, suggested that I file a monthly report on animal welfare in Britain for his Fund for Animals bulletin. This went along merrily – it was easy money – until Amory buttonholed me on a visit to London.

'I understand,' he growled in his ursine way, 'that you are also writing a column for a blood-sports paper?'

'*Field* sports, we say over here. And I am actually writing on *heritage* matters – you know, the stately homes of England – all that malarkey . . .'

'But the *Field* is dedicated to the slaughter of innocent creatures!'

'I assure you, Clip—'

'Cleveland, or on second thoughts Mr Amory to you, son.'

'If I may explain the paradox – as Mark Bence-Jones and I have tried to do in our new book, *The British Aristocracy* – the love of the true sportsman for animals and his love for the sport are not only compatible but complementary. Indeed, sport far from being the enemy of wildlife is on the whole its best friend . . .'

'Bullshit, my friend. You're fired.'

In turn, my position on the *Field* came under threat after I rashly repeated some of Uncle Peter's stories about the late Duke of Gloucester in a book review for *The Times*. 'My dear,' admonished Monsignor Gilbey at the club, 'you'll never be forgiven for that scurrilous piece – it reads like an inside job.' Philip Howard, the Thunderer's literary editor, who had always been generous to me during my time on the genealogical series, stood firm ('My old master, Sir William Haley, used to say that he didn't want *The Times* to be "too damned courtierly"'), but I was told the paper's management, in the persons of Brigadier Denis Hamilton and Charlie Douglas-Home, wanted my head on a spike. I had the novel experience of being deluged with angry letters – some of them, I suspected, ghost-written by my old friend Hugo Vickers, who was relishing the row – and I learned how the Establishment bites back. Some apparatchik from the Commonwealth War Graves Commission demanded that the *Field* sack me forthwith. I was warned to mind my step in future.

While *The Times* was off the street – shut down because of union troubles – in the late 1970s, I made approaches to the *Daily Telegraph* to see if they could, at last, be persuaded to take the opportunity of setting up a proper obituaries column – the lack of which was cruelly exposed by the Thunderer's absence. *The Times* obits had long been a source of great pleasure. It was an esoteric taste I particularly shared with Vickers, who was exceptionally hospitable after my divorce. We would compose spoof obits of various figures, including ourselves. His scabrous one of me read (more or less) as follows:

MR HUGH MONTGOMERY-MASSINGBERD
Man of Unquenched Lusts

MR HUGH MONTGOMERY-MASSINGBERD, whose delight at seeing his name in print will unfortunately this morning be denied him, was a

heavily scented figure with a grossly excessive
appetite. Massingberd was an author, though he
will be remembered more for ideas mooted and
occasionally commissioned than for the few works
which passed the presses. He was a feverish editor
often working through the night to meet a deadline
long passed, and a cruel reviewer who, if he
bothered to read the books submitted to his
scrutiny, defaced them with pathetic obscenities in
his habitual blue felt-tip pen. He wrote weekly
columns in various periodicals which few purchased
and fewer still read. Though far from being a
military man, he adopted the pseudonym
'Enobarbus'.

Montgomery-Massingberd encouraged the
misconception that he was a member of the landed
gentry. Without justification he assumed the
superfluous Massingberd by deed-poll. Yet it was
widely known that Massingberd was an
impoverished hack who dwelt in a basement flat in
south London where conditions were lamentably
bleak. From this humble abode he emerged from
time to time, attired in a weary grey suit, bound for
some house of unspeakable vice. For, besides
possessing an appetite of such magnitude that
friends counted him three men at their table, he
was the slave of an unquenchable (and unquenched)
lust for female flesh. He once confessed that giving
a lecture was to him so powerful an aphrodisiac
that he repaired at once to an establishment
equipped to afford him all too instant ease in a
variety of bizarre fashions.

Occasionally he would become the emotional
victim of an unscrupulous woman, upon whom he
would squander lavish sums in theatres,

restaurants and taxis – a pursuit best left to those
with unchallenged access to expense accounts.
Consequently, at his demise, his bank manager's
relief has been dampened by knowledge of an
unresolved deficit of astounding proportions.

Massingberd was a cricketer of no distinction
and an incongruous figure of the Turf. He was the
least travelled member of his club. A fanatic of the
television, he was able to recognize even the most
passé ham actor. Blessed with talents as a mimic,
he lacked the confidence to make use of this art. He
took no part in the real world. Instead he wove
round him an elaborate fantasy of his own creation,
which he only laid aside briefly in the 1970s.
Furthermore, he was a distinctly impractical man,
unable to turn a key in the simplest of locks. All his
life he remained in the care of a nanny.

H.R.V.

If only, one might say.

'As with all signed obits, my dear Hugo,' I told him
when he handed me the piece, complete with an execrable
caricature, 'it tells us rather more about the person who
wrote it – yourself – than it reveals about the ostensible
subject. When I have my own obits column in the
Telegraph . . .'

'Another of your absurd daydreams, Massingberd.'

'When I am in charge, all the obits will be properly
anonymous.' My own attempts at a Vickers obituary
always seemed to cross over the boundary marked 'Joke',
and the game was abandoned. As the generally silent
Scottish psychotherapist I was visiting rather fitfully in
Clapham pointed out, I appeared to have 'trouble with
integrating hostility into my personal interactions'. Or,

in plainer English, as Jim Lees-Milne said to me after reading some of my intemperate book reviews, 'Your lack of self-assertiveness may explain the occasional aggressiveness in your writing.'

Yet Hugo was right about the *Telegraph* daydream. In a genial interview with its then editor, Bill Deedes (already past the conventional retiring age), it was explained that the Berry family, who owned the paper, were 'not all that keen on death'.

'Would that be on account of their being of Welsh Baptist stock?' I asked impertinently.

'Up to a point, Lord Copper,' said Bill, grimacing; he was fond of quoting Evelyn Waugh, having himself inspired aspects of William Boot of *Scoop* in the 1930s. 'At the *Telegraph* – or "The Cenotaph", as Bron Waugh called it in one of his novels – when somebody hands in his dinner pail [Bill was now switching idioms to Wodehouse] – it is treated purely as a news story. The obit will stick strictly to what's in the cuts – "In 1934, he was appointed Postmaster-General. In 1937, he was arrested for indecent exposure" – you know the formula?'

'But,' I blurted out, 'that's hardly a genuine obit, is it? Surely, with *The Times* out of action this is the perfect moment for the *Cenotaph* – I mean, the *Telegraph* – to, well, cash in?'

'Rather bad form, dear boy, to take advantage of the absence of "Another Newspaper". These are stirring times.'

'Yet I have a vision of all the "illustrious obscure" figures from the Raj, the Empire and the Services, the legions of dotty dowagers and sterling squires from, as one of our old school songs put it, "the great days in the distance enchanted" [Bill was a fellow Harrovian, after all, even if, like Churchill and Baldwin, he had sent his own offspring to Eton] who could adorn the obituaries page of the *Telegraph*.'

'*Page!* Steady the Buffs – you were only talking about a *column* for the nonce. There is such a consideration as space, you know. And I am sure Michael Hartwell would never countenance devoting news pages to the chatty life stories of nonentities no one had ever heard of.'

So it proved, and I slunk away down Fleet Street towards the Ritz, where Denis Hart, an affable Irish journalist on the *Telegraph* weekend magazine who had arranged my interview with W. F. Deedes, was waiting in the bar. At Denis's suggestion, I was compiling a social history of the hotel (David Watkin was looking after the architectural side), which was affording me ample scope for daydreaming. Like my hero Peregrine Worsthorne of the *Sunday Telegraph*, I fed at the Ritz, then shabby and very much the light of former days, 'not on oysters and champagne but on memories of a past world'. I populated the empty, threadbare spaces in my imagination with the luminaries of yesteryear like the old Aga Khan, Michael Arlen (author of *The Green Hat*), Tallulah Bankhead, Noël Coward, Nubar Gulbenkian (the luxuriantly bearded Harrovian whose basketwork taxi could turn on a sixpence – 'whatever that is'), the 'Poor Little Rich Girl' Barbara Hutton, Mrs Keppel, King Zog of Albania, Nancy Mitford and Evelyn Waugh – who had been flattered by the way the old porter always knew which hat belonged to him. Then, one day, in the porter's temporary absence, he discovered a label on his hat in the cloakroom bearing the legend 'Florid'.

Fortunately some of the great names from the hotel's history were still around – such as Lady Diana Cooper, the ageless Edwardian beauty. I sat on her bed in Little Venice and gazed into her limpid eyes as she recalled how her mother, the Duchess of Rutland, had allowed her as a debutante to go unchaperoned to the Ritz because it was 'so beautiful, a palace'. A few minutes later, I stopped for a sandwich in a pub on the Edgware Road where my reveries about the elegant splendours of la belle époque were interrupted by a tannoy announcement: 'Just to say, gents, that Mandy, our stripper for today, wants to apologize for the spot on her bum – anyone want to come up and squeeze it?'

Someone who, by most accounts, might have been game for this type of horseplay was Douglas Fairbanks Junior, who caused consternation by telephoning the rented farmhouse in the Nadder Valley, where I had found temporary refuge after my divorce ('your commune', as some of my smarter friends referred to it).

'It's Douglas Fairbanks here – can I speak with Mr Hugh Montgomery-Massingberd?'

'And I'm Greta Sodding Garbo,' said the resting actress, who lived in the back wing.

'Really? I didn't know you were over, Greta—'

'Piss off – I'll get Monty.' Then to me: 'There's some nutter for you pretending to be Dougie Fairbanks.'

'Oh yes,' I replied airily. 'I was hoping he might ring.'

The range of expressions on the actress's face would have melted the stoniest casting director's heart.

Peregrine Worsthorne, a devotee of the old Ritz Bar, alerted me to its louche reputation during the Second World War and introduced me to the bachelor dandy Felix Hope-Nicholson, who lived in great state at More House on Tite Street in Chelsea. 'Oh yes,' recalled Hope-Nicholson in his capacious inglenook by the fireplace, 'it was outrageously queer. The regulars included Colonel Cutie from the War Office—'

'That's an unusual name.'

'It was his *nickname*, you fool. He was known as

"Colonel Cutie" because he called everybody "cutie". He had an insatiable mania for meeting young second lieutenants. Then there was Paddy Brodie, who mistook the bar for the *pissoir* . . .'

'Wasn't he the model for Evelyn Waugh's character the Hon. Miles Malpractice?'

'I believe so – and, of course, Brian Howard was also a fixture there. Once, when he was in his aircraftsman's uniform, he was carrying on in such an outrageous way about the shortcomings of Churchill and so forth that finally a high-ranking officer sitting nearby rose to his feet and demanded to know the speaker's name, number and station. "My name," said Howard over his shoulder, "is *Mrs Smith*."'

When I went to see Worsthorne – an inspiration since his dandified cameos on television chat shows in the 1960s and who, unlike his fellow performer, Norman St John-Stevas, did not disappoint in the flesh – at the Telegraph building, he told me, in his attractive drawl, that Laurie Ross, the legendary barman, had offered him his memoirs for serialization in the *Sunday Telegraph*. 'Imagine my disappointment,' said Perry (as I didn't dare call him for another ten years),'when the first sentence of Chapter 1 read: "Mr Thomas Driberg was a gentleman of the old school . . ."'

Yet, as Worsthorne put it in an appreciation of Laurie when I finally eased myself into the obits chair at the *Telegraph*, 'while at his bar, and under his aegis, one felt oneself to be the most elegant, important, amusing person in town'. I am glad to say that I can vouch for this myself, as I used to creep into the Ritz while Laurie was still in harness – and make believe that I was Nick Jenkins in *Dance* waiting to meet Mark Members, J. G. Quiggin, Peter Templer or Bob Duport. Like Jenkins, I used to muse on the golden nymph in the Palm Court: 'Although stark naked, the nymph looked immensely respectable; less provocative, indeed, than some of the fully dressed young women seated below her.'

One evening, a few years before the bar closed on Laurie's retirement in 1976, I was chatting to Christine in a corner when we were accosted by a drunk, who proceeded to blow a revolting raspberry at our primness. Spotting that matters were verging on the personal, Laurie smoothly intervened. 'Not in the Ritz Bar, sir, please,' he admonished. '*Not* in the Ritz Bar.'

Laurie's diplomacy would also have been welcome at the book's launch party during an altercation between Margaret Duchess of Argyll and Alastair Forbes, the witty and waspish book reviewer whose 'rediscovery' by John Gross in the *TLS* had prompted my own badgerings.

'Mr Forbes,' simpered the Duchess in her disingenuous little-girl manner. 'You gave my book a very unkind review, considering the hospitality you have enjoyed at my expense.'

'Dear Margaret,' he drawled, 'if you really think a couple of indifferent dinners would influence me to puff your ghost-written drivel, you are very much mistaken . . .' Then, in an all-too-audible aside to me, while the Duchess diverted her attention to procuring a free copy of the book ('I'll pop in and pay for it tomorrow'), Forbes muttered: 'Her father may have been able to give her some fine earrings but *nothing* to put between them. What? As James Ancaster observed, after sitting next to her one night: "she don't tell many jokes, do she?"'

I had met 'Ali' Forbes with Hugo Vickers at the weekend cottage in the Chilterns of Laura Duchess of Marlborough (with whose racy memoirs, *Laughter From a Cloud*, Hugo, a sought-after figure on the 'Dowager Dateline', was lending a helping hand). I found Forbes immensely funny and entertaining – an infinitely more cultivated and charming character than the long-winded name-dropping snob some of his readers imagined – and he duly joined my gallery of gods. He proved a most sympathetic friend, as did Laura Marlborough, and I learned that one could wish for no better tonic than Ali as a hospital visitor. I thrilled to his stories of blazing rows with Randolph Churchill. 'Once we had such a corker at East Bergholt,' he recalled, 'that I found myself heading back down the drive before I had removed my case from the boot.'

As well as the *TLS*, Forbes adorned the books pages of the *Spectator* – a favourite periodical of mine since the 1960s – and in my daydreams I, too, was a *Spec* regular, especially as the weekly was now enjoying a stylish renaissance under the inspired editorship of Alexander Chancellor. The reality was harder to achieve, but eventually the literary editor, Geoffrey Wheatcroft (who, in an earlier incarnation as a publisher had, so the bosses assured me, narrowly pipped me for a job with Cassells, when I was desperately trying to escape genealogy for the mainstream), did the decent thing. He sent me Hugo Vickers's book on an earlier Duchess of Marlborough, Gladys – pronounced *'Glaydis'*, don't you know. Literary London: corrupt, incestuous? Perish the thought.

Reviewing books for the *Spectator* in what I liked to regard as its golden era was certainly a dream come true. Just as at *Books and Bookmen* I had paid homage to the 'house style' of the Ilk and Bron Waugh, for the *Spectator* I sought an admixture of more Bron (now the guru of Doughty Street), Ali Forbes, Richard Ingrams (whose caustic television column was my first port of call in the magazine) and Wheatcroft himself. Once I had got into my stride, as it were (we discovered that we shared a passion for the Turf and a friend-in-common in Tobias Rodgers, a louche yet learned antiquarian bookselling chum of Conynghame's), I entertained Wheatcroft to lunch at the club. We began in the bar with a lengthy discussion of the ideal ingredients of a proper Bloody Mary. Wheatie seemed to be omniscient. His claim that a journalist should be capable of writing about any subject, together with his slightly Wagnerian good looks, put me in mind of Gert Frobe's assertion in *Those Magnificent Men in Their Flying Machines* that: 'There is nothing a Prussian officer cannot do.' Eventually the guillotine was applied to the Bloody Mary topic. 'That way madness lies,' pronounced Wheatie.

Over the claret, he told me that Jeff Bernard, the *Spectator*'s 'Low Life' columnist was not expected to survive the night. 'What an obit he would make,' I mused, still brooding about the *Cenotaph* column. 'In a sense,' countered Wheatcroft, 'he writes his own obit every week – and sometimes it bears a remarkable similarity to the previous week's.'

As it turned out, of course, Bernard lived for nearly two more decades after this dire prognostication. I later learned, on the sound principle of 'a watched pot never boils', that people supposedly at death's door usually take an unconscionable time to pass through it – whereas hale and hearty types are liable to drop dead without any warning, as my much-missed eccentric Uncle Esmond did on the Royal Tennis Court at Hampton Court soon afterwards.

Jeff Bernard – whom I preferred to admire from afar – was to become a fan of the *Telegraph*'s new obits column and I once persuaded him to 'dictate' an appreciation of his old Maltese racing chum Charles St George, down the hotline from Doughty Street. Propped up by the experienced hands of Simon Courtauld (the long-serving deputy editor of the *Spec*), Bernard began promisingly: 'Charles St George ... was the fucking kindest man I ever knew . . .' *Crash. Voices off.* 'Steady, Jeff.' *'Fuck!* Are you still there, you cunt?'

'Yes,' I stammered nervously. 'Er, carry on . . .'

'Charles Saint-*Wots 'is face* was the fucking *kindest* man I ever knew . . . Got that?'

'Yes, I've got that. Anything else, um, at all, er . . . we could add, perhaps?'

'Shit! What more d'you want, you fucking cunt?'

'Um, didn't he visit you in hospital?'

'I said that, didn't I? What the fucking hell . . .'

'What did he bring you?' I heard myself barking.

'Put two hundred quid under m' pillow – said: "You'll need some money for toothpaste."'

'Good. That's more like it. Anything else?'

'He was the fucking best friend I ever had . . .' *Crash. Wallop.*

'That's enough, Ed.' It was Courtauld's brisk voice. 'The optimum time is after two double vodkas but before the sixth – you won't get any more sense out of him now. You'll have to make the rest up, Hugh.'

Following my lunch with Wheatcroft, I was asked to a *Spectator* lunch on the top floor of the Doughty Street offices cooked by the redoubtable Jennifer Paterson. Overcome with nerves, I asked Alexander Chancellor tedious questions about the circulation. 'It's gone up since you've started writing for us,' he wheezed in his irresistible schoolboy giggle (it was no surprise to learn that an absent-minded Somerset squire had recently asked him whether he was still at Eton). 'That byline of yours certainly catches the eye.'

With his wolfish charm and his engagingly laid-back approach to life, Chancellor made the *Spectator* seem like a comfortable yet stimulating club to which everyone appeared welcome. We talked of how embarrassing 'upper-class' accents sounded on television. 'When I was a

reporter on ITN,' he recalled, 'I was always being told to
tone it down a bit.'

As Wheatcroft was preoccupied with his principal
guest, the Earl of Harewood (by now looking the spit of
his grandfather, King George V), in a discussion of operatic matters, I renewed my uneasy acquaintance with
Michael Heath, the cartoonist, whom I had met with the
Cunliffes in Brighton, when Marcus and Lesley (since
divorced) were working on the *Presidential Families of the
USA* for my genealogical series. At least, I found it uneasy
as I suspected that Heath – like everyone else it seemed
– was in love with Lesley. In any event, some time after
my own agonizing affair with her, she and Heath pursued
a long, erratic relationship. 'Of course she was far too
young to marry that old professor,' he said.

Also, like every other hack who came near Doughty
Street, I fell head over heels for the soft voice and statu-
esque beauty of Wheatcroft's assistant, Clare Asquith,
but was far too tongue-tied to pay court. I made a complete and utter fool of myself by not only addressing a
billet-doux to her as (through some crazed aberration)
'the Hon Clare', instead of her correct style of 'Lady Clare',
but then compounding matters by telephoning her to
apologize for my crass solecism. None the less, she gra-
ciously consented to let me take her out to lunch in
Bloomsbury but the occasion was doomed when Jennifer
Paterson buzzed us on her scooter with graphic hand
gestures and shouts of '*What ho!* Monty-Massivesnob and
the Lady Clare, by Gad! Where are you two lovebirds off
to?' After this I was too shy to utter, and blushed continu-
ally in her presence. The only time I plucked up enough
courage to give her a peck on the cheek was some years
later at the club – for my second wedding reception.

I sublimated my loneliness and frustrations, and the
ever-gnawing loss of my children, in my various reviews,

copiously larded with autobiographical diversions and indecipherable coded messages. Once, up in Scotland on a research tour for the *Field*, I dictated the whole of Chapter 13 of the First Epistle of St Paul to the Corinthians (this was before Tony Blair got in the act) to a bemused telegram operator for transmission to Lesley. 'Have you finally flipped?' Lesley asked on the telephone. 'Or did you get stuck in a hotel room with a Gideon Bible? But there's something in *Private Eye* which will cheer you up on your return to the smoke.'

She was right. A parody of the *Spectator* in the *Eye* included a book review which spoofed both Forbes and myself, and gave me the first boost of confidence I had felt since the halycon days of the genealogical series. By now, I was 'well earthed' (as one of my former 'commune' friends put it) in John Powell's basement in Kennington and more than ever addicted to hopeless daydreaming, sloth, gluttony and watching television. Mary Killen recommended that a colleague of hers should telephone me to discuss my telly addiction for an article on couch potatoes. I denied this hotly. 'But,' said Mary afterwards, 'your denial would have earned more conviction if she had not heard, in the background and before you replaced the receiver, the unmistakable chords of the *Neighbours* theme tune.'

What I could not, alas, deny was Mary's lurid account to all and sundry of how I organized the typing of my potboiler books on royalty, the heritage and the like. 'To keep Hugh up to the mark,' Mary would say, 'I send a bike to fetch his daily ration of manuscript. But on most days the bike comes back with an envelope full of blank pieces of paper. He hasn't been able to face telling the biker that there's nothing to collect.'

Many of my worst flaws found their way into a stereotypical profile in the *Tatler* of 'Hugo – The Gentleman

Hack', a contemptuous portrait of a bungling, bullshit-
ting, idle amateur freelance journalist incapable of original thought, industry or insight, let alone the basic
ability to type. Or so, at least, it was related to me. I
could not bear to read the piece. It would have been too
painfully close to the truth.

When, a few years later, Alan Watkins identified the
species of 'Young Fogey' in the *Spectator* after Charles
Moore had taken over the editorship, I readily recognized
some of my own prejudices in his incisive definition: 'He
is conservative but has no time for Mrs Margaret [surely,
Denis, Watneys, old boy?] Thatcher . . . He is a scholar of
Evelyn Waugh . . . He dislikes modern architecture . . .
He laments the difficulty of purchasing good bread, Ched-
dar cheese, kippers and sausages . . . He enjoys walking
and travelling by train. He thinks *The Times* is not what
it was and prefers the *Daily Telegraph* . . .' Yet while in
my daydreams I might have aspired to sound fogeydom,
the reality was that I was far too flaky. Much as I revered
and worshipped, say, A. N. Wilson (a photograph of whom
sporting a trilby on a bicycle in Doughty Street became
the defining icon of the phenomenon), Gavin Stamp, John
Martin Robinson, Dr John Casey, indeed Charles Moore
himself (though the distaste for Mrs Denis Thatcher certainly didn't apply in his case), I could not remotely aspire
to their intellectual rigour.

Much closer to home was Craig Brown's monstrous
character, Wallace Arnold, a smug, stout, self-satisfied
old 'phoney-gent' of the Street who wrote a column in the
Spectator called 'Afore Ye Go' and spread himself liberally
('dread word', as he would say) over other organs. A
complacently blokeish, pipe-smoking crasher and name-
dropper, Arnold's ghastly prose style – larded with such
truly dread words as 'agreeable', 'civilised', 'esteemed',
'disobliging' and so forth – bore many uncomfortable

similarities to my own cod-*Speccie* persona. Moreover, his own corpus of 'slim volumes' supposedly included – besides such works as *A Man for All Seasons: A Biography of Prince Philip, Those Marvellous Mitfords* and *Only Too Delighted, Ma'am: Fifty Years of Royal Broadcasting* – an anecdotal history of the club entitled *Bottoms Up!* When I buttonholed Master Brown in this august establishment where I had done him the honour of putting forward his candidature, forsooth (Arnold-speak is horribly contagious), my old quaffing partner pointed out that 'when it comes to irony and parody, satire and fondness are very closely linked – indeed they are often fighting against each other.'

The end of the Chancellor era at the *Spectator* brought about unexpected repercussions at the *Field*, where I was still churning out my weekly 'Heritage' column. Simon Courtauld, Chancellor's deputy, was appointed editor of the country weekly with a brief to revitalize its by now rather musty flavour and brought along the captivating John McEwen, the *Spectator*'s former art critic, for the ride. At our first meeting, the deceptively brusque Courtauld, who had begun life as a barrister, came straight to the point. 'Your present column reads like a *Telephone Directory*. I know from the *Spec* that you can do better than that. What's going on?'

'The trouble is, Simon, that the old regime didn't like jokes of any description. I have been under orders to keep a straight bat and play it back down the wicket. The chief sub, a former prep-school matron, knows a nun who reads the mag avidly every week and she weighs up all the copy with that in mind.'

'We'll soon put a stop to that,' barked Courtauld.

Under his excellent editorship, the *Field* blossomed as never before. Suddenly all the style, authority and witty writing one had always longed to see – a sort of '*Spectator* of the Hedgerows' – arrived in full measure. While the appeal was sympathetically broadened, the traditional character of the magazine – dealing in rural realities, unlike the sleek and suburban *Country Life* – was not only preserved but enhanced. In my daydream world, the *Field* was once more reassuringly redolent of the leathery scents of the tack room, the whiff of cordite and the freshness of the river-bank. The tone was friendly and robust, the conversational prose evocative of taproom and county club.

Candida Lycett Green, John Betjeman's daughter, wrote on gardens; another *Private Eye* doyenne, Elisabeth Luard, did the cookery column; Geoffrey Wheatcroft studied form; Max Hastings sounded off on his days out; Alan Watkins chipped in a rugby column; and a host of estimable countrymen such as Phil Drabble, Humphrey Drummond and Robin Page gave us the benefit of their rural wisdom. In the back half, Johnny McEwen recruited such inspired hero-figures as William Douglas-Home and Peter Fleetwood Hesketh, a still raven-haired '20s dandy from the club who memorably inveighed against the iniquitous new 'HeathCo' counties: 'non-historical, unnatural, illogical, far from practical, as well as being offensive to the people'. McEwen also installed his old Cambridge chum David Langlands, a learned and mordantly funny friend-in-common of Richard Conynghame's, as restaurant critic. Our jolly lunches together cheered me up no end.

Once more Conynghame had materialized at a turning point in my life in his role as *deus ex machina*. Emotionally washed-up (an unwise one-night stand had threatened to anticipate the feverish plot of *Fatal Attraction*) and struggling to make ends meet as a freelance hack, I reluctantly accepted an invitation to a scratch Sunday supper at Conynghame's temporary chambers in Lennox

Gardens. 'I have got *just* the tonic you need, my dear fellow,' he said when I shuffled mournfully across the threshold. He then introduced me to my second wife, spirited daughter of a raffish baronet.

Being averse to basements, she soon insisted upon our leaving Kennington – a particular wrench for me, as I had developed a new hero worship at the Oval for Monte Lynch, a free-scoring batsman in the most cheerful Caribbean spirit – and heading for the country. Hugo Vickers kindly fixed us up with a Hansel-and-Gretel cottage on his family's estate on the Berkshire/Hampshire borders, not far from our new friends, Simon and Philippa Courtauld.

Courtauld – notwithstanding his *Private Eye* nickname of 'Lavish McTavish' – gave me a contract with the *Field*. This was just as well, for by now I had finally severed all my links with the genealogical series (which seemed to have dispersed to the four winds) and my fantastic plans to write social histories of homosexuality ('the Confraternity'), preparatory schools, meritocratic dynasties and other heavyweight projects had foundered much in the way Hugo had predicted in his outrageous obit.

Above all, Courtauld encouraged me to go on the road in search of the squires still surviving in their dim 'Family Seats' (as the weekly series was called), a quest that had long been close to my heart. It proved an exhilarating journey at a crucial time of change in the increasingly materialistic '80s. Following, in many ways, in the footsteps of my hero Jim Lees-Milne, I was in my element listening sympathetically to the woes of a seemingly doomed class of smaller landowners. Endearing eccentricity abounded. One seat in the still blissfully unwrecked Herefordshire housed a pair of elderly twins and their spouses, with household duties apportioned according to their skills – the accounts, for instance, were handled by

a former deputy governor of the Bank of England. Up in
the Highlands, a Scottish baronet carefully placed his
false teeth on the table in front of him during our interview and – as I could not understand a word he was
saying – my eyes became fixated on these gnashers in the
conviction that they might begin to utter of their own
accord, thereby possibly making more sense than their
owner.

Jokes, though, continued to be frowned upon by the
Matron, of whom I became very fond. 'Look, Monty, we're
not having this,' she said one day after I had referred to a
stalwart estate worker in Staffordshire as having made
'invaluable efforts with his plunger'. 'I wasn't born yesterday, you know,' she continued. 'I know how smutty you
boys can be.'

'I assure you, Matron, that was an entirely innocent
remark. It's always you prudes who have the most prurient minds.'

In fact this last barb proved unjustified when I alluded
in another piece to the Cockney epithet of 'berk' being
based on rhyming slang for the Old Berkeley Hunt. 'What
do you mean, Monty? What does it rhyme *with?*'

'Well, Matron, er, um . . . *Hunt.*'

'*Hunt?* I can't think of anything that rhymes with
that.'

'Perhaps Jeffrey Bernard could enlighten you?'

As a clever young journalist called David (or Lewis)
Jones, who worked with 'the McEwen' in a darkened room
and rejoiced in the title of 'poetry editor', put it to me over
a glass or three (oh dear, Arnold is back again) at a
drinking club near the *Field*'s old-fashioned offices off
Fleet Street: 'We're really "Under the Greenwood Tree"
on this gig, aren't we?'

Yet the inevitable foe of 'winter and rough weather',

foretold in *As You Like It*, all too soon put paid to our revels. The insensitive management, stoutly resisted by *El Caballero* (another Courtauld nickname, on account of his Hispanophilia), demanded that the country weekly become a monthly. And then, in a sacking brutal even by the standards of 'the Street of Shame', Courtauld was ejected from the chair. Together with virtually all the other regular contributors – apart from a pseudonymous hangover from the previous regime whose column was generally chock-a-block with glutinous invocations of chivalry, honour and loyalty – I resigned in sympathy and showered the management with imprecations.

It was, I suppose, easy enough to make such lofty gestures, however sincerely and passionately felt, because, at last, I had finally landed the catch of my dreams – the obits job at the *Daily Telegraph*. I had continued to badger Bill Deedes over the years, but there was nothing doing. Then, shortly after Max Hastings became editor of the paper in the spring of 1986, I had lunch with Charles Moore at the Gay Hussar in Soho to discuss some pieces for the *Spectator* on the changing class structure of the modern Tory Party ('more Estonians than Etonians', as Harold Macmillan observed), the forgotten gentry of Northern Ireland and other fogeyish topics. As we strolled down Greek Street (by now bereft of strip clubs), I said to Charles, as casually as I could: 'D'you think the Blue Max is going to do anything about obits at the *Cenotaph*?'

'Why? Might you be interested in some sort of consultancy role?'

'Oh, much more than that – I would actually love to take on the whole shooting match, head-on. It's the one job I've been longing to do for the last ten years.'

'Really? Good heavens!' Charles laughed in his

courteous way, but his eyes were registering sharp interest. 'Leave it with me,' he mused in more measured tones. 'I'll have a word with Ferdy Mount.'

Ferdy, already a hero-figure as an exceptionally sympathetic literary editor of the *Spectator* and an admired novelist (one of his characters rejoiced in the name of Gunby), promptly earned my undying gratitude by recommending my services to Max. I was duly summoned to the editorial presence. An alarmingly gangling figure – who, on reflection, could only have been an inch or two taller than me but appeared to be twice my height – was prowling restlessly about the palatial editorial suite in Fleet Street. Tieless, he seemed in the last stages of manic exhaustion and was evidently working round the clock to kickstart the old 'Torygraph' into new life. Glancing nervously at his bespectacled visage, I thought of Frankie Howerd's *TW3* crack about Robin Day – 'and, *ooh*, those cruel glasses – *cruel*, yesss, aren't they, missus?'

'Ah yes, Massingberd. Thanks for coming in. I think you've met my wife in the Pytchley country. Take a pew. I understand you want to have a bash at the obits. God knows, we need someone. We can't hope to compete with *The Times*, of course, but it's worth a try. Salary's pretty basic, I'm afraid.' He broke off this rapid-fire monologue in order to consult a list, and then grunted a figure which sounded like untold riches to a freelance hack badly in need of a job.

'Right. When can you start? In the meantime, let me have a piece on how country houses are not remotely in such a bad way as their owners like to make out. Twelve hundred words.'

The interview was at an end. I had opened my mouth a couple of times but could not recall any sound having emerged.

When I reported for duty, Max was having a well-deserved break and no one seemed to be expecting me. The deputy editor, who appeared to prefer semaphore to speech ('Handjive Hutch', as he was referred to by David Jones, who joined the obits desk soon after, and who eventually succeeded me), eyed me warily before taking me along to meet 'the obits editor'. I had been under the impression that was to be *my* job description, but, as things turned out, my predecessor and I rubbed along easily enough in tandem sharing the same title until his retirement a few months later. I learned to swallow my pride when he introduced me to his coevals as 'my new assistant' for he was a wise old bird from south London, well versed in the ways of Fleet Street – which struck me as quite unchanged since *Scoop*.

As he sat serenely at his desk like a Buddha in a safari suit (it was high summer), Augustus Tilley gently warned me that running the obits desk, while reporting to the news editor, was 'a peculiarly stressful job'. He advised me to learn how to relax – he was a practitioner of the Alexander technique – so as to be ready for emergency action, and to turn down extraneous work. To my shame, I inwardly chortled. Who would ever consider the *Cenotaph* obits as being injurious to one's health?

The day got off to a promising start when I noticed among the draft death announcements that my schoolboy hero Henry Blofeld's father, dear old Tom, the Norfolk squire whose surname had been appropriated by Ian Fleming for the Bond villain, had handed in his dinner pail. I scribbled what I thought was a lively little piece and showed it to 'Gus'.

'Jolly D,' he said. 'Bash it out and then try to sell it to the chief sub in the news room.'

'Um, I'm afraid I don't type.'

Gus raised his eyebrows expressively. 'Are you a member of the NUJ?'

'Er, no.' The 'gentleman-hack' had been humiliatingly exposed. My fellow obituaries editor looked pensive.

'All right,' he said and sighed. 'Give it to me. And fetch some blacks, would you?'

'Blacks?'

'*Carbon paper*. Don't you know anything about this game?'

It was like being an articled clerk again, in my forties. I thought back to Lady Mountjoy's share prices, and wondered if I was going to blub. In the days that followed, I constantly found myself biting my lower lip as my other new colleagues treated me rather less gently than Gus. I met either open hostility – 'Call yourself a fucking journalist?' – or sniggering contempt: 'What on *earth* made you want to work on obits? Don't you know it's the newspaper equivalent of Outer Siberia? Are you a necrophiliac or something?'

My attempts at 'selling' my wares to the subs were a nightly exercise in ritual humiliation. 'What's all this rubbish . . . ? We're not going to give space to that crap . . . Fucking hell, this used to be a *newspaper* . . . Bloody amateurs.' When Osbert Lancaster, one of my great heroes, died, I felt very proud of the obit I had commissioned from Gavin Stamp, only to see it butchered by the subs.

'But he's the editor's stepfather,' I protested.

'So bleeding what? This isn't an Old Boys' Club, Mr Massivesnob.'

After much moaning to Max – or as much as I could insert into nanosecond encounters – it was decreed that from September 1986 the obits could have two roped-off columns of their own (though still subject to the shears of the fearsome old Fleet Street news subs). As luck would have it, the 'Big Bang' (as Gus called it) threatened to start with a whimper. Nobody of any note died on the day in question. Max ventured round to rally the troops: 'Come on, *Gus!*' he roared at my partner on the desk as I sat silently, feeling foolish.

'What d'you expect me to do about it?' returned the great Augustus, by now demob-happy. *'Go out and shoot somebody?'*

Yet gradually we began to raise the dirigible off the ground. From time to time Max delivered rockets for being 'uncharitable' about the assorted Wodehousian peers I was over-eagerly celebrating – 'I won't have you making the column into a private shooting gallery,' he would say, or 'Mental illness is *not* a subject for levity' – but the hitherto neglected obits began to be noticed with puzzled amusement by some of the hard-nosed hacks. I began to feel more confident of our progress when, with the enthusiastic assistance of David Twiston Davies (a cousin of the National Hunt trainer Nigel), we began to assemble a trusty team of specialists who could be relied on to turn in regular copy on sailors, airmen, clergymen, lawyers, schoolmasters and so forth.

Yet I worried that the column might be in danger of becoming too 'worthy'. We knew that there must be cracking adventure yarns of dash and derring-do crying out to be told in the straight-from-the-shoulder manner of the *Boy's Own Paper*, but who could provide them? Fortunately, by chance, at a party given by the *Telegraph*'s literary editor, David Holloway (himself a lightning-fast obituarist of bookmen), I met the ideal candidate in Philip Warner, paragon of the *Boy's Own* School of Narrative Historians and a survivor of barbarous imprisonment by the Japanese.

'What about it?' I shamelessly importuned. 'When can you start?'

'I can't think of a worse job,' said the ever-modest Philip. 'I'm not your man at all.' Some months later over lunch at the club, after he had finally relented to our desperate pleas, he confided in me that his initial reluctance to take on the task had been concern that he would have to intrude on the private grief of the widows and families of the soldier he was writing about in order to elicit the information he needed. 'But once I had taken the plunge, I discovered that, in fact, it *wasn't* an intrusion at all – they longed for the opportunity to talk to me about their husband's or father's lives. I soon struck up hundreds of delightful new friendships over the telephone.'

However early I telephoned Philip, who swiftly became the most vivid and vital of my real-life heroes, I always seemed to catch him in his bath at Camberley (across the road from Sandhurst, where he had been a senior lecturer). 'Warner!' His name would echo down the line amid the lapping and splashing of the bathwater. 'What have you got? . . . Oh yes, I remember Slasher – damn good chap. I'll let you have something on him. We'll give the old boy a good send-off . . . Who else? A DSO, eh? What year? . . . Ah, that would have been in Italy. I can fill in the background there. Have you got the widow's number?'

Splish-splash – and before you knew it, Philip would have 'filed' a brace of perfect short stories, brimful of action, vigorous narrative, shrewd assessment and beautifully understated deadpan humour. What a thrill it was to be publishing the lives of, say, 'Speedy', the Gurkha commander who would sit at his desk naked from the waist down and when he heard someone about to enter would step briskly into the crisp shorts standing erect in the corner, which had been starched to perfection by the faithful *dhobi wallah*. Or of the subaltern in Srinagar who went after black bear – he was bitten on the buttocks but it was the bear who expired – and on his return to the regiment was 'advised to stick to duck-shooting'. Or of the young officer who had taken part in the Siege of Spin Baldak in 1919 – the last occasion when a British Army unit used scaling ladders and an operation that, as Philip observed, could only have succeeded if the enemy had been chloroformed before it took place. Philip entranced us with his hilarious yarns of soldiers riding ostriches, organizing fox-hunts at the Front, ejecting monocles upwards and then catching them again in their eye sockets. He chronicled the well-dined major-general trying to light his cigar with a geranium – and succeeding after a tactful ADC had inserted a lighter from the other side. Then there were the naked, head-hunting Nagas in the jungles of Burma, who 'regarded throwing hand grenades as effeminate'.

And who could forget Philip's tribute to the insouciant Digby Tatham-Warner, who strolled nonchalantly about the 'Bridge Too Far' at Arnhem sporting an old bowler hat and a tattered umbrella. 'That thing won't do you much good,' observed a comrade-in-arms.

'But what if it rains?'

All of us on the desk adored Philip, with his wonderful combination of strength and gentleness, grace and uproariously infectious joie de vivre. We knew that 'the Moustaches', as we called them (the nickname derived from Lady Rumpers's remark in Alan Bennett's farce *Habeas Corpus* that her late husband, 'Tiger', had gone into the Army only 'in order to put his moustache to good use'), were the pride and joy of the obits column. Philip immortalized what Kipling called 'The Legion that never was listed'. It was a case of the subaltern transfigured, the simple soldier raised to glory.

Generally backward-looking, I left Fleet Street with

scant regret when the *Telegraph* moved to Docklands in the late 1980s. For the first, and only, time in my life I felt full of confidence. Ignoring Gus Tilley's sage advice, I felt flattered to be asked to chip in miscellaneous other pieces for the paper. After years of being ignored as a freelance fogey, I was suddenly in demand. Thanks to David Jones's brilliant mastery of the form – he took over from Twiston Davies as my deputy soon after we arrived on the Isle of Dogs, when 'the Twister' moved to letters – the obits were going along swimmingly. For four happy years Jones and I were once more 'Under the Greenwood Tree'. This time nothing could go wrong.

Would I like to take on the 'Peterborough' column on the paper in addition to my other commitments? Well, why not? Might it not be just a little too much work? (Certainly my fellow obituarists argued strongly against this unwise move.) Oh no, I could handle it.

I soon learned that, in fact, I could not. It was a painful and public humiliation. ('Massivesnob cocks up Peterbore.') My limitations had been exposed; the rubber band had been stretched to the point where it finally snapped.

The confidence seeped away, the amusing outside commissions dried up, even my sturdy 'Heritage' column (transferred from the *Field*) came under threat – 'That's enough stately homes. Stick to the kiddies' attractions.' I clung tenaciously to my beloved obits – though as Tony Powell noted in his *Journals* after bumping into Geoffrey Wheatcroft in the West Country: 'Hugh Massingberd is said to be hanging on by his eyebrows.' (A singular feat, as I am rather lacking in the eyebrow department.)

There were mutterings from the management and the marketing wallahs that the obits were verging towards self-parody. I was told to tone down the use of nicknames such as 'Buster' and 'Biffer' in the headlines. ('But I'm not *making them up,*' I protested.) In fact, come to think of it, surely we were featuring far too many bristling brigadiers who had tangled with the wily Fakir of Ipi. There even seemed to be some hare-brained notion in the Canary Wharf ether that the obits page (as I now liked to think of it) contained too many '*old* people', and that this did not chime with the paper's trendy new youth-oriented image. 'Perhaps,' I ranted a shade too hysterically, 'you would like me to go out and cull some bright young businesswomen who better fit the new readership profile?' Paranoia was beginning to get a grip.

My attempt to adopt a lower profile by quietly dropping 'Montgomery' from my increasingly embarrassing byline blew up in my face when, to my amazement, this piffling matter suddenly became a cause célèbre. Even E. J. Thribb in *Private Eye* turned his versifying towards this thorny talking point. Columnists such as Alexander Chancellor in the *Independent* magazine gravely considered the question. Chancellor expressed himself pleased that I had come to my senses at last, having made a ridiculous fuss when a similar abbreviation was perpetrated at the *Spectator* some years back. Not wanting the facts to spoil the heroic Alexander's amusing story, I suffered this travesty in silence; but, in truth, it had been Patrick Marnham, the mischievous literary editor, who had agitated about the enforced change of my byline through the exigencies of redesigned typography. I had told Marnham that I did not care a hoot about having 'the full Monty'.

With mock-gravity, Max Hastings boomed across the obits desk: 'I am profoundly concerned about your future, Massingberd. This craven surrender of "Montgomery" strikes me as a very bad career move.'

'Oh dear,' I murmured. 'Perhaps he's right.'

As for the comfort blanket of obits, what had previously been a doddle, handled with insouciant panache (or so I liked to think), turned into a neurotic obsession. The quest for perfection took on an alarmingly psychotic element – though at the time I thought I was merely doing my job. I would drive Jones and my long-suffering colleagues up the wall by fussing late into the night over whether some mildly uncharitable statement would cause trouble, or whether every minute detail of someone's curriculum vitae was absolutely correct.

By the end of 1993 I was beginning to feel burned out. My nerves were not improved by the hijacking from a Post Office van of the only complete copy of the manuscript for a picture book on great houses which I had produced with my new boon companion, Christopher Sykes (nephew and namesake of Uncle Hugh's old friend from Berlin days). After a manic trip to Ireland to interview Lady Cusack-Smith, the doyenne of the Galway Blazers, for the *Sunday Telegraph*, I felt overcome by tiredness and depression. Not even the gamey old bawd's confirmation, over four dozen oysters, of the story of her celebrated exchange with her groom ('The old horse is sweating up a bit, Lady Mollie'; 'So would you be, my man, if you'd been between my legs for six hours') could cheer me up.

The day after New Year's Day 1994 I found myself, apparently floating away into the ultimate dreamland from which no traveller returns, in the Casualty Department of Roehampton hospital. 'Do you know what's happening to you, squire?' asked the duty medical officer in eerily conversational tones, as his 'crash' team busied themselves about my extremities.

I mumbled incoherently, much as I had done in less dramatic circumstances throughout my life. It had long been a fantasy of mine to be addressed as 'Squire' before my demise, but these were not quite the circumstances I had envisaged.

'You're having a heart attack, squire.'

TWELVE

Stage-door Stalker

'*THINK OF YOUR MUSE,*' goes one of Charles Hart's witty lyrics for Andrew Lloyd Webber's ravishingly romantic musical *The Phantom of the Opera*, '*and of the queues / Round the Th-ea-t-re*' (lip-smackingly pronounced with all four syllables intact in the original production by John Savident, otherwise the butcher Fred Elliott in *Coronation Street*). As I drifted in and out of consciousness, during the aftermath of what the medics called 'an extensive arterio-lateral myocardial infarction' and the consequent quadruple coronary bypass graft surgery, I thought of little else during my drug-induced daydreams.

Somehow I found it 'restful' (shades of Major Fosdick) to imagine myself as an actor-manager/composer/lyricist, the master of the West End. Besides a polished version of Lloyd Webber himself, there were elements of Tim Rice (a genial cove, whom I had once interviewed at Lord's about his picture book on its treasures), Noël Coward, Cole Porter and my schoolboy crush Michael d'Abo in this curious hybrid cross. There were also elements of Alan Bennett and Terry Rattigan; the impeccably aristocratic trio of actors Jeremy Clyde, Jonathan Cecil and James Villiers; the more raffish charms of Charles Gray, Ronald Fraser and Gerald Harper (never to be forgotten for his smooth portrayal of the revived Edwardian dandy Adam Adamant, not to mention the Yorkshire squire Hadleigh); and the bell-like vocalists Michael Ball, David Kernan (of *TW3* memory) and Paul Jones, d'Abo's predecessor with Manfred Mann. Choreographing this bizarre thespian admixture in my delirious imagination afforded me months – years, or even decades come to that – of the keenest pleasure.

My most fevered anxiety after the operation was whether I would be fit enough to take my long-reserved place in the stalls of the Adelphi Theatre to see the mesmerizing Patti LuPone's farewell performance as Norma Desmond in the original production of Lloyd Webber's haunting musical version of *Sunset Boulevard*. As had become my extravagant custom, I had already seen the show several – all right, numerous – times before my heart attack, though occasionally the star was 'indisposed'. (In the best prima donna traditions her relationship with the producer/composer was reported to be on the stormy side.) Perhaps, I suggested, I could be rushed to the theatre in an ambulance – as had happened when the ultra-dedicated Michael Crawford rose from his hospital bed to take over from his stricken understudy (who had twisted his leg when falling through a trapdoor) in *Phantom*. Unfortunately, indeed to my eternal regret, I had not been present to witness this classic showbiz moment – though I would have paid any price to have participated in the standing ovations which saluted Crawford's courage. And, as erratic fibrillation detained me in hospital, it became inevitable that I would also miss La LuPone's swansong.

My by now grown-up children (a maturing process radically hastened by intimations of their father's mortality) were deputed to attend the epic occasion on my behalf. Tears ran uncontrollably down my face – the heart attack seemed to have released my hitherto pent-up emotions, much to the consternation of the various old friends I attempted to enfold in a close embrace – as

Harriet and Luke regaled me with a blow-by-blow account.

'You would have been in heaven, Daddy. Every time she came down the staircase all these luvvies in front of us would stand up and screech: "*We love you, Patti!*"'

'And then the scenery got stuck, so she started cracking jokes and singing other songs to keep everyone amused. It was all terribly cheesy.'

'You should have seen the *weirdos* at the stage door afterwards. Real nutters. But we got her autograph for you, and we explained that you hadn't been able to make it – so she added a few extra kisses on the programme. Offstage, she's quite a dumpy little thing, but she was very friendly.'

As I howled with happiness, I mused inwardly that it had taken a near-death experience – I remember feeling as if I were about to take off in an aircraft towards a blinding light, probably merely the result of being rushed along a corridor under strip lighting – for my innermost instincts to come to the surface. At last it had dawned on me that I had been wasting my time fantasizing about triumphs on the pitch or over the sticks, aspiring to be a gentleman of letters and all the rest of that malarkey. My place should have been in the theatre.

Surely that would have been the most practical means of headlong escape for a daydream believer? My shyness and self-consciousness had precluded such an adventure, though study of the stage had taught me that quite a few actors were similarly afflicted. John Gielgud, for example, had memorably confessed to being 'a very timid, shy, cowardly man', and pointed out that: 'Acting is half shame, half glory – shame at exhibiting yourself, glory when you can forget yourself.'

Looking back, I suppose I became stage-struck when

my beloved Biddo used to take me every Christmas to see
the pantomime at the Theatre Royal, Windsor, an intim-
ately Georgian-style candybox. Indeed it was so thrillingly
intimate that I found myself blushing, as if the whole
magical show was being put on exclusively for my benefit
– shades of the 'Dream King' Ludwig of Bavaria, otherwise 'Mad Ludwig', though we will pass swiftly on from
that aside. I found that my enjoyment was intensified if I
focused intently on one particular member of the cast
with whom I could most readily identify. My chosen alter
ego would not tend to be one of the generally fairly insipid
principals – though I made exceptions for the old Sandhurst smoothie Patrick Cargill and the hilariously camp
'dame' Julian Orchard – but rather an unobtrusive chorus
boy. By the end of the afternoon or, as I grew older (hardly
'up'), evening performance, I had transmogrified myself
into this unknowing hero. Yet perhaps, I liked to fanta-
size, he derived an inkling from my enthusiastic applause
when he walked down the staircase at the end.

The Windsor Theatre, then run by the Counsell
family (who turned out to be friends of Hugo Vickers),
continued to play a potent role in my daydreams, which
embraced a stint as actor-manager on its boards. Uncle
Peter's thespian comrade-in-arms told me he had once
portrayed a New Zealander in a John Counsell production
there, and that when he asked for guidance on the accent
was told: 'Just a bit "off", old boy.'

Three of the most enjoyable evenings I have ever
experienced in a theatre took place at Windsor – an
exhilarating rendition of *The Boy Friend* by Sandy Wilson
(who knitted socks for 'our boys' during wartime classes at
Harrow and was later a cherished contributor to my obits
column); Gerald Harper's luxuriantly spoken Professor
Higgins in *Pygmalion*; and the exuberant Etonians Jeremy
Clyde and Jonathan Cecil who more than compensated

for the presence of the Harrovian bore Michael Denison ('Densely Michaelson') and his wife Dulcie Gray ('Gracie Dull') in *The School for Scandal*.

My own acting ambitions as a boy remained almost entirely unexpressed. I was very taken with a sighting at a cricket match of Willie Fox ('James Fox', the actor), a schoolfriend of my half-brother Antony, who had apparently been a child star. He struck me as the most glamorous boy I had ever seen, and I longed to be like him. At my prep school I felt a frisson of excitement when being made up by the youngish assistant matron to play Demetrius in *A Midsummer Night's Dream* (the swain's role savagely cut in favour of the rude mechanicals) and rejoiced in the discovery that you could blush unseen underneath the layers of slap. Many years later, when being made up for a television chat show (Frank Delaney, I fear, not Parky), I surprised myself by engaging the make-up artist in an earnest conversation about the contrasting merits of Leichner and Max Factor – though not nearly so much as I surprised Nigel Nicolson, whose eyebrows were twitching in the next chair.

At Harrow I summoned up enough courage – as artistic activity was always discouraged in my house – to attend an audition for one of the school's Shakespeare productions in its mock-up of the Globe, but lost my nerve when it was my turn to give tongue.

'Speak up, Monty. Pretend you are on the parade ground.'

'*Mumble, mumble . . .*'

'Thank you . . . *Next!* Ah, Dundas . . .'

It was at least some consolation that he, too, failed to land the part, especially as he subsequently turned professional and was given a juicy role in the excruciating '60s film *Prudence and the Pill*. Although the picture was widely panned, the *Tatler*'s critic gushed about a fine performance from 'Lord David Dundas, younger son of the Marquess of Zetland'. Dundas, whose subsequent career I naturally followed with rapt interest, later, like d'Abo, wrote advertising jingles, including *Jeans On* which remarkably made it to the top of the hit parade. His beguilingly passive performance of this catchy number is still sometimes shown on *Top of the Pops 2*.

My own prudence as a schoolboy dictated that I did not adorn my bedhead at Harrow with my male heroes but with a glossy photograph of Hayley Mills, supplied by her fan club (in Leicester, as I recall), which I had joined after seeing *Whistle Down the Wind* at the Plaza Cinema in Maidenhead four times in a week. As the Poona colonel remarks in the mess, when a junior officer enquires whether the monkey cohabiting with their comrade-in-arms Carruthers is male or female: 'Oh female, of course. Nothing wrong with old Carruthers.'

After leaving school, for some reason I could not quite understand, I took to loitering around the stage doors of West End theatres. Even in my dreams, I did not see myself as a sort of Edwardian Stage-Door Johnny decked out in top hat, white tie and tails with a cape carelessly tossed over one shoulder as I swilled champagne from an actress's slipper (ghastly thought), leering the while and elaborately raising an eyebrow – in the manner of the young Roger Moore ogling Jean Kent in the film *Trottie True*. It was more a case of viewing the stage door as embodying every romantic cliché about the theatre: a gateway to fantasy.

It is also, at the end of a performance, an exit to reality. Spotting the minor players – with their ubiquitous shoulder bags and studiedly unconcerned expressions – as they struggle through the waiting fans and disappear into the anonymity of the street became a never-failing source of pleasure. Frequently I would rubberneck at players departing from a performance I had not even witnessed.

After a long wait, which I find curiously therapeutic (I use the present tense advisedly, as I am still addicted to the habit), comes the buzz of anticipation. *'Here he comes!'* goes the cry, and everyone – apart from me, of course – rushes eagerly forward. I remain in the shadows, on the sidelines as an observer – others might substitute 'voyeur' – in order to savour the atmosphere of the star's aura.

If I have managed to persuade someone to accompany me in this bizarre vigil, I will now plead with him or her to 'push in there and get the autograph'. Naturally it is not the actual autograph that matters but the fact that my companion has been in propinquity with the star. In case I have not eavesdropped successfully I will beg a blow-by-blow account of the dialogue.

'Miss Webb, please may I . . .'

'You did say "Miss Webb", *not* "Marti"?'

'Yes, yes . . .'

'Good. That makes all the difference.'

When I confided in Uncle Peter about these strange stage-door rituals, he suggested to my parents that such inchoate theatrical yearnings could be a pointer to a future career on the boards. My mother, whose own uncle had been something of an Edwardian Stage-Door Johnny, stuck firmly to the view that a proper profession would be a more reliable course of action. My half-sister Juliet took pity on me and arranged for me to accompany her when she went 'round' to see her old schoolfriend the actress Amanda Grinling at the Savoy Theatre where she was appearing with Andrew Cruickshank (the growling Dr Cameron in the original *Dr Finlay's Casebook*, Biddo's favourite television programme) in *Alibi for a Judge*. Although thrilled by the contrast between the glittering art deco 'front of house' and the shabby seediness of

'backstage' – evocative of a third-rate hospital, or abattoir
– I felt overcome with embarrassment once we reached
Mandy's dressing room. As a blundering adolescent, I
could not cope with the gushing choruses of 'Darling, you
were *marvellous . . .*'

In future I resolved to stay in the shadows, keeping
my distance from the surly gaze of the stage-door keepers.
One night I experienced the odd sensation of being almost
knocked over by the redoubtable Joan Hickson (later the
star of *Miss Marple*) as she scurried for the Brighton train
immediately after a performance of *Forget-me-not Lane*
by Peter Nichols. The star, the genial Anton Rodgers, was
'off' that night and his understudy, Peter Dennis, went on
to play Gerald Harper's camp butler sashaying around
the button-leather sofas in *Hadleigh*. In my trainspotterish way, I also tabulated the West End debut of the
momentarily topless teenager Stephanie Lawrence, later
star of several Lloyd Webber musicals, who came to a sad
end in her early fifties. Yet the show was chiefly memorable for the tingling type of *coup de théâtre* that I love
(echoes of Desmond Leslie and Bernard Levin on *TW3*)
when, following the baring of Miss Lawrence's breasts, a
seemingly irate punter suddenly advanced from the stalls
to denounce 'the filth' on stage. For a split second I had
the wild surmise that it was my own father. In fact, it
turned out to be Michael Bates, playing a part based on
Nichols *père*.

Much as I loved the theatre and the end-of-show
vignettes, I do not think I became a fully-fledged stage-
door stalker until the miserable aftermath of my divorce
at the end of the 1970s. By way of escape into fantasy, I
started the habit of 'adopting' certain shows that I would
revisit on an obsessively regular basis. I began to wonder
whether I was turning into the Dudley Moore character
in the 'Royal Box' sketch in *Beyond the Fringe* who con-

fesses to his neighbour that he has 'seen this show, let me see 300, no I tell a lie, 497 times'.

The first show to which I became really addicted was Edward Duke's Wodehousian tour de force of a one-man show, *Jeeves Takes Charge*. The enchanted Eden conjured up of gentlemen's gentlemen, the Drones Club and country houses populated by bibulous butlers and demon aunts proved just the stimulus my daydreaming needed. As Evelyn Waugh had written of the Master: 'Mr Wodehouse's idyllic world can never stale. He will continue to release future generations from captivity that may be more irksome than our own.'

In my daydreams, needless to say, I *became* Mr Duke. His irresistible joie de vivre and brilliantly goofy tap-dancing had me in raptures two or three times a week. I never dared to address him as he left the stage door afterwards: I merely gazed in awe. I was so infatuated with his charms that I heard myself devoting most of my speech at the launch party for my book *The London Ritz* to urging everyone present to flock to the Fortune Theatre.

Only when I had finished this passionate advertisement did I notice the bemused looks on the faces in front of me. 'Hugh, my dear,' one concerned friend said as he guided me behind a column in the dream-like restaurant, 'I think you are in urgent need of psychiatric help.'

Was I really going off my rocker? I took soundings in the club. Robin McDouall, comforting author of my favourite culinary work *Cooking for the Greedy* (and notorious for remarking of his sexual bouts, 'I don't mind paying for it, but he has to be a *gent*'), reassured me by reminiscing how he had been captivated by Sandy Wilson's musical of *Valmouth* by Ronald Firbank. 'The box-office manageress used to say to me: "Your *usual* seat, Mr McDouall?"'

Uncle Hugh's friend 'the Vanishing Viscount', Pat

Barrington, confided that he, too, was in the habit of constantly revisiting *Daisy Pulls It Off*, with its bevy of schoolgirl nymphettes in black gymslips, and that he had become familiar – 'not *too* familiar, you understand' – with some of the cast.

I remained faithful to my hero, the 'tall, dark, slim and stately' Mr Duke (as my future *Telegraph* colleague Eric Shorter described him) and continued to haunt the show's revival at Wyndhams a few years later. After his tragically early death in 1994 – the news was gently broken to me when I was myself in intensive care – I went so far as to enquire of his agent what had happened to the rights to *Jeeves Takes Charge*. The daydream he nobly inspired lives on.

My stage-door stalking properly got into its stride during the all-too-short run of *Windy City* at the Victoria Palace. This jaunty musical version of *The Front Page* had a lot going for it – including deft lyrics by Dick Vosburgh and melodious tunes by Tony Macaulay (who wrote the catchy '60s hit 'Build Me Up Buttercup' with Michael d'Abo) and particularly amusing performances by Anton Rodgers and Victor Spinetti. The dialogue in which Rodgers (the fearsome editor Walter Burns) orders a minion to tell Spinetti's prissy character that 'his poetry stinks – and kick him down the stairs' became a mantra on the *Telegraph* obits desk, endlessly employed by David Jones and myself. In the original play, Burns also threatens this minion: 'Unless you brace up, Duffy, I'll send you to *Obituaries*.' Indeed I rather think my addiction to the show fuelled my possibly unwise longings to work on the Street.

Yet a peculiar part of the show's charm was that the star, Dennis Waterman, seemed oddly ill at ease and vulnerable in the role of Hildy Johnson, the ace reporter. Seeing so many performances I could hardly fail to notice the tensions within the company. One night a bolshie Waterman threw the contents of a glass of stage whisky in the face of the musical director. Another night, the actor playing the mad murderer on the run, Robert Long-den – once met years ago when he shared a flat with my then genealogical deputy, Charles Kidd – hurt his foot falling through a skylight. The corpulent John Blythe, playing the Sheriff, was manifestly unpopular with the rest of the cast and subjected to so many ad-libs that he was reduced to whining: 'If we could just stick to the script . . .' Longden, an engagingly eccentric character prone to blowing flamboyant double-handed kisses at the stage door, was always ready to take advantage of Bly-the's discomfiture when the Sheriff's gun failed to report. 'Go on,' he would taunt, '*point* me to death.'

I would cite such evidence of the joys of live theatre when people sneered at me: 'But it must be awfully *boring* seeing the same thing night after night after night . . .' Finding companions to take along was fraught with diffi-culties. One girl fell asleep, others gave me sidelong glances of pity or contempt when I let slip that this was the nineteenth or twentieth time I had seen the show. Fortunately my future second wife saw the point of the exercise ('You'll be back', as the closing chorus had it, 'you'll be back . . .') and she added an extra dimension to the evening's entertainment by tackling the cast both by the stage door itself and in the pub of that name opposite for their autographs, while I took up my customary lurk-ing position.

When she told the surprisingly mild-mannered and bespectacled Dennis Waterman – then at the height of his fame in the title role of *Minder* on television – how many times I had seen the show, he replied: 'Blimey! He must know the bleedin' script better than me.' I experienced a voyeuristic frisson.

Being infinitely braver than her future husband, she also introduced me to the thrills of the standing ovation at the end of the performance. With her leading the way, we regularly stood and cheered ourselves hoarse – a quite novel sensation for me. On *Windy City*'s last night we took a box and invited Richard Conynghame and Hugo Vickers to join us. I donned the show's T-shirt (such musical marketing merchandise then still in its infancy) and Vickers armed himself with some wilting flowers to chuck at Waterman's feet during his curtain call. Earlier in the performance, the star had something else thrown at him – the assembled hacks emptied their glasses in his face. Other end of term pranks included the orchestra holding up scorecards marked '0' at the end of Johnny Blythe's soft-shoe shuffle. When Blythe (one of the most cordially disliked men in showbiz, I was later assured by Uncle Peter's actor friend) snarled at the murderer: 'I've got you, Williams', the cheeky Robert Longden answered back: 'You've got me by the *Williams* – how very uncomfortable!' Well, you had to be there . . .

Whereas *Windy City* ran for only six months or so, the next show that I became hooked on, *Me and My Girl*, Stephen Fry's joyous reworking of the old Noel Gay musical, packed them in at the Adelphi for nearly nine years. Another addict of the 'Lambeth Walk Musical' (which also featured Robert Longden as 'the Hon Gerald' in a silly-ass role), David Shepherd, the wildlife artist, told me that he took a family party into the stalls virtually every week and that it was 'the best tonic' he knew. My wife and I cautiously joined forces with them one night but felt obliged to slip away when they started a conga leading from the stalls round to the cast's dressing rooms.

I preferred my stalking to stick to the stage door, where I tried to turn a blind eye to the plaque recording a murder there in the nineteenth century. Throughout the marathon run of *Me and My Girl* I never tired of singing along with the stirring sentiments of 'Noblesse Oblige' or of laughing uncontrollably during 'The Family Solicitor' song, which was just as well as it was performed year in and year out – in increasingly surreal fashion – by the selfsame actor, Roy Macready. When my wife finally succeeded in dragging me out of the shadows to be introduced to this courteous and modest actor in the last week of his nine years of warbling '*As the family solicitor, my advice to you* . . .', he told me that he always tried to bring 'something fresh' to the role. I assured him that he had triumphantly succeeded.

It was not so much 'something fresh' as 'something exciting, *for a change*' that my twelve-year-old daughter demanded one Saturday afternoon in the autumn of 1986 when we had to fill in some time while her brother attended a friend's birthday party. What happened next shifted my hitherto fairly restrained addiction to full-scale dependency. By chance we happened to be walking past Her Majesty's Theatre in the Haymarket (next to the lamented site of the old Carlton Hotel, now replaced by New Zealand House, which is very much more than a bit 'off'). On a wild surmise, noticing that the returns queue for the matinee of a new musical by Andrew Lloyd Webber (starring his new wife, Sarah Brightman, and Michael Crawford) did not seem impossibly long, I suggested that we join it. Not being especially enamoured hitherto of either Mr or Mrs Lloyd Webber (though on our first proper date my second wife and I went to see *Cats*), or even Crawford, I could not account for this instinctive impulse.

I had plenty of time to ponder on my rashness but to my surprise found the experience of standing in line strangely serene. It induced a sense of camaraderie with one's companions and a positively craven respect for authority in the shape of the Queue Marshal. 'Perhaps,' I

said to a bemused Harriet, 'they should bring back ration-
ing.' The tension mounted, climaxing in the exhilaration
of being finally vouchsafed our tickets.

'This *is* exciting, Daddy,' said Harriet.

The show itself was enchanting: lush romantic music,
spectacular sets and a series of old-fashioned special
effects that were pure theatre. The wonder of water, fire
and disappearances in puffs of smoke took one back – a
short journey in my own case – to the magic of childhood.
The greatest thrill of all was the magnetic, extraordinarily affecting performance of Michael Crawford. There
is nothing finer than seeing somebody extend himself far
beyond his supposed capabilities. His operatic voice and
febrile stage presence were a revelation. When he walked
downstage to take his bow at the end I found myself – for
the first time in my life, without my wife's lead – standing
in the stalls, cheering, crying, choking.

Although I did not quite manage to emulate another
refugee from Fleet Street – a printer called Eddie – who
notched up 100 visits in the first nine months of *Phantom*'s run, and was permitted to jump the returns queue
on the centenary, I soon lost count of my more or less
weekly fixes. Most of our fellow junkies in the returns
queue tended to be single women of a certain age nursing
an unrequited passion for Michael Crawford. One friendly
woman, who lived in hope of insinuating her toy terrier
called Fang (kept under her coat) into the theatre, invited
me to join a society called OGRE (Opera Ghost Returns
Enthusiasts).

'By and large,' she assured me, 'we are as pleasant a
group of harmlessly certifiable lunatics as you could ever
expect to come across.'

I was duly sent an OGRE badge with an injunction to
guard it well. 'Should this command be ignored,' ran a
quotation from the show, 'a disaster beyond your imagin-

ation will occur.' I did not guard it well, and sometimes wondered when things later went awry, whether the Curse of the Phantom was to blame.

As my workload at the *Telegraph* increased I could no longer spare the time for queuing and formed a fruitful friendship with a tout who seemed to have strayed from the Winchester Club in *Minder*. Unfortunately (for him) officious policemen outside Her Majesty's tended to move in to feel the tout's collar before the full amount he was asking had changed hands.

One constable took me away for a quiet word. 'Are you really prepared,' he asked, with a look of ill-disguised loathing, 'to pay *three times* the face value of this ticket, sir? Of your own free will?'

'Certainly, officer. We live in monetarist times – and, in a free market, I can assure you it's worth every penny.'

Such bravado on my own part did not disguise my terror that I would subsequently be arrested in the stalls and dragged off to the cells. Yet I continued to do brisk business with the tout for several happy years. Many was the time he came to my rescue with seats for *Les Misérables* and such emotional last nights as Michael Ball's departure from *Aspects of Love* and Jonathan Pryce's farewell to *Miss Saigon*.

Phantom, though, retained my primary loyalty. Such was my one-track mind on the subject that when Craig Brown arranged for me to participate in a pilot for a teatime television chat show, I insisted on steering the conversation round to my favourite musical. As Craig poured contempt upon my 'incredibly naff' taste, I lost my head completely and proceeded to warble songs from the show. Fortunately the programme was never transmitted – so my children were spared the indignity of having it confirmed that their father really had sung on the telly – and, hardly surprisingly, a series was not commissioned.

Craig's marriage to Frances Welch coincided with Michael Crawford's last night in the London production of *Phantom* and though I had, alas, failed to secure a ticket I did not hesitate to walk out of the wedding party in the Polish Hearth Club to take up my stalking post by the stage door of Her Majesty's. Yet there was something strangely unpleasant in the atmosphere that night. When the perfectionist star with a mesmerizing appeal to his followers (perhaps they, or rather we, recognize a fellow obsessive?) eventually emerged, framed in the doorway, a crowd cheered hysterically. '*We love you, Michael*,' shouted a female chorus in unison. Crawford smiled and waved.

Then an eerie silence descended on the gathering, broken by a bespectacled, stoutish woman in a bulky overcoat who was standing next to me. 'Well,' she snarled at the suddenly slight and vulnerable figure in our midst, '*say something*, can't you?'

The wretched actor whispered hoarsely that he had lost his voice, his hands imploringly placed around his throat. The tension lifted. For a moment, though, there had been a bat's squeak of menace in the air, an unmistakable whiff of the mob ready to turn on its idol and tear him apart. The fickleness of fandom had been alarmingly exposed. As if for the first time I looked at my fellow fans and did not like what I saw. I shuddered, and thought of the evening I had happened to walk past the Dakota building in New York a few hours before John Lennon was shot on that very spot. I felt a distinct chill.

Doubtless I should have abandoned my stage-door stalking there and then. Yet, following the familiar formula of 'I am a fan; she is a nutter; he is a celebrity serial killer', I convinced myself that this had been an isolated phenomenon. Soon I was back in my old haunts.

One night my wife achieved a right and left by cornering both Peter O'Toole (who kept doffing his trilby to her) and Donald Pickering, one of my special heroes since his ramrod-straight portrayal of the adjutant in *Conduct Unbecoming* on the stage in 1969 and his spot-on realization of the gossipy, languid 'Dolly' Longstaffe in *The Pallisers*, scripted by Simon Raven for television.

'You must be so exhausted, Mr Pickering,' I overheard my wife saying from the shadows of Soho. I desperately tried to communicate by semaphore that, in fact, he had not had that much to do in his comparatively small part.

'It was frightfully hot in there tonight, for some reason,' the suave Pickering responded tactfully.

My principal pin-up, Jeremy Clyde, Pickering's dashing co-star in both *Conduct Unbecoming* and *The Pallisers*, was subjected to a pincer movement that his ancestor 'the Iron Duke' of Wellington would not have disdained. As he emerged from the stage door of Sadlers Wells I decided that this was the moment that I had finally to show some guts and (in the Great War, as opposed to the theatrical, sense) 'go over the top' myself.

'Um . . . Mr Clyde?'

The elegant dandy with the bouffant hair looked startled as he noticed this middle-aged moon-faced balding butterball lumbering towards him out of the darkness. He jumped back involuntarily on his well-sprung trainers, as if expecting physical assault. 'Er, yes?' he said nervously.

'Sorry to buttonhole you like this.' I took a deep breath. 'I just wanted to say how deeply I have admired you since the '60s when you used to sing in that duo with Chad Stuart. And then you were in the musical of *Passion Flower Hotel*, weren't you? And I'll never forget your superb performance in *Conduct Unbecoming* at the Queen's, with Paul Jones and Donald Pickering. Or that sparkling *School for Scandal* at Windsor, with Jonathan Cecil—'

'And, of course, Gabrielle was in that, too,' said my hero chirpily.

I looked nonplussed. 'Gabrielle?'

'Gabrielle *Drake* – you've just seen her in there in *Cavalcade* – or at least I presume you have?'

'Oh yes, of course, I'm so sorry. You were absolutely marvellous – and so was Miss Drake. Please would you sign this, for my wife?'

The following day we were in the King's Road when I spotted the bouffant hair moving slowly past in an open-topped Triumph Herald of some antiquity. 'Good Lord,' I said to my wife. 'There's Jeremy Clyde.'

It was the work of a moment for her to dart out into the traffic. 'Hi! Mr Clyde! You very sweetly signed your autograph for me last night. My husband over there—'

I waved respectfully from the safety of the pavement.

'He's your biggest fan.'

Jeremy Clyde, inspecting my bulk, probably did not doubt it. He smiled his ravishing smile and drove off, shaking his immaculately coiffed head. 'I bet he's thinking we're a right pair of raving nutters.'

Having taken the plunge, I became a little bolder in my stage-door stalking. I was brave enough to buttonhole Jim Broadbent (whose portrayal of the compulsive glutton in Woody Allen's film *Bullets Over Broadway* could almost have been based on me), but funked saying anything to Rex Harrison, when I found myself standing behind him in the Gents at Brooks's, where he was carefully brushing his hair in a vain attempt to cover a bald patch. I encountered the magnificently larger-than-life figure of Charles Gray (whose fruity delivery of Blofeld's line 'Tiffany, my dear, we seem to be showing rather more *cheek* than usual . . .' was a constant part of my repertoire) on the great staircase at Christie's. He appeared to be taking up all the available space and my several attempts to circumnavigate him earned me the growled rebuke '*Do make up your mind.*'

I dropped hints to a neighbour of his in Ennismore Gardens that I longed to meet this camp *monstre sacré*, but he was reluctant to throw another dinner party in Mr Gray's honour. The last one, apparently, had ended in disarray when the old ham announced to his host: 'Where do you find these boring cunts? I'm buggering off home.'

Frogmarched by Andrew Barrow, whose prize-winning novel *The Tap Dancer* had a strong showbiz theme, I made daring raids into the dressing-rooms of Barry Humphries and Ken Dodd, who amused Barrow by addressing me as 'young man'. Backstage at the Palladium, the great Doddy gave us a thoughtful hour-long lecture on the theory of 'Tickleology'. He explained how he worked to a rigorously monitored schedule of seven laughs a minute: 'my assistant stands in the wings with a stopwatch'. To my regret I have never managed to persuade my wife or my children to accompany me to see this majestic upholder of the music-hall tradition perform at Skegness on our trips to Lincolnshire; he is infinitely better live than within the confines of television.

Through working for the *Telegraph* I was fortunate enough to meet many of my stage idols. Joss Ackland – who quite unselfconsciously granted me an interview while having his hair dyed for his role as Clarence Darrow – sweetly telephoned me afterwards to say that he had enjoyed our chat and would like to meet again, but I fear that I was too shy to follow this up. The exceptionally sympathetic and intelligent David Suchet gently encouraged me to go on a diet while we breakfasted at the Ritz. After my heart troubles, I asked for a reminder of his regimen at the stage door after a preview of his sensitive show about Sid Field, the now largely forgotten comic. Poor Susan Fleetwood, who was to die young, struck me as uncomfortably neurotic; Juliet Stevenson was touchy about being reminded of her having been at school with Fergie; and Lauren Bacall scared me to pieces over lunch at San Lorenzo in Beauchamp Place. Penelope Keith did not care for my crass attempt to link her rise and fall with Margaret Thatcher's; but her giggly *Good Life* co-star, Felicity Kendal, was as sweet as pie and disarmingly tactile.

Stephen Fry was the soul of tolerance and good humour as I idiotically parroted the best lines of a part he had actually played himself in the revival of Alan Bennett's *Forty Years On*. In the company of an endearingly insecure Hugh Laurie, I longed to shed the inhibitions that had hobbled me emotionally since my prep-school days and enfold the Etonian rowing Blue (how Wodehouse would have approved such a qualification to play Bertie Wooster) in a chaste embrace. When I took my children, ardent fans of *Blackadder*, backstage to meet Laurie after his tour de force in *Gasping* at the Haymarket, we disgraced ourselves by being utterly tongue-tied. (The sins of the father . . .)

During my interview with Simon Gray at English's Oyster Bar in Brighton the banquette was so cramped that he had to put his arm around me in order to conduct the conversation.

'This is as bad as Binkie Beaumont's lift,' I quipped.

We did the only thing open to Englishmen in such intimate circumstances: we talked about cricket, in particular the pleasure afforded by an apparently involuntary late cut.

'There is nothing to beat it, is there?' I gushed.

'I can think of a few things,' murmured Gray, who evidently does not take the summer game quite so seriously as his fellow playright Harold Pinter.

Much as I enjoyed these interviews, I had no burning

ambition to be a clever-dick critic seeking to trip up my
subjects, tempting them into indiscretions and then show-
ering them with irony for the delectation of cynical editors. I remained happiest in the role of fan. Just to meet
my heroes and bask in their aura was all I asked.

Some of the most enjoyable afternoons of my life were
spent in the company of Jonathan Cecil, James Villiers
and Ronald Fraser. At one of our memorable lunches,
Jonathan told me that he was the recipient of an authentic Gielgud 'brick' when auditioning under Sir John's
direction for *Halfway Up the Tree* by Peter Ustinov in the
1960s.

'I have seen lots of young men for this part,' Gielgud
told him. 'All very talented, very good looking. The problem is that they have to go to a lot of trouble to try to
appear ridiculous. Whereas *you* . . .'

Jonathan also worked with Frankie Howerd and
Terry-Thomas; his affectionate mimicry of them exceeded
any daydreams. I could not hear enough of his hilarious
anecdotes. Cast as an eccentric earl in a film made in
Canada, he was given the line: 'You must come up to my
place. Best grouse-shooting in Surrey!' He had to point
out that there are not actually many grouse on the Purley
Hills. Then, when the guests arrived at his 'place', the
butler emerged and announced: 'Good afternoon, I am
Shepperton, the butler.' The guests gave their names and
the butler said: '*Charmed!* Let me show you to your
rooms . . .' Jonathan mused: 'I was rather sorry when that
bit was cut out of the film.'

Above all, Jonathan Cecil is the supreme Wodehousian. As Richard Briers observed, when I buttonholed him
at the BBC to thank him for the pleasure his own interpretation of Bertie Wooster had given me: 'I am afraid I
was far too middle class for the role. Jonathan was born
to play it.'

Jonathan and his wife Anna Sharkey (I remember seeing them together in the blissful *Cowardly Custard* revue at the Mermaid in the early 1970s) perform a delightful two-hander entitled *Plum Sauce* which features the songs and stories of Wodehouse and the music of Jerome Kern. The evening I caught it at Guildford, with Jonathan centre stage in straw hat and monocle, transported me to Wodehousian paradise.

The most refreshing thing about Jonathan Cecil is that while obviously highly literate and intelligent (his father, Lord David, was Goldsmith Professor of English Literature at Oxford; his mother the daughter of Sir Desmond MacCarthy, the critic), he has a delectably light touch and a love of broad comedy. So many modern thespians are priggish pseudo-intellectuals who take themselves far too seriously and have no sense of humour. That could never have been said of Jimmy Villiers and Ronnie Fraser, with whom I was privileged to carouse in the Coach and Horses.

At Wellington, Villiers told me in his richly old-fashioned tones, he was 'never brainy enough' to be allowed to act with the Gravediggers, the college's dramatic society. Happily he had already become hooked at his prep school in Worcestershire.

'I came on in a play called *The Crimson Coconut*, spoke my line and suddenly everyone started pissing themselves with laughter. I thought: I rather like this.'

'Do you ever get fed up with being typecast as a gent?'

'No,' he replied. 'After all, I suppose I *am* one.'

As if on cue, a chirpy cockney shouted out: ''Ere, Jimmy, have a glass for *The Ruling Class*!' This was the film in which he starred with his old oppo 'Pedro' O'Toole.

'No thanks,' said Villiers equably. 'I've already got one.'

In the corner of my eye I noticed Ronnie Fraser
surreptitiously emptying the remains of several glasses
into his own. Tragically, Ronnie had lost most of his
savings (from his starring role in television as the
doughty retired Empire-builder 'Badger' in *The Misfit*) in
an ill-fated restaurant venture. As they advanced in years
neither of these two stalwarts was being given nearly
enough work.

'Look here, old cock,' Ronnie said, grabbing my arm.
'You're meant to be a writer, aren't you? Why the fuck
can't you write something for me and Jimmy here?'

'I wish I could. I always think of you two as a natural
partnership. I remember when you played Apthorpe in
Evelyn Waugh's *Sword of Honour* and Jimmy was Lord
Kilbannock; and then you were Colonel Pickering to his
Higgins. What fun that must have been.'

Ronnie Fraser did one of his celebrated eye-rolls. 'Yes,
yes. You can cut the crap – that's all in the past. Most of
my old mates who liked a cocktail are dead – Burton,
Niven, Huston, Robert Shaw, John 'Le Mes' [urier] . . . I
often feel like Justice Shallow. And the ones who are still
around – you know, O'Toole, Connery, Harris and Co. –
are all bloody superstars. Yet when we were at the Court
I was the one hailed as the bright new star – where did I
go wrong?'

'You'll always be a superstar to me, Ronnie!'

'Bullshit,' he said as he punched my stomach.

'Oi, Jimmy – I've just had lunch with Paddy Ryecart
and he tells me he's got something in the pipeline which
will give all his muckers a nice little earner.'

'I'll believe it when it happens,' said Villiers
mournfully.

'Anything else in the offing, then?' asked Fraser.

'I've been offered a job at Windsor but the money's not
up to much.'

'You must insist upon the Ivor Novello Suite at Skindles, dear boy.'

The two old chums fell into reminiscing about the knockabout days of the '50s, hanging around in actors' pubs like the Salisbury and playing footer in the park. Ronnie recalled his stint as Wolfit's dresser for *King Lear* ('Fraser,' he intoned, 'I know there was an *artist* on the wind tonight') and the time he understudied for Rachel Roberts as a witch in 'the Scottish play'.

'It can't be as much fun as it used to be,' I suggested to them.

'No, it certainly isn't,' said Villiers. 'Frankly, I now find the business of acting more and more terrifying. I think you do as you get older . . .'

'The trouble is,' said Fraser, 'that none of these ruddy teenage casting "directors" have the foggiest fucking *clue* as to who you are or what you've done.'

'Couldn't you revive dear old Badger?' I ventured.

'Nothing I'd like better,' chortled Fraser. 'This time we'd transplant him to the European Sodding Community – you can imagine what he would have to say about the Krauts, Frogs, Wops . . .'

Sorrowfully I took my leave of the two old quaffing partners and only wished that I had a smidgin of Craig Brown's creative genius in order to have written a script for them both. Craig himself asked me along to watch the recording of his BBC Radio 4 series in which Wallace Arnold (played by Harry Enfield) bade listeners *Welcome to My Wireless*. Beforehand it was arranged that we should have lunch with the star. In a scene of pure farce, I was taking a telephone call (from Jeremy Paxman, as it happens) at the restaurant's reception desk when the great comedian arrived.

'No, I'm sorry, Jeremy. I really *can't* come on *Newsnight* to talk about the Royal Family. I am afraid I shall

be tied up all day in a studio at Broadcasting House.'
(Well, I had been promised a grunt and a spit during the
recording.)

'Ah, Mr Enfield.' I stuck out my hand, which unfortunately still contained the telephone. 'A great honour, I am
an *enormous* admirer . . .'

Looking distinctly bemused, Harry returned my hand
and the instrument. He could see I was enormous, and it
was also clear that he thought I was the maître d'.

'Er, table in the name of . . .' he said softly. 'Oh,
terribly sorry, I can't remember the name. You must
think me completely bonkers.' (Craig, as a restaurant
reviewer, had booked the table under a pseudonym which
Harry had, quite understandably, forgotten.)

'Not at all, not at all.' I could barely restrain myself
from rubbing my hands together and bowing my neck in
the traditional maître d' manner. 'Just follow me.'

'But, hold on, how on earth do you know who I'm
supposed to be lunching with?'

Happily by now Craig had come to the rescue. 'Hello,
Harry – I see you've already met Hugh. He's a tremendous fan of yours.'

I put out my hand again. 'A great honour . . . *enormous*
admirer.'

'I think we've done that bit, haven't we?'

I took my place at the table.

'Oh, are you joining us? I thought you worked here. I
am so sorry.'

'Not as sorry as I am. I feel like a cross between your
characters the gormless publican Leslie Norris and my
fellow Harrovian Tim Nice-But-Dim.'

Harry turned out to be everything one hoped for in a
true hero: modest, self-deprecating, mildly unsure of himself, refreshingly open and down to earth – and, of course,
wonderfully funny. Everything went swimmingly until

Harry rebuked Craig for a personal crack in one of his columns about the Pinters. Craig looked somewhat miffed.

'Surely,' said Harry, 'we're not here purely to heap praise on each other, are we?'

This was news to me, at least. Harmony was soon restored and once we were in the studio I had to stuff a handkerchief into my mouth to suppress the *fou rire* that Auntie's microphone must not pick up. Becoming ever more slurred and maudlin over his reminiscences of the 'dread decades', Arnold, sucking revoltingly on his pipe, recalled how he was the only person to have chosen 'My Way' twice among his eight *Desert Island Discs*, and also claimed the record for having collapsed into tears eleven times during his interview for *In the Psychiatrist's Chair* with Dr Anthony Clare ('Big blow now . . . That's better, isn't it?').

Inebriated with mirth and happiness, I presumed to go so far as to advise Enfield on how to improve his mimicry of Ted Heath's *veowel seounds* and heard myself offering my own imitation. Eventually I was offered the ultimate accolade of approaching the microphone myself in order to supply a few hearty 'chuckles' (as directed) to accompany jovial 'Uncle Bob' Robinson's leaden quips in a spoof of *Stop the Week*.

My passion for showbiz found a handy outlet in the *Telegraph* obits column where the supposedly 'useless information' I had lovingly tabulated over my years as a couch potato and stage-door stalker turned out to be surprisingly useful. All those hours watching, say, *Coronation Street*, *Crossroads* and *On The Buses*, not to mention *Stars on Sunday*, proved grist to the mill when their respective stars dropped off the perch. As the effervescent obits secretary Teresa Moore put it, when she was reminding me of the incident in *On the Buses* when

Olive's sidecar becomes detached from the morose Arfur's motorbike: 'This is better than working, isn't it?'

When the ubiquitous 'other rank' Victor Maddern went to the great barrack room in the sky, I could recall the time in dear old *Dixon of Dock Green*, then transmitted live, when this redoubtable supporting player, cast as a villain, had to say the line: 'It's down at Dock Green nick.' Instead viewers were treated to the following farrago: 'It's down at Dick Green Dock . . . It's down at Dock Green Dick . . . Who writes these bloody scripts? Can't I just say "down at the nick"? Fuck Dock Green!'

And when Gordon Jackson, the upright butler Hudson in *Upstairs, Downstairs*, died, I remembered Stanley Baxter's spoof in which an outraged Mrs Bridges admonishes her kitchen maid for referring to 'the old Queen', which she had mistaken for an allusion to Mr Hudson.

After nearly handing in my own dinner pail I very reluctantly gave up the obits chair ('You've heard of the expression,' my doctor said, 'I'll do this job if it kills me . . .'), which I still grievously miss to this day, and sought a less stressful existence in the Lincolnshire Wolds – where unfortunately the roof of our rented cottage soon fell in, both literally and metaphorically. Knowing my love of showbiz, the *Telegraph* suggested that I might care to become their new five-days-a-week television critic.

'It's always the job they give the crocks,' a colleague helpfully pointed out.

I jumped at the chance to fulfil my long-held fantasy of being paid to watch the box night and day – though Craig Brown and David Jones, both former television reviewers, wisely warned me that the remorseless volume of serious programmes demanding detailed attention would weigh heavily. So it proved. Watching the telly ceased to be a relaxing pleasure but an onerous, extraordinarily demanding chore.

I became swamped in videotapes and obsessively worried that I should study every one of them in exhaustive detail – just in case orders came down from on high that I had to cover such-and-such a documentary. I scribbled away, but the old insecurities were as bad as ever, the lack of confidence even worse. After eighteen months of writing five columns a week, I ground to a complete halt. I collapsed in a heap in front of a blank computer screen – or should that be 'terminal'? It nearly was for me. To head off yet another journey to intensive care, I took early retirement on medical grounds from the paper.

Freed from the wearisome responsibility of being a critic, I retreated once more to John Powell's basement sanctuary in Kennington and drifted back into dreamland. At the Oval I formed a dedicated attachment to the thrilling Surrey batsman Alistair Brown, known as 'Lordy' by his teammates as he bats like a lord – an irresistible recommendation for any hero of mine. Away from the haven of the Bedser Stand, Wodehouse, as ever, proved the perfect pick-me-up and before long I was regularly stalking outside the stage door of Alan Ayckbourn and Andrew Lloyd Webber's idyllic musical, *By Jeeves* – which is more or less where we came in.

THIRTEEN

Forty Years On

IN THE LATE 1990s my ultimate daydream merged with the surreal when the opportunity arose to loiter on location for the filming of *A Dance to the Music of Time* by Channel 4. On arriving at Knebworth – the pinnacled Gothic pile in Hertfordshire, which represented Thrubworth, family seat of the narrator Nick Jenkins's in-laws, the Tollands – I deduced from the authentic drabness of the set that the saga had reached the mid-1950s. I experienced a strange feeling of being transported backwards in time. It was particularly disconcerting to realize that these years of my own boyhood four decades ago now had to be carefully dressed 'in period'. The fleet of motor cars drawn up beside the church (for the funeral of Jenkins's brother-in-law the quixotic Earl of Warminster) were now evidently regarded as 'vintage'.

The flavour of the '50s was heightened by that splendidly craggy actor Bryan Pringle ('I'm playing the drunken butler, Smith'), whom I knew to be an old mate of Jimmy Villiers and Ronnie Fraser, taking me aside on the set and, cocking his head conspiratorially in the direction of two other members of the cast, rasping: 'You do realize, old cock, that in real life those two are both *baron-ets!*'

The Barts in question were that suave duo of gentlemen-actors Johnny Standing (Nick Jenkins) and Jeremy Child (Jenkins's brother-in-law, Roddy Cutts, a Tory MP). Their easy Etonian banter enlivened the proceedings.

'Remember,' Child said to a woman from the wardrobe department, 'Roddy Cutts would not be seen dead in a naff shirt. This is the '50s, don't forget.'

I introduced myself to Child, an old school friend of Bill Deedes's son, Jeremy, the managing director of the Telegraph Group. 'I remember,' I told him, 'seeing you play racquets at Queen's Club one freezing afternoon in the early 1960s wearing a loose, long red cardigan with buttons down to below your knees. It caused quite a stir up in the gallery.'

'Oh, *fuck*,' snorted Child genially, and we settled down to an enjoyably gossipy chat with Standing and Pringle. I was reminded how much I relished the company of actors. Yet again I regretted that I had not attempted to be of their number. Perhaps even now I could give it a go?

'So you want to do a turn, eh, Massingberd?' said Child. 'Never too late, is it, Johnny?'

I had, in fact, recently sent off for an application form to the Webber-Douglas Academy of Dramatic Art in South Kensington, where I believed that another of my cherished gentlemen-actors, Moray Watson, was on the governing body, but had yet to fill it in and send it off. I mused about possible audition pieces. Naturally *Forty Years On*, which I still knew by heart, would feature in my programme.

At the next location – an even loopier Gothic monstrosity near Henley – my daydream 'cup ranneth over' when I learned that Alan Bennett himself (doing what Sir Jeremy would call 'a turn' as Sillery, the snobbish, scheming left-wing Oxford don) was going to be on set. To meet Bennett would give me the full pack of cigarette cards, as it were. (I felt I could count Evelyn Waugh, as Bron Waugh and his wife Teresa had generously entertained me to lunch at Combe Florey, where I made a pilgrimage to the great novelist's grave.)

Bennett, though, is known to be wary of being button-holed by importunate hacks and I felt extremely apprehensive. Fortunately, the flamboyant photographer Michael Roberts was taking stills of some of the cast and he turned out to be an equally enthusiastic fan of Alan Bennett, whom he jollied along. 'You know Napier Miles, don't you?' he asked me, alluding to an Etonian chum of Craig Brown's. 'Like you, he's got most of Bennett's gems off pat.'

To my delight, the great man in full 'Sillers' make-up complete with white wig, soup-strainer moustache and tweeds, turned out to be geniality personified, while being the soul of modesty and unassuming good manners. On being introduced he asked me: 'That's a Lincolnshire name, isn't it?'

'Yes, that's right. Do you know that vast, dim county at all?'

'Well, my grandfather was a farm labourer at North Rauceby.'

To my surprise and pleasure, he saw genealogy, like Anthony Powell himself, not as a snobbish pursuit but merely as 'an expression of interest in other people'. He took me to his trailer for a homely cup of tea, which he brewed himself with practised efficiency. He tackled the procedure of dishing it up in a brisk, schoolmasterly manner. 'Milk? Sugar? Help yourself.' Seeing his 'Sillers' get-up I half expected him to add: 'Have a rock bun.'

My usual form when meeting my heroes is to spoil everything by seeking to impress them with my intimate knowledge of their work. I took the plunge: 'I am sure you remember that in your marvellous play *The Old Country* that know-it-all Arts Council type (portrayed by John Phillips) refers to Anthony Powell having "probably pulled it off"?'

'Oh yes,' replied the playwright in a gratifyingly flattered way. 'He was rather a Noel Annan character.'

'May I ask what tone of voice you are using for Sillers, bearing in mind his habit of occasionally lapsing into stage cockney?' (God, I sounded like a priggish prat.)

'I'm just doing the usual high-fluting Harold Acton-type voice,' he replied evenly. I suppressed the urge to say something cheeky like 'Don't you mean Thora Hird?' and asked: 'Did you like being an Oxford don yourself?'

'No, not really. I remember feeling rather threatened by my pupils.'

Later, in between takes, some of the cast and crew were standing around chatting and Michael Roberts joshingly encouraged me to recite the 'Telegram' sketch, a particular favourite of mine from one of Bennett's turns for an Amnesty International charity fund-raising revue. 'I hesitate to do so before the man who wrote and performed it.'

'I've got a poor memory,' Bennett said, laughing. 'How did it go?'

Blushing furiously, I stammered my way through a very rough version of the original sketch, but tried to ham up the best lines – such as the caller, on learning that the telephonist's name is Doris, saying: 'We seem to be drifting into a state of redundant intimacy.' When the caller explained that the signature of 'NORWICH' at the bottom of the telegram addressed to his girlfriend signified 'Knickers Off Ready When I Come Home', I risked an extra beat in the pause before continuing: '*Yes*, I know "knickers" has a "*k*" – I was at Oxford. That was one of the first things they taught me.' And by the end I was managing to achieve some momentum: 'BURMA? No, I am not familiar with that particular acronym . . . "Be Upstairs Ready My Angel" . . . Yes, yes . . . The only problem is that my girlfriend lives in the *basement* flat and the upstairs flat is occupied by a window dresser for

Bourne & Hollingsworth, so she wouldn't care for that –
and he *certainly* wouldn't.'

The crew were now downstairs and readying themselves for the next scene in a mock-up of the House of
Commons dining room. I spotted Bennett sitting rather
forlornly among a group of extras at a large trestle. He
was surreptitiously reading a book under the table.

Later, I nosily asked him the name of the book. He
held up a paperback of *The Debt to Pleasure* by John
Lanchester, a friend of his on the *London Review of Books*
(who had passed through the *Telegraph* obits desk). 'The
extra sitting next to me,' he said, 'was reading Frank
Harris's pornographic memoirs *My Life and Loves* as if
they were perfectly run of the mill. Have you noticed that
in the north extras are usually real people, but in the
south they tend to look like psychopaths?'

I laughed at this spot-on observation. Eventually Bennett had a line to deliver (not in the novel) about 'dining
with Diana Cooper'.

'Did you ever meet Lady Diana in real life?' I asked.

'Yes, once. She came round to my dressing room
during the run of *Forty Years On*. She asked me why I
had chosen to write about all her men friends who had
been killed in the Great War.'

'Edward Horner, Raymond Asquith, Shaw-Stewart
and the Grenfells ... they were not passionately concerned with the shortcomings of the world. It was still too
rich and enthralling a place for them to find fault with
it ...' I recited from the play.

'I am flattered by your knowledge of my work,' said
Bennett, before adding slyly: 'I remember Lady Diana
admiring herself in the mirror – rather in the way Peter
Cook used to do.'

Emboldened, I heard myself blurting out that

Anthony Blunt (subject of Bennett's ingenious play *A Question of Attribution*), who had accompanied my uncle Peter to see the original production of *Forty Years On*, had found the allusion to Virginia Woolf's suicide ('filling her pockets with stones, walks into the River Ouse . . . with her hat still firmly on her head') to be in what he described as 'rather bad taste'.

'It probably was,' said Bennett.

I mentioned to Bennett that I was planning to read a speech from his much underrated play *Enjoy* at a memorial service for Lesley Cunliffe, who had recently died of cancer. Nearly twenty years earlier I had taken Lesley to the first night (where we were deafened by Robert Morley's laughter and spotted the ghostly figure of Laurence Olivier up in a box), and I remembered her clutching my arm when the social worker – in fact the elderly couple's son in drag – described the assorted objects on their mantelpiece. 'Pure poetry,' Lesley enthused.

'That *is* a tribute,' Bennett said gently. 'At the time the idea in *Enjoy* of placing a back-to-back in a museum was dismissed as far-fetched, but exactly that sort of thing was being done only a few years later.'

Although I felt uplifted by the experience of spending the day with such a sympathetic genius, mention of Lesley's death reminded me of the darker side of Powell's great novel sequence. 'The *Dance* is the *danse macabre*,' explained the screenwriter Hugh Whitemore, 'the Dance of Death.'

The Grim Reaper was not only in constant attendance in the novel and film. For Bryan Pringle brought news of Ronnie Fraser's recent funeral. 'Jimmy Villiers was there looking terribly upset.' Soon Villiers himself (slightly miscast as the chillingly 'chic sailor' Buster Foxe in the film of *Dance*) followed him to the grave. Suddenly the pantheon of my heroes was beginning to crumble: Jim

Lees-Milne died; Willie Rushton and John Wells died; Charles Gray died; and then, early in 2000, E. W. Swanton, my cricketing mentor, departed to the great pavilion in the sky.

The magisterial Jim had mellowed since the days when he treated me as a recalcitrant schoolboy in the late 1970s, when we worked together on an encyclopedia of the summer game. 'I'm not speaking to *you*,' he once growled at me after ignoring me all morning in a tiny office provided by our patrons.

'So I couldn't help noticing, Jim. What have I done wrong?'

'You passed a proof without my permission.'

'I don't think I did.'

'*Don't* answer me back! I may be an old man [he lived for another twenty years, and kept his eye on the ball to the end], but I am still in charge.'

'Of course, Jim. I'm very sorry.'

But that was all in the past. We eventually became the best of friends and I grew very fond of my old hero. Indeed he kindly dedicated his last book to me – a collection of his cricket obits.

Later in the year the *Telegraph* obits page also lost its chief adornment, Philip Warner, who was everyone's hero. Dear Philip kept the obits coming until the last day of his extraordinarily active life – and the superb standard never slipped a millimetre. Then he went up to bed, read the *Spectator* (which contained a book review by him), as well as his customary chapter of Wodehouse, and died peacefully in his sleep, aged eighty-six.

I had the honour of paying tribute to this exemplar of the old breed at a service of thanksgiving at Sandhurst. Unfortunately the Commandant of the Academy told me afterwards that he had not heard 'a ruddy word'. The story of my life, I mused. Also in the course of 2000 I found myself in the pulpit to deliver doubtless equally inaudible addresses about two more heroes – the Reverend Henry Thorold, the Lincolnshire antiquary, and, of course, Anthony Powell, the Sage of the Chantry. Pondering 'last conclusions, please' in his memoirs, Tony had considered '*If*, on the rocks, without soda.'

For my part, living up to Kipling's ideal of a Man has never been a conceivable option. The line 'If you can dream – and not make your dreams your master' ensured an early fall. I am still enmeshed in my daydream fantasy world (the actor-manager scenario remaining to the fore), but now that so many of my heroes are no longer around I feel rather in limbo.

The death of Auberon Waugh early in 2001 was a devastating blow. As Michael Wharton ('Peter Simple') put it, Bron truly deserved to be 'enrolled' in the 'Great Hall of Heroes'. For me, his brilliant wit, wisdom, courage and bracing honesty made him the greatest journalist of all time. He was always extraordinarily kind to me and I regretted that the last time I had seen him, on the street in Bayswater (where my wife and I had settled yet again), I had not taken more trouble to come to his aid when, in a sadly confused state, he was hoping to find a cab. I would also have liked to have told him something of what he had meant to me – for his writing had a liberating, inspirational quality which somehow seemed to make life worth living.

Without Bron's guiding light of dissidence, I have my doubts on that score. My beloved wife calls me 'the Incredible Sulk'. Yet she feels that one encouraging sign that I may at last be growing up a little is the unexpectedly easy and relaxed friendship I have struck up in middle age with A. N. Wilson. In an earlier incarnation I could only ever have contemplated approaching him on all fours. Thanks to Andrew's enchanting encouragement and magical confidence-boosting, I have made a little more effort to re-enter the real world.

My stage-door stalking now seems largely confined to pursuing the reformed Manfreds rhythm-and-blues group around their gigs. Two of my heroes, the apparently ageless Paul Jones and Mike d'Abo, now share the vocals, and the richly nostalgic old numbers sound better than ever. They end their shows with Mike Hugg's yearning lament (from *Whatever Happened to the Likely Lads* television series): '*What became of the people we used to be . . .*'

Indeed the evocative lyrics are not dissimilar to d'Abo's and my old school song, 'Forty Years On':

> *When you look back, and forgetfully wonder*
> *What you were like in your work and your play . . .*

Looking back myself, I feel more strongly than ever that I really should have tried to be a teacher, like my mother and my daughter. What affords me some satisfaction is that many of the younger writers with whom I once worked on the genealogical series, the cricket encyclopedia and other assorted projects, as well as on the obits desk, blossomed so successfully – though I am not presuming to claim any credit whatsoever in the matter. Step forward, Hugo Vickers, Charles Kidd, George Plumptre, Mary Killen, David (Lewis) Jones, James Delingpole, Robert Chalmers, Damian Thompson, Dean Godson, Aurea Carpenter, John Lanchester, Martin van der Weyer, Hugh Fearnley-Whittingstall, Will Cohu, Kate Summerscale, George Ireland and the three 'Glorious Granddaughters' – Claudia FitzHerbert (Evelyn Waugh's), Imogen Lycett Green (John Betjeman's) and Georgia Coke (Anthony Powell's).

I decided to write this book, for what it's worth, as a cautionary tale after something Kate Summerscale told me when she was in the obits chair at the *Telegraph*. An enthusiastic fellow had come in for an interview for a possible vacancy on the desk. 'What,' Kate asked him, 'do you *really* want to do in life?'

'I want,' he replied, 'to be the new Hugh Massingberd.'

On hearing of this exchange, I squirmed and writhed with embarrassment, much as my own heroes must have done over the years. I thought, too, of the haunting conclusion to the film *All About Eve*, as the latest ingénue on the block eyes her chances of taking over from her idol.

Subsequently, though, I learned that the young shaver had decided against this baffling ambition. Instead, he entered the priesthood. My uncle Hugh would have approved of his priorities.

As E. E. Bowen put it in the Victorian theme song of this concluding chapter, 'Forty Years On':

> *Then it may be that there will often come o'er you –*
> *Glimpses of notes, like the catch of a song;*
> *Visions of boyhood shall float them before you,*
> *Echoes of dreamland shall bear them along.*